The Myths of National Security

The Myths

of

National

Security

The Peril

of

Secret

Government

Arthur Macy Cox

BEACON PRESS BOSTON

353.00996
C83m
95398
nov.1975

9 8 7 6 5 4 3 2 1

Grateful acknowledgment is made to the following for use of material
in this book: *Foreign Affairs, An American Quarterly Review,* for
"The Sources of Soviet Conduct," an article by George F. Kennan, who
appeared anonymously as "X," in the July 1947 issue of *Foreign Affairs,*
copyright 1947 by Council on Foreign Relations, Inc., quoted by permission; and Oxford University Press, for excerpts from *Secrecy and
Foreign Policy,* edited by Thomas M. Franck and Edward Weisband,
published in 1974 by Oxford University Press, reprinted by permission.

Library of Congress Cataloging in Publication Data

Cox, Arthur M.
  The myths of national security.
  Includes bibliographical references and index.
  1. Government information — United States.
I. Title.
JK468.S4C68   353.009′96   75–5288
ISBN 0–8070–0496–0

Contents

The Myths of National Security

1

National Security
—Reality and Hoax

The political demise of President Richard Nixon was devastating evidence of a national illness that has pervaded our society for years. But the first presidential resignation in our history did not arrest the disease; it merely focused attention on the need for a cure. The corruption of Watergate was a symptom of a larger malaise resulting from the use of the "big lie" technique to deceive the American people — countless lies perpetrated under cover of a vast system of executive secrecy, justified on grounds of protecting our national security. Until we understand how this happened we will not be able to restore our democracy to health.

The drafters of the Constitution provided us with an ingenious system of government based on machinery to check and balance the use of power, but they did not anticipate the problem of secret government, nor has that problem been dealt with in subsequent constitutional amendments. Despite a lack of safeguards, a large consensus of the American public since World War II has granted to succeeding presidents extraordinary secret powers to protect the security of the nation. The people felt that in matters of national survival the President should be given total trust — he should be allowed to make decisions in secret to protect our national security.

But democracy and secrecy are incompatible, and it has now become clear that secret powers should never have been delegated without guarantees of accountability to the people's representatives in the Congress. The peril of inadequate accountability is intensified because the American public is often gullible, espe-

1

cially in matters of national security. It took the public until 1968 finally to see through Lyndon Johnson's "credibility gap." He had lied to them too many times about the Vietnam War. Yet the lesson had not been learned — Richard Nixon also lied about Vietnam; and several months after the Watergate break-in he won a landslide reelection in 1972, almost escaping the exposure of his conspiracy. Watergate and the related acts of deception covered up by national security secrecy show how dangerously unbalanced our democratic system has become.

Cynicism and mistrust in government have become rampant because the people have been deceived by their leaders so many times. At the end of 1973 the pollster Louis Harris conducted a massive study entitled "Confidence and Concern: Citizens View American Government" for the Senate subcommittee on Intergovernmental Relations, chaired by Senator Edmund Muskie (D.–Maine). The survey reached two major conclusions:

1. That government secrecy no longer can be excused as an operational necessity, since it can exclude the participation of the people in their own government, and, indeed can be used as a screen for subverting their freedom; 2. That the key to any kind of successful leadership must be iron-bound integrity. The matter of honesty and straight dealing has the public deeply alarmed. It cannot be underestimated. The American people will not rest easy until it feels that integrity in government at all levels is secured.

A growing number of people are now aware that control of information is control of power—that secret government breeds arrogance, self-righteousness, and corruption. Fear, much of it whipped up by government national security managers, has been the central reason for public acquiescence in giving priority to security at the expense of freedom. Confronted by a totalitarian adversary whose system is secret, conspiratorial, and dominated by police control, we have responded by adopting similar methods to protect our national security. In the process of deterring the threat of communism we may be on the verge of losing our democracy.

It is time for us to reevaluate our whole system of national security. Trust will not be restored until better accountability is insured—until our leaders understand that the pendulum of democracy needs to swing in the direction of openness and freedom of information even at the risk of allowing some security advantages to our opponents. The threat of excessive secrecy to the survival of our democracy is far greater than the threat of communism and Soviet power.

In order to understand how and why we lost our way we need to examine all aspects of the national security system and executive secrecy. One of the reasons for so much confusion, manipulation, and distortion is that national security is a very ambiguous term, subject to many differing interpretations. Most people are for it, but what does it mean? We want to protect the security of our nation, but what are we protecting, and how far from our borders does such protection extend? Are we talking about protecting the survival of our nation alone, or do we include the survival of our friends and allies? Are we willing to risk nuclear war for the protection of our allies, and what do we know about the relative danger of such a risk? Such matters involve us all, but because of secrecy and the concentration of executive power they have been decided through the years by a small group of men in and around the White House.

During World War II it became relatively simple to define security issues, especially after Pearl Harbor. If we didn't fight back and win, our very survival as a nation would be at stake. So, it was not difficult to rally the public to mobilize our total resources, human and material, to defeat the forces of Hitler, Mussolini, and Tojo. Popular commitment was so strong that there was almost no disagreement when President Roosevelt announced that we would not stop fighting until we won the unconditional surrender of our enemies. Though the war never reached into the United States, most Americans, whether in North Africa, Asia, or Europe, fought as though they were defending their homeland. There are few ambiguities in total war.

The Truman-Acheson Era

The Cold War was something else. The National Security Act

of 1947 said that the National Security Council should "advise the President with respect to the integration of domestic, foreign and military policies relating to the national security so as to enable the military services and other departments and agencies of the Government to cooperate more effectively in matters involving the national security." Very sweeping powers involving integration of all policies and effective cooperation of all agencies with respect to the national security. What did it mean? Presidents, secretaries of state, secretaries of defense, and national security scholars have been trying to define it ever since.

Walter Lippmann, writing during World War II, said, "A nation has security when it does not have to sacrifice its legitimate interests to avoid war and is able, if challenged, to maintain them by war."[1] This sort of statement seems to make sense until one begins to ask what is a "legitimate interest." Such terms, along with "national interest," "national security," and even "national defense," have a ring of something solid and patriotic until the details are examined. Arnold Wolfers, one of the scholars who has thought most deeply on this subject, said:

> When political formulas such as "national interest" or "national security" gain popularity they need to be scrutinized with particular care. They may not mean the same thing to different people. They may not have any precise meaning at all. Thus, while appearing to offer guidance and a basis for a broad consensus they may be permitting everyone to label whatever policy he favors with an attractive and possibly deceptive name.[2]

That was written more than twenty years before Watergate.

Two other scholars, Frank Trager and Frank Simonie, have defined national security as "the part of government policy having as its objective the creation of national and international conditions favorable to the protection or extension of vital national values against existing and potential adversaries."[3] They define the vital national values as the most fundamental principles on which the social, political, and physical existence of the state is based. It would be worth knowing what fundamental principles they have in mind. Their definition not only calls for the protection but also the "extension" of these vital national values. Presumably this extension would give us license to impose our values around the world in the name of national security. Some of the imperial actions taken by various presidents since 1947 have done just that.

The Cold War has been dominated by two fundamental issues of security: Soviet-controlled international communism and its hostile ideology of Marxism-Leninism, and, slightly later, the development of nuclear weapons with delivery systems which make possible the mutual destruction of the U.S. and the U.S.S.R. Sadly, as we shall see, the threat of adversary communism has been directly linked in the minds of the public with nuclear weapons. Nuclear weapons are capable of destroying us; therefore subversive communism is capable of destroying us. The latter myth was never valid, even before the Cold War began to thaw; but, even today, most Americans don't know it is a myth because their leaders have not told them.

One of the earliest Cold War policy papers dealing with national security was written in September 1946 by Clark Clifford, then a White House counselor to President Truman. Clifford stated:

The language of military power is the only language which disciples of power politics understand. The United States must use that language in order that Soviet leaders will realize that our government is determined to uphold the interests of its citizens and the rights of small nations. Compromise and concessions are considered by the Soviets to be evidence of weakness and they are encouraged by our retreats to make new and greater demands. Therefore, in order to maintain our strength at a level which will be effective in restraining the Soviet Union, the United States must be prepared to wage atomic and biological warfare. . . . The United States with a military potential composed primarily of highly effective technical weapons should entertain no proposal for disarmament or limitation of armament as long as the possibility of Soviet aggression exists.[4]

By 1950, as the Cold War intensified, the National Security Council approved one of its most famous strategic policies, known as NSC-68. According to Secretary of State Dean Acheson,

The paper began with a statement of the conflicting aims and purposes of the two superpowers: the priority given by the Soviet rulers to the Kremlin design, world domination, contrasted with the American aim, an environment in which free societies could exist and flourish. . . . [Our] analysis of the threat combined the ideology of communist doctrine and the power of the Russian state into an aggressive expansionist drive which found its chief opponent and, therefore, target in the antithetic ideas and power of our own country. It was true and understandable to describe the Russian motivating concept as being that "no state is friendly which is not subservient," and ours that "no state is unfriendly which, in return for respect for its rights, respects the rights of other states."[5]

The paper went on to recommend a large, immediate expansion of military forces and weapons. In a speech in Dallas, June 13, 1950, Acheson ruled out a policy of isolationism, saying,

Appeasement of Soviet ambitions, was, in fact, only an alternative form of isolation. It would lead to a final struggle for survival with both our moral and military positions weakened. A third course, euphemistically called preventive war, adopted with disastrous results by other types of people and governments than ours, would take the form of nuclear attack on the Soviet Union. It would not solve problems; it would multiply them. . . . War is not inevitable. But talk of war's inevitability, had, in the past, helped to make it occur.[6]

These were Acheson's great years. This particular speech came at a time when Senator Joseph McCarthy was referring to Acheson as "the Red Dean of Communism."
Acheson believed that

. . . in dealing with the Soviet Union the most useful negotiation was by acts rather than words, and stability was better and more reliable than verbal agreements. . . . [The] NSC-68 program insisted on repairing weaknesses and "creating situations of strength. . . ." [In] the non-communist world [were] large areas of weakness, which by its very nature the Soviet system had to exploit. They presented irresistible invitations to fish in troubled waters. To urge them not to fish, to try to agree not to fish was as futile as talking to a force of nature. One cannot argue with a river; it is going to flow. One can dam it or deflect it, but not argue with it. Therefore, we had been at work to create strength where there had been weakness, to turn our former enemies into allies, to replace the dams that once contained Russia to the east and to the west, to aid growth and progress in the undeveloped areas in the world.[7]

Acheson and the NSC spelled out the details of the policy of containment set forth by George Kennan in 1947.

The Eisenhower-Dulles Era

Acheson's successor as Secretary of State saw it very differently, but only for a while. John Foster Dulles thought that psychological warfare might give us "more bang for the buck." He thought the policy of containment was insufficiently aggressive and probably too expensive for the limited results it might accomplish. Dulles said the new aim must be to make security more effective and less costly

. . . by placing more reliance on deterrent power and less dependence on local defensive power. . . . [If] an enemy could pick his time and place and method of warfare — then we would need to be ready to fight in the Arctic and the tropics, in Asia, the Near East and in Europe, by sea, by land and air with old weapons and with new weapons.

In order to correct this situation Dulles said we would "use the deterrent of massive retaliatory power." We would "depend primarily upon a great capacity to retaliate instantly and at places of our choosing."[8]

This was the doctrine of massive retaliation. In a *Life* magazine piece Dulles referred to it as brinksmanship. We were willing to go to the brink to stop Soviet expansion with nuclear weapons, if necessary. Dulles thought the threat would deter the Soviets from further aggressive action. Instead of money spent all over the world in AID programs to shore up vulnerable nations, the threat of massive retaliation, according to Dulles, would deter the Soviets from adventurous moves. However, there were immediate negative repercussions, especially among our major allies, who were worried that we might start a nuclear war on their territory without their approval. Dulles had stressed the capacity to "retaliate instantly." As the policy moved ahead the United States became more dependent on a nuclear capability that it could not safely use. It soon became clear that alternative policies were needed.

In 1957 Henry Kissinger, then a professor at Harvard, wrote a book sponsored by the Council on Foreign Relations entitled *Nuclear Weapons and Foreign Policy* which provided the intellectual basis for a major shift in the strategic thinking of U.S. leaders. Kissinger asserted that while the United States must retain a capacity to retaliate with all-out nuclear attack, it should also be prepared to retaliate in a more limited manner when the provocation is limited. Kissinger said we must be prepared to wage limited wars with conventional forces or, if necessary, with small nuclear weapons. The limited-war concept challenged the Dulles doctrine of massive retaliation and provoked a sharp debate among strategic planners and thinkers. Kissinger's critics said his approach was unrealistic, because either the U.S. or the U.S.S.R., if it found itself losing a limited war with tactical nuclear weapons, was bound to escalate to strategic weapons. Therefore, it was better to be prepared for all-out nuclear war.[9]

Describing the period leading to this debate a national security scholar, Gordon Turner, said:

There is no question that, in the United States, the total-war school has long been in official favor. The limited-war school, although it has made its voice heard and its influence felt . . . , has been unable to develop either the doctrine or the means to fulfill the nation's security needs. . . . In terms of strategy the total-war school thinks, plans, and talks about massive retaliation, about strategies of deterrence and decisive thrust or about continental strategy. In essence, these terms are interchangeable since they all depend upon the swift and awful striking power of nuclear weapons either to prevent war or to win it quickly. On the other hand, the limited-war school thinks in terms of graduated deterrence, or insular strategy, or what is sometimes called peripheral strategy.[10]

One of the difficulties in understanding national security concepts is the extensive use of gobbledygook. Even if most of it were not hidden under a secrecy umbrella, the average layman could not possibly comprehend what was being said.

At the same time that the debate on limited and total war was being conducted there was debate on communist intentions. A very conservative scholar named Robert Strausz-Hupé, whom Nixon named Ambassador to Sweden, wrote *Protracted Conflict,* a book publicly admired by Acheson, Kissinger, and Admiral

Arleigh Burke of the Joint Chiefs of Staff. It was also praised by Barry Goldwater, who, years later, appointed Strausz-Hupé as foreign affairs advisor for his 1964 campaign. In *Protracted Conflict* Strausz-Hupé stated that

> . . . the Communists are likely to win World War III because they know they are in it. . . . Even if the present parties to the conflict would seek, by mutual consent, to compose it now, the liquidation of the most contested issues would not be completed within the life span of this generation. Hence we must reckon with the extension — the protraction — of the world conflict into the next century.[11]

There was an attempt to link the terror of nuclear weapons to the protracted conflict signaled by communist ideology, in the belief that we could deter Soviet military aggression if we maintained a large enough nuclear arsenal. Edward Teller, the so-called father of the hydrogen bomb, argued that we should not be paralyzed by the fear of nuclear war. He said,

> There is no danger that any atomic bomb of present or future design will ever blow up the earth, the sea, or the atmosphere. This can be stated with all the assurance of which science and common sense are capable. We must rid ourselves of the unreasonable fear of nuclear weapons. These weapons were first used against cities. If military reasons (and considerations of common humanity) prevail, they need never again be used in this fashion. Instead they can be used to neutralize aggression and to provide us with the time in which real solutions can be found to the problems of the modern world.[12]

The Kennedy Era

During the late fifties and early sixties a group of strategic thinkers emerged who had great impact on national security policy. A surprising number of them were mathematicians and physicists — perhaps not so surprising when one looks at the way they think about problems of power and politics. Most were employed, at one time or another, by the Santa Monica, California, "think-tank" known as RAND. The most famous and influential (except for Daniel Ellsberg, who became famous in other ways) was Herman Kahn. In 1960, Kahn wrote *On Thermo-*

nuclear War and followed it with another on the same subject, *Thinking About the Unthinkable.*

While at RAND Kahn had conducted a study of civil defense. He believed it was desirable to take a look at the details of death in an all-out nuclear war. In *On Thermonuclear War* he said:

> It is necessary to be quantitative. . . . [In] describing the aftermath of a war it is not particularly illuminating to use such words as "intolerable," "catastrophic," "total destruction" and so on. Such words would be useful, only if it were really true that in a modern war all possible targets would be overkilled by factors of five or ten.

Kahn did not think that nuclear war would be the end of the world. He believed that with an adequate shelter program and certain other civil defense measures more than half our people could survive the blast and radiation of a nuclear war. He said:

> If we have a posture which might result in 40,000,000 dead in a general war, and as a result of poor planning, apathy, or other causes, our posture deteriorates and a war occurs with 80,000,000 dead we have suffered an additional disaster, an unnecessary additional disaster.[13]

For about a year Kahn's ideas had great impact. When Kennedy became President in 1961 he created a major new civil defense office in the Defense Department. After his meeting with Khrushchev when threatening remarks were made about Soviet intentions in Berlin there was genuine fear of war. As a result, there was a brief spurt of government and private shelter building. When the astronomical costs of a meaningful shelter program were realized, however, most of the enthusiasm vanished. Another influential argument against a massive shelter program was that the process of building such a defense might intensify the danger of a Soviet first strike.

When the arguments for civil defense began to lose ground, the strategy of deterrence was again emphasized. Another RAND man, Albert Wohlstetter, was the architect of a doctrine he called the "delicate balance of terror." Wohlstetter was opposed to sharing nuclear weapons with our allies, the deployment of tactical nuclear weapons, or a large first-strike force and other measures which he felt might be dangerous because they could shift the stability of the "balance of terror." He said,

There are good and bad, that is adequate and inadequate, or stable and unstable deterrents. . . . [The] stability of a deterrent is measured by the shocks it can sustain. A good deterrent is one that works in crises when the risks an adversary might feel in not striking would be very large. We want a deterrent that will make striking with nuclear arms the worst of all possible alternatives available to an adversary, even when the alternatives may look bad. . . . The object of a deterrent is to reduce the chances of war.[14]

Some theorists have claimed that the Cuban missile crisis of 1962 was an excellent example of how the "balance of terror" served to deter nuclear conflict. It is true that Krushchev withdrew his missiles, undoubtedly influenced by the knowledge of our strategic superiority. But what would have happened if Kennedy had not compromised and given his pledge that the United States would not invade Cuba? How important was the human factor — the leadership of the men Krushchev and Kennedy? Krushchev's memoirs contain these revealing statements:

And a compromise over Cuba was indeed found. The episode ended in a triumph of common sense. I'll always remember the late President with deep respect because, in the final analysis, he showed himself to be sober-minded and determined to avoid war. He didn't let himself become frightened, nor did he become reckless. He didn't overestimate America's might, and he left himself a way out of the crisis. He showed real wisdom and statesmanship when he turned his back on right-wing forces in the United States who were trying to goad him into taking military action against Cuba. It was a great victory for us, though, that we were able to extract from Kennedy a promise that neither America nor any of her allies would invade Cuba.[15]

Arthur Herzog, who has studied the whole process of strategic thinking, says,

Where I am forced to doubt analytic thinking is over the question of strategic deterrence itself. As worked out with statistical precision, nuclear deterrence tends to assume that military strategy is itself fearful enough to dominate the logic of the other side. This in turn assumes that fear will keep both sides at nuclear peace at least. There is no doubt that we want to be logical and rational in this situation, but there is a great deal of doubt as to whether we can depend on the mathematics of destruction to keep the peace. Too much of our experience points to illogic and self-destructiveness. The analytic "model" has led it to acquiesce to high levels of nuclear arms as a method of controlling the opponent and managing war. I think those ideas are too narrow and I wonder if the analysts have fought hard enough to change away from the use of military threats.[16]

In *The Necessity for Choice,* Henry Kissinger acknowledged that limited war with nuclear weapons, even tactical ones, was not very practical. He conceded that a strategy of limited conflict with nuclear weapons would be difficult to carry out because we would not be psychologically ready to use them except under such extreme provocation that limited war would be unrealistic, and the aggressor might be tempted to attack because our nuclear threat would not be credible. In order to remedy this problem Kissinger advocated a build up of conventional forces, especially in Europe, which could block attack on the ground. Kissinger said the West should be ready to use nuclear weapons if attacked by nuclear weapons, but the onus for first use should be on the aggressor. This policy still permitted a limited war, but it removed the requirement for using nuclear weapons unless attacked. This new strategy was adopted by the Kennedy Administration.

In a speech in Michigan in early 1962 Secretary of Defense Robert McNamara announced:

The U.S. has come to the conclusion that, to the extent feasible, basic military strategy in a possible general nuclear war should be approached in much the same way that more conventional military operations have been regarded in the past. That is to say, principal military objectives, in the event of nuclear war stemming from major attack on the alliance, should be the destruction of the enemy's military forces not his civilian population. The very strength and nature of the alliance forces make it possible for us to retain reserve striking power to destroy an enemy society if driven to it. In other words we are giving a possible opponent the strongest imaginable incentive to refrain from striking our cities.

McNamara was saying if you don't hit our cities we won't hit yours, but if you do we'll go back to massive retaliation. This refinement on the Dulles policy was hailed as a great improvement, though skeptics pointed out that nuclear bombs don't permit "surgical strikes" because prevailing winds carry lethal fallout to cities.

The major national security problems for the Kennedy Administration though, could not be solved by the strategic arsenal. Four crises erupted — in Cuba, the Congo, Laos, and Vietnam — all involving communist expansion, but none controllable by nuclear power. Former Chairman of the Joint Chiefs of Staff General Maxwell Taylor attacked the Dulles doctrine of "massive retaliation" in *The Uncertain Trumpet* because small wars were much more likely than large ones. Kennedy agreed and recalled Taylor to the White House. In order to deter communist-inspired "wars of national liberation," Taylor, Walt Rostow, Roger Hilsman, and CIA leaders developed a new doctrine known as "counterinsurgency." Counterinsurgency was a whole series of measures, including paramilitary forces, covert political operations, psychological warfare, and economic warfare, designed to assist governments threatened by communist insurgency to defend themselves. Another part of counterinsurgency was the training of special forces, able to be moved rapidly by air and to fight in the jungle or the desert. These forces, called the "Green Berets," were expert in the organization and techniques of guerrilla warfare and were the men who were assigned along with the CIA paramilitary specialists to be the military advisors to the government troops of Laos and Vietnam.

The Johnson Years and Vietnam

The greatest disaster in American history was U.S. involvement in the Vietnam War. That disaster was the logical consequence of misperceptions about U.S. national security which have been amply documented in the *Pentagon Papers* and *The Best and the Brightest* by David Halberstam. The failure in Vietnam had its roots in the strategic doctrines previously discussed and in the early Cold War policies which were adhered to rigidly even though major changes in world affairs had made those policies long out of date. The most fundamental error paving the way to U.S. involvement in Vietnam stemmed from the thinking of John Foster Dulles. After World War II there were two major interrelated forces at work: the bi-polar struggle for power dominated by the U.S. and the U.S.S.R., and the breakup of the European colonial empires.

After Western Europe began to recover from World War II, the Korean War had been settled, and Stalin had died, attention focused on the power vacuums emerging in the Middle East, Africa, and Asia. For Dulles it was very simple: U.S. national security required that the new governments must be anticommunist.

This policy inevitably meant U.S. reliance on rightist, conservative leaders — usually military dictators. But the dynamic force in the newly emerging countries was nationalism, neutralism, and anticolonialism and was sometimes led by communists. Such was the case in Vietnam. Though Ho Chi Minh was a communist, he was first of all a nationalist much like Marshal Tito of Yugoslavia, whom we had the sense to support after he broke with Stalin. The United States had supported Ho Chi Minh against the Japanese during World War II. We shall never know what position Ho would have taken had we supported him in 1954, but we can, in hindsight, make a well-informed guess that he would have adopted an independent position of national communism very similar to that of Tito.

Instead, when the French were defeated in 1954 we gave only lukewarm support to the Geneva Peace Accords and eventually decided to fill the power gap caused by the French departure with Ngo Diem in Saigon. The Geneva Accords had called for a nationwide election in 1956 which everyone knew would be won decisively by Ho Chi Minh. However, we joined with Diem in measures that prevented the election from being held. That was the beginning of the Vietnam tragedy. We acted on grounds of containment of communism and the falling domino theory — i.e., if Ho came to power he would soon take over Laos, Cambodia, Thailand, and so on. Dulles and his advisors had, in the name of anticommunism, decided to block the dynamic spirit of anticolonialism and nationalism. The United States had become the colonial substitute for Japan and France. It was an impossible task then — and still is today.

After the assassination of Diem in 1963, it became clear that a decisive showdown was looming. By 1965 it was apparent that South Vietnam would be cut in two by the Vietcong, and the war would soon be over. So President Johnson began the massive intervention of U.S. forces. It was mistakenly asserted that Ho Chi Minh was a creature of the Chinese. Hanoi's drive was the test case of China's policy of supporting wars of national liberation. If Ho won in South Vietnam the Chinese would press ahead with wars of national liberation throughout Asia, and then Africa and Latin America, so the theory went.

In the face of this danger, contrived by American theorists, the United States took over the war, including most of the fighting, the supplies, and the command. The "whizz-kids" of Secretary McNamara had demonstrated conclusively on their computers that our firepower would provide such a favorable kill ratio that the Vietcong and North Vietnamese would soon be defeated.

We know the rest — bloody, destructive waste, death, and despair resulting in incalculable damage to our nation — our respect for our government, our reputation abroad, and the stability of our economy. Never before in our history have our leaders, as a group, manifested such unwarranted optimism. Some top official — whether the President, the Secretary of State, the Secretary of Defense, or the U.S. Commander in Saigon — was always seeing "a light at the end of the tunnel." The main reason for this was our reliance on military power and our inability — in fact, our blind unwillingness — to look at political reality. The belief and fascination in military power ruled out any serious attempt at negotiation or political solution. The United States gave lip service to negotiations because there was such confidence that victory was in sight. Even when the war became stalemated the answer was never a compromise solution, but always the application of more power. If more troops could be sent and more bombs dropped the enemy would soon be defeated. Unwarranted optimism continued, but the American people were getting fed up; they were beginning to realize that they were being lied to. Then came Tet, the vote in New Hampshire, and the political demise of Lyndon Johnson.

The Nixon Years to the Present

President Nixon and Henry Kissinger did recognize that the Vietnam War was unwinnable, but they took four long years to extricate U.S. troops, during which time thousands of Americans were killed and wounded. They too gave lip service to negotiation, but didn't seriously negotiate until 1971. Instead, they followed the policy of "Vietnamization," meaning that the United States would gradually withdraw its troops while training, equipping, and building South Vietnamese forces so they could defend themselves with continuing military and economic supplies from the United States. The withdrawal of U.S. forces was a very popular goal on the American political scene, and if it could be successfully accomplished during the four-year period it would almost guarantee another four years in the White House for Nixon in 1972.

However, this was a very perilous and tricky course. There was always the danger that as our troop level declined from 550,000 to 350,000 to 150,000, and so on, a point would be reached when the North Vietnamese and Vietcong would attack. A successful attack would endanger our remaining troops and possibly run the risk of losing the war. Therefore, extraordinary precautions were taken, including some that temporarily widened the war. Cambodia and Laos were invaded for short periods of time to break up North Vietnamese supply lines and depots. Cambodia was secretly bombed for months — a secret which obviously was no secret to the communists, but was kept from the Americans through a process involving constant official lying. During the course of the "Vietnamization" process much of South Vietnam was laid in waste in order to protect the orderly retreat of American forces.

Probably the greatest factor though, in the successful withdrawal of U.S. forces, was the changing position of Russia and China. When President Nixon assumed office in 1969 he announced an era of negotiation to replace the era of confrontation, a new approach that paid dividends in many directions. Negotiations were launched almost immediately with the Soviets on strategic arms limitation (SALT). Kissinger and Soviet Ambassador Anatoliy Dobrynin developed an unusually close and productive relationship during these negotiations which became known as the "back channel." Later Kissinger made his secret contacts with the Chinese and the North Vietnamese.

John Newhouse, in a book on the SALT negotiations, *Cold Dawn*, reported on part of the process this way:

> On his twelfth day in office, Nixon instructed Kissinger to look into the possibility of a rapprochement with China. Peking had already sent some faint signals toward the new President. . . . There followed a series of small steps aimed at creating the conditions for a thaw. Washington issued a mild relaxation of trade and travel restrictions. Peking's surprise invitation to the American table tennis team and Premier Chou En-lai's remark that a new page in Chinese-American relations had been turned coincided with the Twenty-Fourth Soviet Party Congress. Soviet leaders must have been aroused by the quickening movement toward the liaison they most feared. And if the handwriting was not on the wall, Kissinger put it there with harsh clarity by suddenly turning up in Peking on July 9, 1971, one day after the start of [the next round of SALT]. Triangular politics had started. Indeed, the United States was playing an old-fashioned Realpolitic, hitherto an alien style. The Salt agreement reached on May 26, 1972, was the product of multiple purposes and forces of which none may have been more critical than Washington's revival of nineteenth-century power politics.[17]

Power politics of the same sort were involved in the negotiations with North Vietnam. The precise details are not yet public, but it is known that both the Soviets and the Chinese pressed Hanoi to work out a truce permitting the completion of the withdrawal of U.S. forces. After months of secret negotiations with Le Duc Tho, Kissinger in October 1972 was able to announce that "peace is at hand." It was not quite "at hand" because Kissinger had been too optimistic about his capacity to deliver the acquiescence of Thieu. Thieu balked at some of the terms, which led the North Vietnamese to hold back. Completely confident of his position, Nixon, after his landslide reelection, launched an all-out bombing attack on Hanoi and Haiphong, and mined the harbor of Haiphong. After ten terrible days Hanoi had had enough, Thieu was satisfied, and negotiations were resumed.

On January 23, 1973, an agreement on "Ending the War and Restoring Peace in Vietnam" was signed by the parties. President Nixon called it an "honorable peace." It was not a peace. It was an agreement which brought an end to the involvement of U.S. forces which, in the period since 1965, had totaled more than 2.5 million men. After the U.S. troop withdrawal there followed what Henry Kissinger called a "decent interval." When the Communists attacked in the spring of 1975 the collapse of the Thieu regime was rapid and total, revealing the awful failure of the policy of "Vietnamization." The consequences of American involvement in Indochina will haunt us for years to come. The future actions of our government, our Congress, and our voters will determine whether we have learned the lesson of this most tragic episode in our history.

Though Vietnam dominated U.S. national security affairs during the years 1965 to 1973 there was some important progress toward relaxation of tensions. The contact with China ended the nonsensical "two-China" policy and provided a basis for normalizing relations with a nation representing one-fourth of the world's population. After so many years of frozen relations and hostility the thawing process undoubtedly will be a slow, step-by-step affair with some reversals along the way.

The even more substantial breakthrough was with the Soviet Union. The several agreements ratified at the Moscow summit in 1972, most notably the interim SALT agreement ending antiballistic missile programs (ABM) and the 1974 Vladivostok agreement limiting offensive weapons, moved the super powers in the direction of detente. Soviet Chairman Leonid Brezhnev has commented that the Moscow agreements and the U.S. withdrawal from Vietnam provide the basis for an irreversible detente.

There can be no question that major changes have occurred in both the United States and the Soviet Union. In the United States, especially, the Vietnam War and Watergate have raised fundamental doubts about the past national security concepts and procedures of our government. As far back as May 1969, less than a year after the Soviet invasion of Czechoslovakia, *Time* magazine and the Harris polling organization asked whether Americans would favor sending U.S. troops to rescue certain of our allies if they were invaded by outside communist military forces; 27 percent said yes if Italy were invaded, 26 percent said yes for West Berlin, 25 percent said yes for Thailand, and 9 percent said yes in the event Israel were being overrun by "Soviet-aided" Arabs.[18] Perhaps the most remarkable of these results is the fact that 74 percent would oppose U.S. military action in West Berlin and 91 percent would oppose such action in Israel. This is a shocking reflex to the Vietnam War, which would undoubtedly be turned around by the right kind of national leadership, but it indicates a dramatic shift away from the Cold War consensus.

Despite the shift, national security managers have resisted changing policy and have perpetuated myths that were inadequately challenged from the outset. The most important was the myth that Soviet forces were planning to invade Western Europe. We now know there was no evidence even in Stalin's time of such intentions. Yet, more than 25 years after the first Cold War alarms were sounded, we still had 300,000 U.S. military personnel in Europe. It had been apparent for years that the primary reason for the Red Army presence in Eastern Europe was not to attack Germany, but rather to defend against attack and to crush independence movements, as occurred most recently in the 1968 invasion of Czechoslovakia.

As it has turned out, the most constructive purpose of U.S. troops in Germany has been to provide a sound argument against the pressures for German rearmament. Now that the Ost-policy of Willy Brandt has brought recognition of East Germany as a new nation and relaxation of tensions between Germany and Eastern Europe, there is even more reason to question the present level of U.S. troops. The main consideration was that we

were negotiating a mutual and balanced force-reduction agreement with the Soviets whereby they would phase out of Eastern
Europe as we phased out of Western Europe. If we reduced our
forces unilaterally our bargaining position would have been
weakened. Valid as these arguments may have been, it has long
been clear that the main function of NATO and the U.S. troop
presence is political and not military.

Another basic myth which lingers on is the threat of monolithic, cohesive communism. The bi-polar world of the two camps
dominated by the United States and Soviet Union has been dead
for more than fifteen years, but the peril of international communism is still raised by national security managers. Actually,
every "revolutionary government that has come to power without
the Red Army has turned out to be ambivalent, cool or even
hostile to the Soviet Union," including China, Yugoslavia, North
Vietnam, Albania, and Cuba.[19]

One of the great ironies of our times is that while we reach out
for detente with the Soviets we continue to hold Cuba at arm's
length. If we restored relations with Cuba we would certainly
lessen Soviet influence and would return to our normal source of
sugar, thus reducing the astronomical price. Perhaps a small
point, but illustrative of the destructive influence of some of the
myths we have lived with for so long.

Another sad aspect of the national security mythology is the
need for maintaining reputation at all costs. American leaders
have recently taken a stance that they should not admit mistakes.
Unlike the refreshing candor of De Gaulle who admitted that
France should not be in Algeria, or of Kennedy who said the Bay
of Pigs was a colossal blunder, Johnson and Nixon could not
acknowledge mistakes. Thomas Schelling, a Harvard national
security scholar, has said, "reputation is one of the few things
worth fighting for." Nixon said we must never be thought of as a
"pitiful, helpless giant." So, in the process of proving we were
not, we persisted in Vietnam to maintain our reputation and
prestige despite catastrophic consequences.[20]

Maxwell Taylor has said:

National security, once a trumpet call to the nation to man the ramparts and repel invaders, has fallen into disrepute. A victim of complications arising from the Vietnam syndrome and from its own internal contradictions, it has come to signify in many minds unreasonable military demands, excessive defense budgets and collusive dealings with the military-industrial complex. Watergate revelations have fueled suspicions that it may be little more than a cover for executive encroachments upon civil liberties and a free press.

General Taylor goes on to define national security as

. . . current assets and national interests, as well as the sources of strength upon which our future as a nation depends. . . . [They] range widely from political assets such as the Bill of Rights, our political institutions and international friendships, to many economic assets which radiate worldwide from a highly productive domestic economy supported by rich natural resources. It is the urgent need to protect valuables such as these which legitimizes and makes essential the role of national security.[21]

General Taylor is undoubtedly correct when he says national security has fallen into "disrepute," but the rhetoric he has used does little toward restoring legitimacy and spelling out essential security needs. The vague expression "national interests" just won't work any longer, and there are real problems with "economic assets which radiate worldwide." The time has come to define our security stakes much more precisely. The American taxpayer is no longer willing to foot the bill for the protection of private investment abroad, whether the protection is accomplished overtly or covertly, as was the case in the CIA activities in Chile on behalf of ITT and the copper companies.

The nation's security should never be dependent on the profit motives of Americans who invest abroad, including such politically sensitive commodities as oil. Lincoln Bloomfield, a political science professor at MIT, puts it well when he says,

A list of what we have been actually doing everywhere . . . is no longer acceptable by even a majority of Americans as enabling them to infer a valid statement of American interests and national purpose for the period ahead. Indeed, we have been badly served by the invocation of something mystical called the "national interest" as a substitute for the hard, painful analysis needed to devise coherent national policies.[22]

The need to know what we mean by national security becomes even more crucial as we move into a national debate about how far and how fast we should move in the direction of detente with the Russians — a relaxation of tensions to reduce the danger of war. We need to assess the changes in Soviet ideology which have occurred since George Kennan wrote the "containment" doctrine. Even today some Soviet spokesmen refer to peaceful coexistence as a "form of class struggle requiring ideological conflict to be intensified during detente." Some Soviet writers assert that the United States will weaken as a result of internal economic and political problems which will inevitably lead to the victory of Soviet power. U.S. critics call Chairman Brezhnev's advocacy of detente merely a tactic designed to lull us into lowering our guard. Despite the reaffirmation of some of the old themes, there has been a noticeable change in the reverence accorded to Marxist-Leninist dogma, especially in the new generation of Soviet leaders. It is time to pay more attention to Soviet action with respect to such things as strategic arms control and operations in the Middle East, rather than the words of a fading ideology.

The Soviets do have an advantage over the United States because their closed society permits them to avoid domestic political repercussions which might otherwise be encouraged by a relaxation of tensions. In the United States however, the rhetoric of detente leads to optimistic assumptions and calls for cuts in the defense budget and unilateral dismantling of "obsolete" Cold War assets. Secretary of Defense James Schlesinger, in an interview with the *New York Times,* said:

Democracies are suffering from their traditional problem — they need an overt manifest threat in order to bring about the appropriate allocation of resources within the society to maintain a defense establishment that continues to deter rather than to rely on the goodwill of potential opponents.[23]

But in stressing the need for "an overt manifest threat" there is always emphasis on the potential dangers and reluctance to pursue the opportunities for detente. As in the United States, there are proponents and opponents of detente in the Kremlin. Soviet military leaders are advancing skeptical arguments almost identical with those coming from the Pentagon. The views of Moscow hawks tend to reinforce the views of Washington hawks, and vice versa.

Some opponents of detente contend that we should not make any concessions for the purpose of relaxing tensions until there have been fundamental changes in the Soviet system. However, such changes will not occur through liberation, nor is revolution a likely prospect. If the only hope for change in Soviet society is through evolutionary processes, then increased contact and negotiation between the adversaries is essential. If Soviet leaders become less fearful of external threats, they may, in time, move more willingly to relax their internal controls, their police state. American opponents of detente claim that a policy of relaxing tensions is inconsistent with our abhorrence of Soviet repression, maintaining that detente gives comfort and respectability to a regime which has no regard for human freedom. In the long run, however, it may be that the only way to end repression is through the gradual elimination of paranoia among Soviet leaders.

The pace and scope of detente has become the subject of a major debate in both Moscow and Washington. There is no consensus in either capitol such as existed during the Cold War, and it will probably take several years to establish such a consensus — especially in the United States. This is the central issue of U.S. national security policy.

American thinking has been influenced by Russian dissidents, especially the Nobel Prize–winning writer Aleksandr Solzhenitsyn, now in exile, the nuclear physicist Andrei Sakharov, and Soviet historian Roy Medvedev. All three are renowned critics of contemporary Soviet society but have sharp disagreement with each other. Solzhenitsyn, in a letter to the Soviet leaders, urged the abandonment of communist ideology, giving up Eastern Europe and the non-Russian republics of the U.S.S.R., turning away from industrial growth, beginning a new society in the virgin territories of Siberia which would preserve old Russian values and the orthodox religion. He said that the government should remain authoritarian since Russians are unprepared for democracy.

Sakharov, in a published response, accused Solzhenitsyn of "religious-patriarchal romanticism" and said his proposals based on "Russian nationalism are alien to me." Sakharov supports detente, but only if Soviet citizens are given the right freely to leave and return to their country. He says:

It would become impossible to retain anti-democratic institutions in this country, it would become necessary to bring living standards in line with those in the West, and the conditions would arise for a free exchange of people and ideas."[24]

Medvedev says the opponents of detente in Russia are the mirror image of Americans who are against relaxing tensions. Speaking of these "reactionaries," Medvedev says:

They are afraid that along with goods and machines, ideas and views will start penetrating into this country from the West. They are afraid that the Soviet people will get from detente not only material wellbeing, but also a different view of reality, different from the many myths of today's propaganda. These dogmatists see only an aggressive imperialist state in the U.S. that wants to impose its power on the whole world and to destroy the Soviet way of life first of all. They would welcome destruction or economic bankruptcy of the U.S., but since they can't achieve that, they want to separate our country from the West and the U.S. by an iron curtain.
The anti-Kremlin radicals in this country on the other hand try to prove that detente and cooperation with the West will only strengthen the Soviet bureaucracy, helping it to solve difficult internal problems with the use of trade and credit from the capitalist states. They think that such a situation weakens the development of opposition movements among the Soviet people and makes the collapse of the hated Soviet system less likely. . . . Detente is a long process and we are still at the start. Each step forward must be accompanied by concessions on both sides, but it is still impossible to expect big concessions, and demands for them will look like ultimatums.[25]

In the United States those who are skeptical about the merits of any substantial relaxation of tensions at this time are led by Senator Henry Jackson (D.–Wash.) and include Secretary of Defense Schlesinger, the Joint Chiefs of Staff, AFL-CIO President

George Meany, Barry Goldwater (R.–Arizona), and some Jewish leaders. The proponents of detente are led by Secretary of State Henry Kissinger, most of the members of the Senate Foreign Relations Committee, and most of the Soviet experts, including former U.S. ambassadors to Moscow Averell Harriman and George Kennan and such scholars as Adam Ulam of Harvard and Marshall Shulman of Columbia.

Senator Jackson does not think that U.S. negotiators like Kissinger have been tough enough in their bargaining with the Soviets. Jackson charged that the interim SALT agreement gave the Soviets an advantage, and he has been a sharp critic of Soviet measures to stifle internal dissent. Charging that the Soviet supply of arms to Egypt and Syria was primarily responsible for the Yom Kippur war in 1973, he asserts that Soviet action in the Middle East demonstrates the speciousness of their claims for detente. His amendment to the trade bill pressured the Soviets to pledge freer emigration for Jews wishing to go to Israel. The pressure went too far, resulting in a Soviet rejection of the trade bill and a sharp decline in Jewish emigration from Russia.

Jackson also challenged the guidelines for strategic weapons limits worked out by Ford and Kissinger with Brezhnev in Vladivostok. He claimed that we should insist on lowering the level of strategic weapons on both sides. Kissinger and his supporters, on the other hand, warned that detente, in these early stages, is very fragile and the opponents in the Kremlin are likely to win out if we demand too much.

Detente is made up of many interrelated issues including strategic arms, conventional forces, weapons supplied to third areas such as the Middle East, trade, human rights, cultural exchange, and clandestine operations. A true relaxation of tensions will involve progress in all of these areas, but by far the most important is strategic arms limitation because nuclear missiles pose a threat to national security on both sides. Secretary of Defense Schlesinger has been opposed to ending the arms race. He thinks it essential that we maintain our weapons superiority because of what he calls the importance of perceptions and asks, "How will others see the balance? Will others not regard imbalances favoring Moscow as a sign of disintegrating American will?"[26] Schlesinger, believing that we must be manifestly superior in weaponry to demonstrate that we will deliver on our world responsibilities, says, "The burden for the maintenance of free societies can only be borne by the U.S. We must accept that. There is no alternative. If the U.S. drops the torch there is no one else that can pick it up."[27]

Schlesinger's remarks are in sharp contrast with the thinking of another Secretary of Defense, Robert McNamara, who in his best speech said,

> . . . neither conscience nor sanity itself suggest that the U.S. is, should, or could be the global gendarme. . . . The U.S. has no mandate from on high to police the world, and no inclination to do so. . . . The plain truth is the day is coming when no single nation, however powerful, can undertake by itself to keep the peace outside its own borders. Regional and international organizations for peacekeeping purposes are as yet rudimentary, but they must grow in experience and be strengthened by deliberate and practical cooperative action.[28]

Schlesinger has received authorization from Congress to proceed with the research and development of what he calls a counterforce to protect the United States from a possible first strike on our hardened missile sites. Leslie Gelb of the *New York Times* says:

> The critics think Schlesinger has gone mad. They see no need for these new weapons systems. They point out that one Poseidon submarine now can strike at 160 different targets, with each warhead having the force of some 60 kilotons, or more than three times the Hiroshima bomb. They cite the fact that there are no more than 40 Soviet cities with populations over 100,000. As to the need for greater missile accuracy for the counterforce option they cite the fact that present accuracies are around one quarter of a nautical mile. They see no end to the nuclear arms race unless Washington is prepared to show some unilateral restraint.[29]

Senator Thomas J. McIntyre (D.–N.H.), who is Chairman of the Senate Armed Services subcommittee on research and development, has vigorously opposed Schlesinger's counterforce proposals. He said:

These counterforce programs will put a hair trigger on nuclear war. The stable nuclear peace that the world has enjoyed in recent years has been secured by the confidence each side has had in the survivability of its retaliatory force — even after all out attack. This stability would be undermined by greater counterforce capabilities on either side. Our threat to Soviet intercontinental missiles might motivate them to strike first in a period of international tension. These programs, therefore, produce an international Wild West filled with fears and dangers of a nuclear "fast gun."[30]

There is still hope that the "hair trigger" situation predicted by Senator McIntyre may not materialize if the counterforce weapons never get beyond the stage of research and development, which will be the case if sufficient agreement is reached with the Soviets during the next few years to end the arms race and begin the slow process of disarmament. It will mean that those who are willing to accept parity with the Soviets, instead of insisting on superiority, win the policy debate. The United States has a three-to-one lead in nuclear warheads over the Soviets. The United States has three times as many strategic bombers, each capable of carrying up to twenty-four nuclear weapons. The United States has quiet submarines equipped with multiple independently targeted reentry vehicles (MIRV) missiles and forward bases in Scotland, Spain, and Guam. The Soviets do not have quiet submarines (they are vulnerable to U.S. sophisticated antisubmarine warfare techniques), they do not have forward bases, and as of mid-1975 they had not yet tested sub-launched MIRV's. It is generally agreed that submarines have become the most important weapon to assure second-strike capability.

In view of these facts, the proponents of detente argue that now is the time to stop building new weapons and to end the arms race. The core problem is that the United States with MIRV has a huge lead in nuclear warheads. The Soviets are not going to agree to disarmament until they have caught up with the United States.

The trouble with the Ford-Brezhnev agreement is that it puts a "cap" of 2400 missiles, 1320 of which may be MIRV'd, for each side until 1985. Since the Soviets won't have MIRV's deployed on their missiles for some time — especially sub-launched missiles — the "cap" agreement means that the arms race will continue until the Soviets feel that they are equal with us, and the incredibly wasteful expenditures will continue. The only way to stop this would be for the United States to agree to hold to a lower MIRV'd missile level and let the Soviets catch up with that figure rather than moving to 1320. On the other hand, if we continue to press for an extension of our present superiority through technological advances and new weapons systems, the arms race will continue indefinitely.

Senator Jackson has argued that we should insist on a lower number of intercontinental ballistic missiles (ICBM's) on both sides. The Soviets have more and larger ICBM's which, when they achieve MIRV, would permit them to have a numerical advantage in this weapon. However, the United States has a counterbalancing lead in strategic bombers and a huge lead in tactical bombers and nuclear weapons in Europe and Asia. The United States is also well advanced on the B-1 strategic bomber, which may replace the B-52, and the gigantic Trident nuclear submarine. Jackson, under the guise of advocating disarmament, is actually attempting to block genuine parity of nuclear weapons. He has been a consistent supporter of U.S. strategic superiority and the continuing arms race.

The dangers of nuclear war have been reduced substantially since the height of the Cold War, but there are still points of potential explosion, such as the Middle East. In addition, a very real new danger exists which affects our national security even more than the threat of war — the state of the economy, the peril of growing inflation, recession, and possible depression. Our defense budget has been bloated for years with the incredible waste of the Vietnam War. But even though that war is no longer ours, our defense budget is higher than ever. The inflation caused by the Vietnam War accounts for part of the increase, though by no means all.

We have a huge defense budget principally because we are still engaging in an unnecessary arms race and maintaining a capacity to fight one and a half wars at once (a concept that dates back to World War II). We can no longer, if we ever could, afford the luxury of this kind of defense budget. When weighing the balance of a defense program which equips us to fight wars that we should never be in, against an economic decline that very definitely threatens our national security, the answer should be obvious. However, as this is written, there is no sign that either the Ford Administration or the Democratic leadership is prepared to take action.

An important reason for this tragic condition is the secrecy surrounding national security. Because of this secrecy a few men are able to make decisions which can affect the lives of us all, with very little accountability to the public. In fact, as we have seen, under the secret cover of national security a President of the United States and a few of his assistants engaged in conspiracy against the American people.

The nonsense of secrecy has reached "Alice in Wonderland" proportions as illustrated in the following conundrum: The U.S. government used to keep information secret from the American people so that it wouldn't reach the Soviet government, but now the U.S. government keeps information secret from the American people because the Soviet government doesn't want it to reach the Russian people. For example, two parts of the interim SALT agreement were kept secret because, according to Secretary Kissinger, the Russians were willing to share sensitive information with U.S. officials, but not with their own public. Senator Kennedy asked about this problem on a trip to Moscow in 1974 and was told that the Russian people would not understand the drive for detente if discussion of nuclear rivalry and the arms race were associated with detente.[31] Perhaps so, but why should the U.S. government collaborate with the Soviet government in blocking information also from the American people?

Another, directly related, reason for our tragic condition is that national security secrecy has been used, not to protect information from falling into the hands of our adversaries, but to deceive the American people. As Secretary of Defense Schlesinger says, "Democracies . . . need an overt manifest threat in order to bring about the appropriate allocation of resources . . . to maintain a defense establishment." People won't spend money for national defense if they are not afraid. So what has happened through the years is that military leaders, at budget times especially, have contrived a threat. While there has always been some legitimate national security threat, the Pentagon has invariably magnified and distorted it. Thus, we have seen since the midfifties a "bomber gap," a "missile gap," a Soviet ABM system which didn't exist, and more recently a "throw-weight gap." (This means that the Soviets have bigger ICBM's capable of sending larger warheads. We gave up large ICBM's because we found the smaller ones more accurate and efficient.) In all cases the purpose was to scare the American people into the belief that the Soviets had a dangerous advantage.

Senator Thomas McIntyre, one of the few members of Congress who has done his homework on strategic weapons, said in a speech in June 1974:

> When the Pentagon is playing for big stakes it is inclined to print testimony long on scare words and exageration, but short on candor and objectivity. My criticism of the Pentagon has two goals: (1) To help us get the best defense for the dollar — without wasting a single dollar. (2) To help maintain required national security without escalating the arms race or provoking a nuclear catastrophe. Emotion and symbols have replaced fact and trust. Only the emergence of a "responsible center" in the defense debate can bring about a rational defense policy — that "responsible center" would reject both the insanity of a defense policy which would escalate the arms race and provoke nuclear confrontation and the idiocy of unilateral disarmament.[32]

Richard Barnet, a one-time member of the government national security establishment, says in *Roots of War:*

> [A] great root of war is the vulnerability of the public to manipulation on national security issues. People do not perceive where their true interests lie and hence are easily swayed by emotional appeals to support policies that cost them their money, their sons, and their own lives. Because they have been willing to accept uncritically the

myth of the national interest — i.e., the definition advanced by the national security managers — they exercise almost no control over the commitments the managers make in their name. Supposedly the beneficiaries of national security policy, they become its hostages. There can be a foreign policy which really protects the interests of all Americans only if those interests are articulated in the political process.[33]

As we have seen, there are genuine issues of security which do call for adequate protective measures and public support. But one of the most destructive developments of the Cold War has been the deception of the American people. Nothing, including the Russians, has been more damaging to our democracy than the fear mongers, the manufacturers of danger, and the Cold War power manipulators.

Some of the national security managers, joined by certain favored pundits, have cried "wolf" too many times. Because they think the public may not be adequately responsive they have become phony patriots, galloping along, calling, "The Reds are coming, the Reds are coming," unlike Paul Revere, who was warning of the real thing. This manipulation of fear can be just as destructive in national terms as the cry of "fire" in a crowded theater when there is no fire. How much better it would be to risk a little information to our opponents and, at the same time, level with the American people with a fair, full, open disclosure of our security needs — that way there would be public response, trust in government, health in our democratic system, and adequate security. It is true there also undoubtedly would be a sharply reduced defense budget and new ways of looking at our responsibilities abroad.

2

The Growth of the
U.S. Secrecy System

One of the most difficult problems for democratic government is maintaining adequate national security while preserving basic freedoms. All totalitarian regimes emphasize control and security at the expense of freedom. In the United States, until World War II and the Cold War, our government was much more concerned with freedom than security. When confronted by the totalitarian power of Japan and Nazi Germany followed by Stalin's Communism we began to give priority to security — to national survival. The public accepted the argument that secrecy was essential to our self-protection. Secret government depends on broad public trust that leaders are making secret decisions in response to legitimate threats to national survival. When public fear is manipulated and dangers are contrived, trust breaks down, freedom is jeopardized, and responses to real threats to national security are diluted. This we have experienced during the past decade.

Early Secrecy

The articles of war in 1775 prohibited any unauthorized correspondence by soldiers with an enemy, and there has been legislation since 1776 forbidding spying by civilians in time of war.[1] When the Constitutional Convention met in Philadelphia in 1787 the proceedings were conducted in secret, with press and public excluded. Not until 1820 were the restrictions removed, permitting the publication and distribution of the Convention records. Nowhere in the Constitution or any of its amendments is there a provision for secrecy in the activities of the executive or judicial branches of government. However, the so-called house-keeping statute adopted in 1789 as Article I, Section 5, did authorize the House and Senate to publish a journal of proceedings, "excepting such parts as may in their judgment require secrecy." This statute, finally amended by Congress in 1958, was utilized to withhold information from the public on a wide range of government actions extending beyond information relating to foreign and defense policy.[2]

From the beginning of our Republic, the President, under authority of Article II, Section 2, of the Constitution as the Commander in Chief, has restricted the dissemination of information relating to defense and foreign policy. The first instance of the use of this authority occurred when President Washington in 1790 presented, for Senate approval, a secret article to be inserted into a treaty with the Creek Indians.[3] The Federalists interpreted the Constitution as providing for executive secrecy in diplomatic negotiation where "perfect secrecy and immediate dispatch are sometimes requisite"; and in "the business of intelligence [where] the most useful intelligence may be obtained if the persons possessing it can be relieved of the apprehensions of discovery."[4]

Despite the recognition that certain secrecy was necessary, there was strong support for disclosure of information. The earliest precedent for leaking secret information occurred in 1794 when Chief Justice John Jay negotiated a treaty with England, attempting to resolve some of the controversies of the Revolutionary War. The treaty called for the obligation of funds, so the House of Representatives sought the instructions to Jay and the documents supporting the treaty. In rejecting the request President Washington said,

. . . the papers called for can throw no light, and as it is essential to the due administration of the government that the boundaries fixed by the Constitution between the different departments should be preserved, a just regard to the Constitution and to the duty of my office, under all the circumstances of this case, forbids a compliance with your request.[5]

Southerners in Congress were incensed at the way the treaty had been handled, and Senator Stevens Mason of Virginia sent the secret treaty to a newspaper in Philadelphia, which published it amidst great furor.

In the War of 1812, "Secret," "Confidential," and "Private" marking were used on military information,[6] but no significant system of secrecy emerged during the entire nineteenth century. In 1844 President Tyler was blocked in his desire to avoid public debate of the annexation of Texas when he tried to gain approval of a secret treaty in the Senate. Senator Benjamin Tappan of Ohio arranged to leak the treaty which was published by William Cullen Bryant in the *Evening Post*. In 1848, when the Senate was debating the merits of the Treaty of Guadalupe Hidalgo providing for an end to the War with Mexico, the *New York Herald* published the complete text. There is no record of the source of this leak. The publication of the Pentagon Papers, in retrospect, seems much less significant than the disclosure of secret treaties still to be ratified.[7]

There was very little preoccupation with systematic secrecy during the period leading up to the Civil War. President Polk in a message to Congress in 1846 said, "I am fully aware of the strong and correct public feeling which exists throughout the country against secrecy of any kind in the administration of government." The emphasis in government was on broad disclosure of public policy and decision making. Even during the Civil War, the gravest crisis in our history, there was no system of official secrecy, no Sedition Act, and no Espionage Act. Lincoln did suspend habeas corpus, and did authorize the censorship of mail and the suppression of some newspapers, because there was a widespread fear of spies and Copperheads. Secretary of State William Seward maintained a network of secret agents to apprehend Confederate spies, collaborators, and sympathizers. But Lincoln in his second inaugural address said, "The progress of our arms, upon which all else chiefly depends, is as well known to the public as to myself."

In 1869 the War Department established the first formal

peacetime security procedures with the following order: "Commanding officers of troops occupying the regular forts built by the Engineer Department will permit no photographic or other views of the same to be taken without the permission of the War Department." As a result of deteriorating relations with Spain which later led to the Spanish-American War, the War Department issued a new General Order in March 1897 which said, in part:

No persons except officers of the Army and Navy of the U.S., and persons in the service of the U.S. employed in direct connection with the use, construction or care of these works, will be allowed to visit any portion of the lake and coast defenses of the U.S. without the written authority of the Commanding Officer in Charge.[8]

Quite clearly the security precautions were minimal and did not infringe on civil rights or public participation in the process of government.

In 1912 the War Department directed that certain records would be considered "confidential," including submarine mine projects, land defense plans, tables, maps and charts showing defense locations, number of guns, and character of armament. But it was not until the United States had entered World War I that the War Department adopted in November 1917 a system, patterned after those of the British and French, calling for classification of information as "Secret," "Confidential," and "For Official Circulation Only." Material designated "Secret" could not be disclosed; material designated "Confidential" could be circulated to persons known to be authorized to receive it; and "Official Circulation" material could be circulated to official sources, but not to the press or public.

The Espionage Act became law in June 1917. The Act provided, among other things, that it shall be unlawful to disseminate information relating to vital military or naval installations or equipment or "classified information" relating to cryptographic and communication systems and facilities. The law also provided for imprisonment or the death penalty for

. . . (a) communicating or transmitting a document or information relating to the national defense to any foreign government, faction, citizen, etc., with intent or reason to believe that it is to be used to the injury of the United States or to the advantage of a foreign nation; or (b) in time of war, with intent that the same shall be communicated to the enemy, collecting, publishing, communicating, or attempting to elicit any information with respect to the movement, numbers, or disposition of armed forces, ships, aircraft, or war materials or military operations, plans or defenses or any other information relating to the public defense which might be useful to the enemy.

The Espionage Act did not make reference to the military classification system, and there was no provision for different levels or degrees of security classification. Though codes and cryptography were given special attention in the Espionage Act, the protection of secrets seemed so unimportant by the late twenties that Secretary of State Henry L. Stimson disbanded the codebreaking section because "gentlemen do not read other gentlemen's mail."[9] Robert Murphy, former Undersecretary of State, wrote in his memoirs that there were "practically no security precautions in the State Department prior to the war."

Though the Espionage Act was designed for conditions of war, the Army issued a regulation in 1935 dealing with so-called "restricted" military projects. It read:

Restricted: Notice — this document contains information affecting the national defense of the United States within the meaning of the Espionage Act. The transmission of this document or the revelation of its contents in any manner to any unauthorized person is prohibited.[10]

In 1937, Army regulations specified, "to reveal secret, confidential, or restricted matter pertaining to the national defense is a violation of the Espionage Act." These regulations were issued without any clear statutory authority, and were not tested in the courts.[11]

World War II and National Security

Widespread use of secrecy to control the dissemination of information emerged for the first time in U.S. history in World War

II. As the threat from Nazi Germany became more apparent each day, President Roosevelt issued Executive Order 8381 in March 1940 which

> . . . controlled all official military or naval books, pamphlets, documents, reports, maps, charts, plans, designs, models, drawings, photographs or specifications marked under the authority of the Secretary of War or the Secretary of Navy as secret, confidential or restricted.

President Roosevelt maintained that the substance of his order was already provided for in an Act of Congress (Public Law 418, January 1938) which called for criminal action against violators and a $1,000 fine and/or imprisonment of up to one year.

With the shock of Pearl Harbor and U.S. entry into the war came a growing preoccupation with secrecy. In September 1942 the Office of War Information issued a regulation controlling the identification, handling, and dissemination of sensitive information. It defined three categories of classification:

> *Secret information* is information the disclosure of which might endanger national security, or cause serious injury to the Nation or any governmental activity thereof; *Confidential information* is information the disclosure of which although not endangering the national security would impair the effectiveness of government activity in the prosecution of war; *Restricted information* is information the disclosure of which should be limited.

The authority for this OWI regulation has not been identified by historians nor was the term "national security" defined, but this classification system for the first time in our history went beyond military and defense information. Soon most of the government was using the classification system.

As the war progressed, the public was made aware of the importance of secrecy by a very effective campaign mounted by the OWI. The public was briefed constantly on the dangers of espionage. The ruthless techniques of Otto Himmler and the Gestapo were soon part of the American consciousness. The "Fifth Column" was known by most Americans as one of the Gestapo methods for penetrating foreign countries. Effective movies appeared, showing how spies could listen to an innocent conversation and pick up valuable information about troop movements. One of the most memorable posters showed a stern Uncle Sam with his finger on his lips; the caption said, "A slip of the lip can sink a ship." Families became aware that they must not talk about the whereabouts or experiences of their soldier sons. It was not long before secrecy became equated with patriotism.

Americans came to understand that their national survival was at stake — the country was in greater danger than at any time since the Civil War. It was not surprising, therefore, that there was so little protest over censorship of the mails and the press. Often letters would be received from overseas almost unreadable because censors had scissored out so much of the contents. But Americans did not grumble about the security measures because they understood and trusted their leaders' explanation of the necessity for secrecy. In fact, most Americans took great pride in successful security. The value of secrecy was most dramatically demonstrated when the Nazis were unable to ascertain the time and place of the Normandy invasion. And in October 1974 the world learned for the first time that the British, helped by Americans, had broken the German code in 1943, thus having access to most of the battle secrets of Hitler and his field commanders. That this secret was held for more than thirty years was a fantastic accomplishment.

World War II also marked the baptism of U.S. participation in the murky world of clandestine operations and espionage. Six months before Pearl Harbor, President Roosevelt created the Office of the Coordinator of Information (COI) led by William H. ("Wild Bill") Donovan, a World War I hero, Wall Street lawyer, and Republican politician. After the United Stated entered the war the propaganda functions of COI were split off and added to OWI, with the Donovan organization renamed the Office of Strategic Services (OSS). The United States had some limited experience in military intelligence and naval intelligence, but Americans were babes in the woods when it came to clandestine operations and espionage. Roosevelt was persuaded by Donovan that the United States needed an arm to combat the Gestapo and to provide support and encouragement to potential resistance movements in Nazi-occupied countries. At that time the British had the finest secret service in the World. So, much of what was learned by oss agents came from British tutelage, but a significant part came from the inventiveness and imagination of Donovan and his lieutenants.

By the end of the war Donovan had put together an organization of more than 12,000 men and women. They made some serious blunders and wasted a considerable amount of money, but they also provided some extraordinarily vital information and conducted some very successful operations, including the arrangement for the surrender of all German forces in Italy. The oss carried out some of the most sensitive operations in U.S. history — usually classified "Top Secret," a category which had been added to the U.S. classification system inspired by the British marking of "Most Secret." The oss had five major functions, including: secret intelligence (si) or espionage; secret operations (so), aid to resistance movements, blowing up bridges, troop trains, etc.; counterintelligence (ci); morale operations (mo), black propaganda and deception operations to break down enemy morale; and research and analysis (r&a), the division which analyzed all the information, including open sources, and made intelligence estimates.

Representing the most secret side of the war, and with a nickname of "Oh So Secret," in fact, most of the operatives of oss were not enamored with secrecy. Most of them were mavericks, swashbuckling adventurers who found it appealing to be able to fight a war without being tied up in the military routine and bureaucracy; or they were professors and thinkers who found in oss the only means to use their training and talents to help the war effort. The oss was made up of a strange combination of prominent businessmen, labor leaders, athletes, ex-criminals and Mafia, society ladies, and communists. Whatever their background, many of them had talent, courage, and tremendous motivation to defeat the Axis powers. Morale was very high in oss.

Speaking of communists General Donovan once said, "I'd put Stalin on the oss payroll if I thought it would help us defeat Hitler."[12] The oss employed known communists who were often effective links to the resistance movements.

Donovan found that political leftists were often the most valiant field officers in his espionage and sabotage branches. When the FBI demanded the ouster of three communists from the organization, Donovan responded, "I know they're communists; that's why I hired them."[13]

On another occasion Donovan was accused of using a man who was on the honor roll of the Young Communist League. "I don't know if he's on the communist honor roll," the General replied, "but for the job he did in Africa and Italy he's on the honor roll of oss."[14]

The oss was operating under instructions to carry out clandestine operations which would undermine the enemy and hasten the end of the war. Some of the most effective resistance movements were being led or aided by communists. That is why oss agents and supplies were parachuted into Tito's "Partisans" in Yugoslavia, or Italian, French, and Greek resistance groups led by communists, or to Ho Chi Minh and other Asian communists fighting the Japanese. Stalin was our ally, and the courageous record of the Red Army on the Eastern Front was acknowledged with admiration by Americans everywhere. The war ended with a mood of euphoria and anticipation of an era of peace.

The Cold War and the National Security Act

It was with considerable shock that the public gradually became aware in late 1945 and 1946 that the communists considered us to be "imperialists" and enemies. The agreements which Roosevelt and Churchill had made with Stalin at Teheran and Yalta were being violated. The Red Army, instead of moving out of Eastern Europe, was remaining and installing, by force, communist regimes in Poland, Rumania, Bulgaria, and later in Hungary. There were already communist governments in Yugoslavia and Albania which provided bases for the Greek communist guerrillas waging civil war against the government. In Iran the Soviets encouraged the organization of a communist party called "Tudeh" (Masses), and Soviet forces were withdrawn from Iran only after great diplomatic pressure and UN action, two months after the agreed deadline.

In 1947 Moscow announced the formation of the "Cominform," an association of the communist parties of the Soviet Union, France, Italy, and six Eastern European "popular democracies." The "Cominform," a sort of successor to the "Comintern," was run by Moscow and provided a mechanism for centralized propaganda and political-action guidance. It soon became apparent that the communist resistance leaders who had been supported by the United States during the war were agents of Moscow, with loyalties to the Soviet Union rather than to their own countries. For example, French and Italian communist leaders did not represent legitimate national political parties; their first loyalty was to Moscow and the expansion of Soviet power through political subversion. Even in the United States some communists openly admitted their allegiance to Moscow-led international communism.

It was in this atmosphere that the "Truman Doctrine" was launched in March 1947, setting forth U.S. programs to stop the advance of communism in Greece and Turkey through economic and military assistance. In July 1947 George Kennan, head of policy planning in the State Department, in his famous "Mr. X" article enunciated the policy of "containment." Essentially Kennan said that it should be the policy of the United States to contain communism throughout the world, to keep it within existing boundaries, and to build our resources and those of our allies to block expansion of communism anywhere. The "policy of containment" became the strategy of the U.S. government for dealing with communism throughout the Cold War.

At the same time that the "policy of containment" was being explored in public discussion, Congress was adopting President Truman's recommendations for a National Security Act. The Act, passed in July 1947, provided for a substantial reorganization of national security affairs. It created, for the first time, a National Security Council (NSC) to be presided over by the President to provide "integration of domestic, foreign, and military policies relating to the national security so as to enable the military services and the other departments and agencies of the Government to cooperate more effectively in matters involving national security."

The Act also established the Department of Defense to replace the former separate War and Navy Departments. Under the Secretary of Defense are a Deputy Secretary and three new departments of Air, Navy, and Army, each with a Secretary in charge but reporting directly to the overall Secretary of Defense. A fundamental purpose of this part of the Act was to unify the armed services. This was further developed by the creation of a Joint Chiefs of Staff composed of the chiefs of staff of each of the military services, with a chairman appointed by the President with the advice and consent of the Senate.

The National Security Act was the authority too for the creation of the Central Intelligence Agency (CIA). The duties of CIA, under the direction of the NSC are:

(1) to advise the National Security Council in matters concerning such intelligence activities of the government departments and agencies as relate to national security;

(2) to make recommendations to the National Security Council for the coordination of such intelligence activities of the departments and agencies of the Government as relate to the national security;

(3) to correlate and evaluate intelligence relating to the national security, and provide for the appropriate dissemination of such intelligence within the Government using where appropriate existing agencies and facilities:

Provided, That the agency shall have no police, subpoena, law enforcement powers, or internal security functions: Provided further, That the Departments and other agencies of the Government shall continue to collect, evaluate, correlate and disseminate departmental intelligence: And provided further, That the Director of Central Intelligence shall be responsible for protecting intelligence sources and methods from unauthorized disclosure;

(4) to perform, for the benefit of the existing intelligence

agencies, such additional services of common concern as the National Security Council determines can be more effectively accomplished centrally;

(5) to perform such other functions and duties related to intelligence affecting national security as the National Security Council may from time to time direct.[15]

The National Security Act has remained in force to the present time. It served to formalize a peacetime role for military and intelligence leaders in U.S. foreign affairs that did not exist before World War II. This was explained primarily by the growing concern over national security which resulted from the emerging Cold War, but also by the fact that U.S. planners already could see that the United States would have increasingly important responsibilities as the greatest power in the world. The Act is essentially legislation providing for major organizational changes and does not attempt to define national security.

The National Security Act gave special authority to the Director of Central Intelligence for statutory secrecy that had not existed before by making him responsible for "protecting intelligence sources and methods from unauthorized disclosure." The authority for protecting secrecy of methods has been used by CIA to withhold information about many operations which would not ordinarily be thought to be intelligence methods. In fact, the most controversial aspect of the CIA mandate is the so-called "fifth function," calling for the performance of "such other functions and duties related to intelligence affecting national security as the National Security Council may from time to time direct." That function has been used as authority for CIA's so-called "dirty tricks" — the covert operations of political, psychological, and paramilitary warfare. Through the years several members of Congress have questioned whether these activities are directly related to intelligence as required in the "fifth function." They have asserted that they had no intention of authorizing such things as the covert overthrow of governments, the buying of elections, or clandestine military operations and sabotage.

Nevertheless, in 1948 after the Czech coup which put communists in control of Czechoslovakia, replacing the last democracy in Eastern Europe, there was a demand for covert operations to counter the communists' aggressive moves. So an NSC policy paper known as 10/2 established a new organization responsible for secret political and psychological operations within CIA, but also under the joint authority of State and Defense. (This organization and another which had been assigned the clandestine espionage role were merged in January 1951 under the operational control of CIA). Already launched near Munich, Germany, was the headquarters of the spy organization of General Reinhard Gehlen, who had served as Hitler's chief of Soviet intelligence and had become the most important source of Soviet intelligence for CIA. (The Gehlen organization is discussed in greater detail in the chapter on CIA.)

The Cold War was expanding rapidly as Stalin's aggressive moves were countered by U.S. plans and operations. In addition to the Czech coup, the Soviets had blockaded Berlin and were pumping money into the communist parties of Italy and France in anticipation of gaining control through popular fronts and coalition governments. All of Western Europe, but especially France and Italy, had been economically devastated by the war. The American response was the Marshall Plan (the European Recovery Program), which was probably the most imaginative, farsighted, and successful program in the history of U.S. foreign affairs. That same summer Marshal Tito broke with Stalin and pulled Yugoslavia out of the Communist Bloc, marking the first challenge to Moscow domination of world communism.

The summer of 1948 also produced the startling revelations of Elizabeth Bentley which led to the dramatic confrontation before the House Un-American Activities Committee of Whittaker Chambers and Alger Hiss. It was during these sensational hearings that Richard Nixon, as a junior congressman from California, began to build his reputation as a champion of anticommunism. Hiss was later tried and convicted of two counts of perjury. The Hiss case, along with others before and after involving such names as Judith Coplan, Klaus Fuchs, and the Rosenbergs, fostered a sort of spy hysteria. International communism was a dangerous, mysterious threat which seemed to be spreading throughout the world, including the United States.

When the Soviets exploded their first atomic bomb in 1949 news stories everywhere reported that they had made the breakthrough as a result of espionage. Actually U.S. atomic scientists have stated that the Soviets had the necessary information through their own resources. Nontheless, the spy mania was increasing. The mood of anxiety was greatly exacerbated by the successful completion of the takeover of China by Mao Tse-tung. Mao was part of the communist camp, loyal to Stalin. Extremists in the United States began blaming the "loss" of China on the U.S. government, especially the "old China hands" of the State Department.

There was almost unanimous support in Congress for the North Atlantic Treaty which became effective in August 1949, after Senate ratification. The Treaty provided for the collective self-defense of many of the countries of Western Europe and the United States. The signatories agreed that an armed attack against one or more of them in Europe or North America shall be considered an attack against them all. The North Atlantic Treaty Organization (NATO) provided the basis for keeping U.S. troops in Europe, mostly in Germany, a practice which continues to this day, after thirty years. There are still about 300,000 U.S. military personnel in Europe.

As the Cold War proliferated, the fear of communism, espionage, and conspiracy grew in the United States like the most luxuriant of weeds. Out of this atmosphere emerged Joseph McCarthy, an obscure junior senator from Wisconsin, who discovered that the fear and mystery surrounding communism could be manipulated and whipped up to a frenzy. Posing as an authority on how to "wipe out communism" McCarthy realized that he had the key to incredible power. By the spring of 1950 he had become a towering figure. "No man was closer than he to the center of American consciousness or more central to the world's consciousness of America."[16] McCarthy began by making speeches claiming that he had evidence that there were 57, 81, or 205 (the figure fluctuated in various speeches) card-carrying communists in the State Department. With each speech he obtained bigger headlines and more TV coverage. Soon McCarthy was "finding" communists in the Defense Department and CIA.

McCarthy's power increased rapidly as he held hearings claiming that he was exposing the depth of communist penetration in the U.S. government. He didn't produce a single communist, but he did damage and smear the reputation of many innocent Americans. The hysteria was so great in the United States during those years that he got away with it for almost four years. Incredibly, he was able to capture headlines while making totally destructive remarks about U.S. leadership. He called Secretary of State Dean Acheson the "Red Dean of Communism." General George Marshall, whom President Truman had called "the greatest living American," was referred to by McCarthy as, "a man steeped in falsehood . . . part of a conspiracy so immense and an infamy so black as to dwarf any previous venture in the history of man . . . invariably serving the world policy of the Kremlin."

The technique of vicious smear, linking public officials with communism, became known as "McCarthyism." The Senator claimed that "McCarthyism is Americanism with its sleeves rolled."[17] McCarthy held such power that from 1950 to 1954 presidents Truman and Eisenhower were often unable to take effective action. He had great influence on American foreign policy setting the tone of the Cold War. The McCarthy era, next only to the Vietnam War and the last two "Watergate" years of Richard Nixon, was a low ebb in American history. The country lost its balance, infected by a manipulated fear of communism from which it has not yet recovered.

Fuel was added to the fire of "McCarthyism" in June 1950 when the North Korean army struck into South Korea, beginning a bloody war which saw the United States shouldering most of the burden. The UN served as a "fig leaf" for the defending forces, but the United States was responsible for command and for supplying most of the troops, supplies, and money. The Cold War had become a hot war, at least in Asia, and Stalin had clearly given his approval to the aggression. (The North Koreans, at that time, were most loyal to Soviet hegemony.) The fear of communist aggression was at a peak in the United States, and McCarthy and Nixon, among others, used that fear for full political advantage.

This was the period in U.S. history when the secrecy system began to grow from bud to blossom. After the National Security Act of 1947 the NSC was given responsibility to make recommendations to the President for protecting sensitive information. An Interdepartmental Committee on Internal Security (ICIS) was created to examine the problem. In 1950 President Truman issued Executive Order 10104, which superseded Roosevelt's Order of 1940 dealing with, "Definitions of Vital Military and Naval Installations and Equipment." The Truman Order kept the earlier three categories of classification and formalized the additional designation of "Top Secret." In September 1951 President Truman issued a new Executive Order 10290, which extended the security classification system within nonmilitary agencies as well as the defense agencies. It permitted any executive department or agency to classify information on a uniform basis and defined security information to mean "official information the safeguarding of which is necessary in the interest of national security, and which is classified for such purposes by appropriate classifying authority."[18]

This Order was strongly criticized by some members of Congress and the press for its vagueness and potential abuses. It permitted secrecy to be used in hundreds of domestic departments and agencies with no clear limits or controls and no definition of "appropriate classifying authority." The directive did not have any specific constitutional or statutory authority. Instead, President Truman relied on such implied constitutional powers as the "faithful execution of the laws" clause.[19] The fact that Truman's Order was not seriously challenged in Congress, while unfortunate, was not surprising in view of the times and the willingness of the public and their representatives to grant almost any kind of authority demanded by the executive branch in the name of national security. Not only was 1951 a year of "McCarthyism," widespread communist aggressive moves, and the continuing Korean War, it was also the year the United States exploded the hydrogen bomb, an event which terrified millions of people throughout the world.

This terror was increased in 1953 when the Soviets exploded their own first nuclear weapon. But 1953 was also marked by two other very important events which began the slow process of thawing the Cold War. Perhaps most important was the death of Stalin in March, bringing to an end the rule of the most ruthless and dangerous dictator of modern history, possibly excepting only Hitler. Malenkov, who succeeded Stalin, moved rapidly to ease world tensions. He renounced Soviet claims on Turkish territory which had first been advanced in 1945 and '46, he moved to relax the tension between the Soviet Union and Yugoslavia, elsewhere he launched what was called a "peace offensive," and in July an armistice ending the Korean War had been concluded.

President Dwight Eisenhower, during his campaign for election in 1952, had pledged an early end to the unpopular Korean War. The war probably could have been settled earlier had it not been for the destructive influence of McCarthy. The Democrats were afraid of losing too much further ground to McCarthy's charges of being soft on communism. After the settlement, President Truman said, "I would have been crucified for that armistice."[20] But the war was over, Stalin was dead, and the most dangerous peak of the Cold War had been scaled.

In the fall of 1953 President Eisenhower replaced Truman's controversial Executive Order with his own Executive Order 10501. This Order narrowed the sweeping term "national security" to "national defense," reduced the number of agencies authorized to classify information, eliminated the "Restricted" classification, and refined the definitions of the other three categories:

Top Secret: . . . information the unauthorized disclosure of which could result in exceptionally grave damage to the nation such as leading to a definite break in diplomatic relations affecting the defense of the United States, an armed attack against the United

States or its allies, a war, or the compromise of military or defense plans, or intelligence operations, or scientific or technological developments vital to the national defense.

Secret: . . . information the unauthorized disclosure of which could result in serious damage to the Nation, such as by jeopardizing the international relations of the U.S., endangering the effectiveness of a program or policy of vital importance to the national defense, or compromising important military or defense plans, scientific or technological developments important to national defense, or information revealing important intelligence operations.

Confidential: . . . information the unauthorized disclosure of which could be prejudicial to the defense interests of the Nation.[21]

Though this Order clearly improved on the Truman classification program it was still very ambiguous, granting wide discretion to those given the classification powers within the bureaucracy. When secrecy could be justified as information "jeopardizing the international relations of the U.S., or endangering the effectiveness of a vital national defense program or policy," the inclination to err on the side of secrecy was not surprising. How is jeopardy or effectiveness measured? The Cold War system of secrecy had become a far cry from the World War II standards based on our national survival. As in the Truman Order, Eisenhower's legal advisors seem to have been relying on implied constitutional powers. The Order provided no basis for disciplinary action against individuals who mishandled or disclosed classified information without authority, and no attempt was made to correct these inadequacies.[22] Yet, this Order, as amended, served as the basis for security classification for almost twenty years, until President Nixon replaced it in 1972.

Through the years the classification system, with one important exception, has been handled through executive orders handed down by various presidents, without any congressional oversight. The exception was the Atomic Energy Act of 1954, which established the Atomic Energy Commission and a Joint Congressional Committee on Atomic Energy. The Act provided that atomic energy information would have a special security classification known as "Restricted Data," which was defined as follows:

The term means all data concerning (1) design, manufacture, or utilization of atomic weapons; (2) the production of special nuclear material; or (3) the use of special nuclear material in the production of energy, but shall not include data declassified or removed from the Restricted Data category.[23]

The Act requires the Commission and the Department of Defense to keep the Joint Congressional Committee fully and currently informed on matters relating to development and application of atomic energy. It is somewhat ironic that Congress has, for twenty years, maintained oversight of information relating to nuclear weapons, generally acknowledged to be the most sensitive information, while having no oversight of other executive branch material classified as "Top Secret" and "Secret." There has never been a leak of "Restricted Data" atomic energy information from Congress.

In 1954 the McCarthy era came to an end. Joseph Welch, a gentle but courageous attorney for the defense, bested McCarthy in the nationally televised Army–McCarthy hearings. Edward R. Murrow, the TV newscaster for CBS also attacked the foundations of McCarthy's credibility. Finally, his peers in the Senate voted 67–22 to condemn him on two counts. The demagogic power of Joseph McCarthy had collapsed. But the damage had been done, and the tragic effects of McCarthyism are still felt in such places as the foreign service of the State Department. The techniques of deception and irresponsible exploitation of the fear of communism have been used in the era of Nixon's Watergate with the same destructive impact as when they were used in the McCarthy era.

As the McCarthy era faded in Washington, post-Stalin changes were shaking Moscow. The new party chairman, Nikita Khrushchev, was consolidating his power, culminating in the ouster and execution of the dreaded chief of secret police, Lavrenti Beria. In 1955 Khrushchev ordered the withdrawal of Soviet troops from Austria, returned the naval base of Porkkala to Finland, announced that Yugoslavia and other socialist states could follow their "own paths of socialism," and, most important of all, recognized the government of the new German Federal Republic. In

July he went to Geneva for a summit conference with President Eisenhower where there were announcements of "open skies," "peaceful coexistence," and possible disarmament talks.

But the Cold War was not over and the "Geneva spirit" was short-lived. In Hungary, where one of the most oppressive Stalinist regimes was in power, the people rebelled in late 1956, especially in Budapest. Most of the "freedom fighters" were young communist university students. When it looked as though a Titoist named Imre Nagy would install a new government the Soviet Red Army moved in with tanks and crushed the uprising. The failure of the "Hungarian revolution" also marked the end of a phony U.S. policy pledge.

Shortly after John Foster Dulles had become Eisenhower's Secretary of State in 1953 he announced a so-called "policy of liberation" for the captive peoples of Eastern Europe. It was hoped that through various psychological and political pressures from outside the people of Eastern Europe would be helped to liberate themselves. There were radio broadcasts from Radio Free Europe and Radio Liberty, U.S.–financed exile organizations, balloon-launched leaflets over Eastern Europe, and various clandestine operations. However, when the Hungarian "freedom fighters" called for U.S. help, none was forthcoming and the absurd policy of liberation was dropped. Though Dulles had vigorously attacked Kennan and the policy of containment as a do-nothing policy, it remained the basic U.S. Cold War policy.

Meanwhile, the secrecy system was growing in Washington with no control in sight. Alarmed by the growing unauthorized disclosure of secret information, Secretary of Defense Charles Wilson, with President Eisenhower's blessing, in late 1956 created a five-member Committee on Classification Information under Charles Coolidge. The Coolidge Committee found that a primary reason for leaks and the casual attitude about the system was the overclassification of information. The Committee recommended a determined attack against overclassification, making clear that the system should be used only to protect national security information and should not be used for administrative matters. The Committee also recommended a sharp reduction in the number of people authorized to classify papers "Top Secret."

At about the same time, Congress created the Wright Commission on Government Security, composed of six Republicans and six Democrats with four of the members selected by the President, four by the Senate, and four by the House. After nearly two years of work the Commission issued a massive 800-page report in 1957. The Commission recommended that the classification category "Confidential" be abolished because too much information was being classified. This would have meant that 76 percent of all State and Commerce information would have become public, and 59 percent of all Defense information. Unfortunately this recommendation was never implemented. The Commission also emphasized the negative impact on national security of the classification system, pointing out that too much secrecy had set back our scientific and technological progress, thus depriving the country of the advantages that come from the free exchange of scientific ideas. This observation took on special relevance when the Soviets launched their "Sputnik," apparently taking a commanding lead in outer space.

The most controversial aspects of the Wright Commission report were allegations that the press often breached security by using classified information in news stories. The Commission urged Congress to "enact legislation making it a crime for any person willfully to disclose without proper authorization, for any purpose whatever, information classified 'secret' or 'top secret,' knowing, or having reasonable grounds to believe, such information to have been classified." A fine of $10,000 and a jail term of up to five years was recommended for those convicted of such security violations. These recommendations created strong objection from the press and were not further pursued in Congress.

The House meanwhile had created a Special Government Information Subcommittee of the Government Operations Committee. Chairman John Moss (D.–Calif.) has been a champion of an open society and an advocate of as much disclosure of information as possible. His Committee concluded in 1958:

Never before in our democratic form of government has the need for candor been so great. The nation can no longer afford the danger of withholding information merely because the facts fail to fit a predetermined "policy." Withholding for any reason other than true military security inevitably results in the loss of public confidence — or a greater tragedy. Unfortunately, in no other part of our government has it been so easy to substitute secrecy for candor and to equate suppression with security. . . . In a conflict between the right to know and the need to protect true military secrets from a potential enemy, there can be no valid argument against secrecy. The right to know has suffered, however, in the confusion over the demarcation between secrecy for true security reasons and secrecy for "policy" reasons.[24]

This excellent advice was given little attention either in Congress or the Executive Branch.

The public and the Congress had become accustomed to executive secrecy and to granting to their presidents the unfettered right to withhold information in matters of national security. The secrecy system was spreading over more and more information, with literally millions of documents classified each year. Yet the danger of war, the threat to our survival, was receding. The Cold War had crested, but the bureaucracy it had spawned was expanding under the comfortable unbrella of secrecy.

The threat of communism was no longer monolithic. The Chinese had asserted their independence and were following a different path from Moscow's. A new phenomenon had emerged which Italian communist leader Togliatti dubbed "polycentrism." It meant several centers of communist activity and policy and was not limited to the Sino-Soviet split and Tito's independence, but extended to communist parties throughout the world. Chairman Krushchev, having given his secret speech attacking the cult of dictatorship under Stalin and having replaced Malenkov and Molotov, felt secure enough to traved to Washington for the talks with Eisenhower which brought the so-called "spirit of Camp David." It was agreed that the two leaders would meet again at the summit in Paris in 1960 to discuss a broad relaxation of tensions.

The summit meeting, which was to include French President

Charles De Gaulle and British Prime Minister Harold Macmillan in addition to Eisenhower and Krushchev, never got off the ground. A few days before the conference was to start Krushchev announced that an American spy plane had been shot down over Soviet territory. At first, Washington said it was a NASA weather plane that had strayed off course, but when Krushchev announced that he had both the plane and the pilot the State Department admitted it was an intelligence flight that had taken off without authority. However two days later President Eisenhower took full responsibility for the U-2 program. When the summit leaders convened in Paris Krushchev demanded an apology, which he didn't get. He did get a promise of no more flights over Russia, but the damage had been done and the meeting collapsed.[25]

The U-2 flight had been authorized because the high-flying planes were obtaining very valuable intelligence about the Soviet missile system. It was felt that the Paris summit to be followed by Eisenhower's scheduled trip to Russia might produce a detente making future flights inappropriate. Eisenhower never did make the trip to Russia, and he left the White House with his dreams of promoting a lasting peace in a shambles. In an interview with the Knight newspapers in 1962, describing his "greatest regret" as President he said: "The lie we told about the U-2. I didn't realize how high a price we were going to have to pay for that lie. And if I had to do it all over again, we would have kept our mouths shut."[26] That might be one lesson, but surely a more important one is that, under the circumstances, the flight should not have been authorized in the first place.

When John F. Kennedy came into the White House in 1961 high hopes for a new era were rapidly jolted by the Bay of Pigs fiasco. A few days later, "in the worst and most inexplicable speech of his Presidency, he weighed in on the side of secrecy," according to one of his top aides, Arthur Schlesinger, Jr. Among other things, Kennedy told the American Newspaper Publishers Association:

If the press is awaiting a declaration of war before it imposes the self-discipline of combat conditions, then I can only say that no war ever imposed a greater threat to our security. . . . The danger has never been more clear and its presence has never been more imminent.[27]

Kennedy did show concern about the amount of executive secrecy and did amend the Eisenhower Executive Order to set up an automatic procedure for lowering security classifications and declassification of material no longer requiring protection. Secretary of Defense Robert McNamara issued a Defense Department Directive which said, "I suggest we follow this principle: When in doubt, underclassify. In no event should over-classification be used to avoid public discussion of controversial matters."[28] Unfortunately there were no penalties for overclassification so very little was done. The interest of Kennedy and McNamara was soon overtaken by events.

When Kennedy met with Krushchev in Vienna he found a very different man than Eisenhower had dealt with before the U-2. Krushcev was tough, abrasive, and threatening; the "spirit of Camp David" was dead. There followed the Berlin crisis and the erection of the Berlin Wall, and then in 1962 the Cuban missile crisis. The Cold War had returned to a fever pitch similar to that of the Stalin era. But it didn't last long after Krushchev's back-down and withdrawal of his missiles from Cuba. In April 1963 Pope John XXIII delivered his encyclical entitled "Peace on Earth," which is one of the most eloquent documents of the subject ever conceived. It had impact throughout the world, including a favorable response from Krushchev.

Shortly thereafter, at American University, President Kennedy delivered his most memorable speech, entitled, "Toward a Strategy of Peace," in which he said:

Let us focus on a more practical, more attainable peace, based not on a sudden revolution in human nature, but on a gradual evolution in human institutions — on a series of concrete actions and effective agreements which are in the interest of all concerned. . . . Let us not be blind to our differences, but let us also direct attention to our common interests and to the means by which those differences can be resolved. And if we cannot end now our differences, at least we can help make the world safe for diversity. . . . For we seek relaxation of tensions without relaxing our guard.

That speech paved the way to the "hotline" agreement and the partial nuclear test ban. Had Kennedy not been assassinated a few months later the promise of detente might have been fulfilled.

However, detente did not ensue because, in 1965, President Johnson decided to intervene massively with U.S. forces in the Vietnam War. This was the beginning of an era, extending from the Gulf of Tonkin resolution to the Nixon resignation, during which the U.S. public under the umbrella of secrecy and national security was lied to constantly. The war in Vietnam certainly did not threaten the survival nor the national defense of the United States, yet there was more secrecy and deception practiced by the U.S. government during this period than at any time during the Cold War.

There was a proliferation of special clearances for various types of classified information with many documents dealing with the Vietnam War limited to "Eyes Only" distribution to four or five people. There had always been special clearances for "Restricted Data" dealing with nuclear weapons and for certain electronic intelligence and cryptographic information, just as there is special clearance required for certain information obtained from space satellite reconnaissance today. "Top Secret" still was the top classification, but access to certain information had even more special controls. This preoccupation with information control reached its zenith during the Vietnam War. The reason was not security but a series of disastrous White House decisions which were made under the cover of outright fabrication to the U.S. public.

Meanwhile, Congressman John Moss and his subcommittee on government information kept hammering away at the need for information disclosure. On July 4, 1966, after years of work, Congress finally passed the Freedom of Information Act, a law which placed the burden on the government to justify withholding a document. Federal agencies were "required to publish procedures in the *Federal Register* on disclosure of information, and to make available to the public statements of policy, staff manuals and instructions, and final opinions." The law also provided for judicial review if a public request for information was denied by the government. Unfortunately, the law permitted the government to withhold all information "specifically required by Executive Order to be kept secret in the interest of national defense or foreign policy."[29]

But the Act did establish a precedent as far as Congress is concerned. While the Act does permit withholding certain national defense and foreign policy information from the public, Section 3(f) states: "Nothing in this section authorizes withholding of information or limiting the availability of records to the public except as specifically stated in this section, nor shall this section be authority to withhold information from Congress." However, though members of Congress may have access to government information, they may not compel disclosure.

In 1971 Congresswoman Patsy Mink (D.–Hawaii) and 32 other members of Congress requested documents from the Environmental Protection Agency dealing with the planned underground nuclear test explosion on Amchitka Island, Alaska. The U.S. District Court refused to compel disclosure but the U.S. Court of Appeals reversed the decision. However, the Supreme Court overruled, deciding that the documents were properly classified under the Executive Order and involved "highly sensitive matter vital to our national defense and foreign policy." The Court turned down the proposition that exemption in the Act authorizes or permits, in camera, inspection of a contested document bearing a single classification so that the Court might separate the secret from the supposedly nonsecret components. Mink et al. had contended that some of the components were not classified for national defense purposes. Thus it continues to be possible for the government to consider an entire report secret, so long as there is some secret information contained therein.[30] Paradoxically, as the Cold War declined, the secrecy systems burgeoned.

In 1968 Lyndon Johnson, after announcing his intention not to run for reelection, desperately sought to end his term in office with a major step toward peace. The Soviets did agree to sit down for arms limitation talks, but then, at the time of the Democratic National Convention, the Red Army invaded Czechoslovakia to crush "liberal tendencies." Thus, all hope for peace talks vanished.

When President Nixon assumed office in 1969 he announced a policy of negotiation to replace the era of confrontation that had marked the Cold War. After almost four years of negotiations, several agreements were signed at the Moscow summit meeting in 1972 for the purpose of relaxing tensions between the U.S.S.R. and the U.S. The relaxation of tension with Moscow combined with the Nixon visit to Peking and the opening of more friendly relations with China set in motion a mood of peace and talk of an end to the Cold War. This reduction of conflict with the communist powers was generally credited as the greatest achievement of the Nixon years. Though the threat of war was declining, the techniques of secrecy reached their peak during the last years of Nixon's stay in the White House. The justification for secrecy used during the Stalin years based on deep fears, whether fully legitimate or not, had lost all meaning during the Nixon-Brezhnev detente. Yet, the secrecy system had become such a tool of executive power that it spread throughout the Nixon regime, providing a cancerous cover for the most corrupt presidency in our nation's history.

After the Pentagon Papers leak was discovered, President Nixon ordered a review of all security classification procedures. The first chairman of the interagency review committee was then-Assistant Attorney General William H. Rehnquist, later appointer to the Supreme Court and replaced on the committee by David Young, who was soon to become chief of the "plumbers." Related to the study was an order signed by General Alexander Haig requesting a list of all government employees, outside consultants, and private contractors with access to "Top Secret" and "Secret" information. There was pressure to control the secrecy system from the White House. After about a year of study the Committee submitted its recommendations to the National Security Council. A request by William Moorhead, Chairman of the Government Information Subcommittee, to White House Counsel John Dean, for a copy of the draft study was denied. In March 1972 Nixon issued Executive Order 11652 entitled "Classification and Declassification of National Security Information and Material," superseding the Eisenhower Executive Order 10501 which had been the authority for almost twenty years.

President Nixon issued the following statement outlining the "most significant features" of his Order:

The rules for classifying documents are more restrictive.

The number of departments and people who can originally classify information has been substantially reduced.

Timetables ranging from 6 to 10 years have been set for automatic declassification of documents. Exemptions will be allowed only for such information as falls within four specifically defined categories.

Any document exempted from automatic declassification will be subject to mandatory review after a 10-year period. Thus, for the first time a private citizen is given the right to have national security information reviewed on the basis of specified criteria to determine if continued classification is warranted so long as the document can be adequately identified and obtained by the Government with a reasonable amount of effort.

If information is still classified 30 years after origination it will then be automatically declassified unless the head of the originating department determines in writing that its continued protection is still necessary and he sets a time for declassification.

Sanctions may be imposed on those who abuse the system.

And a continuing monitoring process will be set up under the National Security Council and an interagency classification review committee, whose chairman is to be appointed by the President.

The President's claims for improvement in the classification system have been vigorously challenged in both the Senate and House, where several bills have been drafted to provide congressional oversight for the secrecy system. A study of Nixon's Executive Order by the House Foreign Operations and Government Information Subcommittee was critical, claiming the order misconstrued the meaning of the Freedom of Information Act, and by broadening the coverage to "national defense and foreign relations" it provided authority for classifying more rather than less information.[31]

But the secrecy system and the tons of classified documents residing in government safes were not the cause of the Watergate conspiracy. The cause was the arrogance and unchecked ambition for power of Richard Nixon and his men. The secrecy system fostered habits of behavior, acceptance of lying, and a knowledge of the techniques of deception and espionage which made it easier for power-greedy men to move undetected. Under the claim of national security and the struggle with communism these men were able to rationalize the use of CIA techniques in the "plumbers" operations, Watergate, and the national election itself. Nixon used the CIA techniques of covert political and psychological warfare in domestic affairs in order to ensure that he had his way in dealing with the war in Indochina. How far all of this might have gone had it not been exposed nobody knows, but certainly we were moving in the direction of totalitarian government. We had lost the balance of our democratic system which must never again be placed in such jeopardy for want of adequate provisions of accountability from our chief executives. No danger from abroad, however real it may be, should ever again be permitted to justify such an extraordinary grant of power to the President.

3

Executive Secrecy
—Legitimate and Illegitimate

The uproar over government secrecy caused by the Pentagon Papers and the Watergate scandals has inspired demands for change. We know that the secrecy system has, for years, been out of control with far too much information classified. We know too that properly classified information has been withheld from public circulation long after the reasons for security protection ceased to have force. We are learning also that the bloated secrecy system has eroded our democratic society by providing cover for corruption, conspiracy, disastrous decision making, and incredible economic waste and inflation. Under these circumstances some citizens have urged abolition of all secrecy, maintaining that the risks of giving some useful information to our adversaries do not compare with the risks to our democracy from secret government. Certainly the present system, with the present controls, is too much of a risk, as Watergate demonstrates; but there could be a different system providing for the very small amount of essential secrecy and for executive branch accountability as well.

As we have seen, our current secrecy system emerged out of World War II when certain concepts of war and national survival were established. There has been very broad agreement that in time of war, information which could be useful to an enemy should be kept secret. It was recognized that the public's right to know should be sacrificed to the more important goal of defeating the enemy and saving American lives. Nobody questioned the validity of protecting information about our shipping routes from German and Japanese submarines, or keeping our battle plans secret. By the same token, there is very little argument about keeping our war plans secret today. In total war such as World War II the fact that the balance of secrecy was weighted against freedom of information was not an issue so long as the people were accurately informed of the progress of the war. The Cold War, however, was much more complex.

During the Stalin era most Americans and most of their leaders thought we were threatened with a danger almost as great as total war. The fear of international communism combined with a fear of nuclear weapons led to an emphasis on security and a sacrifice of freedom of information. The Korean War was fought under the cover of the United Nations, which the United States dominated at that time. Congress did not declare war, though President Truman declared it a national emergency. The World War II ground rules for secrecy were used even though the Korean War was very limited in terms of geography and national mobilization. The Vietnam War was not declared by Congress nor was it made a national emergency. Yet, the secrecy system proliferated, using the World War II rationale again. Even in the case of Vietnam, which in no way could be compared with World War II, the American people probably would have accepted the secrecy had they not been lied to so many times about the course of the war. So, today we see the secrecy system finally under a challenge overdue for more than twenty years. Today a budding detente with Russia and China makes the security arguments of total war meaningless. Under these circumstances, what are the legitimate boundaries of secret information?

War plans and contingencies will remain secret, though there should be much more rigorous congressional oversight. There should never again be a secret bombing of Cambodia, nor a secret war in Laos involving Americans, without Congress being informed. A strong case can be made that no overt or covert use of American forces in combat should be permitted without the approval of Congress, which has the only Constitutional authority to declare wars. If Congress is not willing to agree to U.S.

involvement in a war, no matter how small, then U.S. forces even under civilian cover should not be used. The war powers act, in its present form, does not deal adequately with this problem.

Three areas, in addition to military plans, require classification protection according to the national security managers. These are secret diplomacy, secret intelligence, and secret military weapons systems, especially in the early stages of development. Undoubtedly, there is a requirement for some security protection in all of these categories, but how much information should be secret and for how long?

Secret Diplomacy

William Macomber, now Ambassador to Turkey, but formerly Deputy Undersecretary of State, was the highest ranking diplomat to testify before Congress during the Pentagon Papers hearings in 1971. He made the following points:

> I think it is important to remember that diplomacy cannot function if we cannot deal with other governments in the world — especially with governments that are not particularly friendly to us, if we cannot deal with them on a basis of confidence — if they cannot speak to us in confidence and have confidence that we will protect from disclosure what they are saying to us. If you remove the element of confidentiality from the diplomatic process you destroy the diplomatic process.[1]

Mr. Macomber was making one of the strongest arguments for secret diplomacy. The point is stressed most vigorously when considering the importance of secrecy in negotiating with adversary governments. If the Russians can't trust us to negotiate in secret, it is claimed, they will not negotiate. Why is the secrecy so important? It is said, for example, that if a negotiating position of Chairman Brezhnev were discussed in the press, the Soviet hawk opposition might mobilize sufficient resistance within the Politburo to block him or even oust him. A close examination of the way the Politburo works demonstrates that this is most unlikely. Actually the negotiating positions of Brezhnev have been much more broadly discussed in the Kremlin than, for example, the Nixon-Kissinger positions for SALT I were discussed in Washington. If a Brezhnev position were reported in the *New York Times* before agreement had been reached what harm would it do? Because the Soviet system is closed it would receive no attention there. It might generate debate in the United States which might make difficulty for our negotiators, but might also be very healthy for the ultimate result.

Perhaps as difficult as negotiating with the Soviets was the Kissinger negotiation with Le Duc Tho of North Vietnam and Thieu of South Vietnam. If his talks with Le Duc Tho had not been in secret Thieu would have blocked progress and vice versa, it was claimed. As it turned out Thieu blocked the original agreement anyhow. Another difficult negotiation was the first-phase disengagement of forces after the Yom Kippur war which Kissinger, with his shuttle diplomacy, worked out between Egypt and Israel and Syria and Israel. Again, it is asserted that the negotiations would have failed if the progress were being discussed openly day by day. Who can know for sure?

Certainly there can be no question that no nation wants its fall-back position, or positions, known in advance of a negotiation. On the other hand, when a treaty is at stake requiring the advice and consent of the Senate by a two-thirds majority, it would seem prudent to have the leadership of the Senate well informed in advance. In a democracy such participation in the decision-making process is important even while the negotiating details are held in confidence. As diplomacy has been conducted during the past decade it is impossible to know whether a better agreement could have been worked out for Vietnam, the Middle East, or in Vladivostok if the negotiating process had been less secret. Macomber said in his testimony, "I am not suggesting that we should have secret agreements secretely arrived at. In the end we must have open agreements. But very often the best agreements, which are open in the end, are arrived at secretly."[2] Undoubtedly Macomber is correct in saying that some good agreements are reached secretly, but he doesn't seem to recognize, nor do most diplomats, that many very bad agreements are also reached secretly. It may be as important to open up international politics as national politics. Just because a totalitarian regime insists on secrecy does not mean that we have to adopt its ways. We can insist on keeping our people fully informed even if our adversaries insist on controlling the dissemination of information to their people.

Speaking to this point, in 1957, John Foster Dulles said,

> In these days there's very little secret diplomacy. Policies have to be worked out with our allies; thus many people come to know about them. They have to be explained to the people and the Congress. This requires speech-making, Congressional presentation, press conferences and the like. . . . It gives certain advantages, at least temporarily, to despotisms which wholly control the news within their own country, and can put out varying propaganda versions of their policy to various parts of the world.[3]

Dulles could have added that background briefings and calculated leaks to the press are other ways information reaches the people in the United States. In a democracy there are compelling advantages in getting the facts to the people as soon and as accurately as possible. Even in the middle of the Korean War, when President Truman fired General Douglas MacArthur the Senate held open hearings which brought before the public most of the prior secret U.S. policy positions in the war. Those hearings served as a catharsis for U.S. politics. They healed a political wound which, if left to fester, could have endangered the nation. More recently we have seen how fully the details of the negotiations of the Cuban missile crisis were reported. That crisis brought us closer to nuclear war than any other event in our history, yet the story has been told. There is no point in keeping the details of an agreement secret after it has been consummated.

Undersecretary Macomber in his defense of diplomatic secrecy said:

> Another area that is awfully important, I think — and it has been lost sight of . . . in the hullabaloo over the Pentagon Papers — is this business of the necessity to be able to insure orderly and effective functioning of the executive branch to be able to assure the subordinates in the various departments that they can recommend

unpopular recommendations, any recommendations that they think are right and not be inhibited by whether they could defend their recommendations if they are hauled before a Congressional committee. We do not want subordinates in the executive branch to be inhibited from giving their best advice, whether popular or not, to their supervisors. . . . [In] the many years I dealt with Congress we always insisted on this principle: When Congress wanted to know who recommended what, we always said, "No, we won't tell you who recommended what. We will tell you what the final decision was and what the various possibilities were that were considered. But we don't want to disclose what were the individual recommendations." Now, that was a battle that we went through in the McCarthy era. I think it is very important not to slip back now. I think it is another reason why confidentiality is so important.[4]

This is a popular argument in support of the secrecy system, but it is misplaced. The confidentiality of individual points of view in government is essential, but it has nothing to do with national security. Unless the material the individual discusses justifies a national security classification it should not be classified. Classifying a document "Secret" to protect an individual opinion is a gross, but common, misapplication of the security system. The views of an individual can be protected merely by marking his opinions "Official Use Only." Furthermore, when subordinates in the executive branch give their best advice to their chiefs they would be wise always to have Congress in mind, even though their views are made in confidence.

Writing about the place of secrecy in foreign affairs, McGeorge Bundy, national security advisor to Presidents Kennedy and Johnson, said:

There is one element in the styles of the last 10 years which, if I am right, will be profoundly out of place in the next 25 years — the apparent belief that there is an indispensable need for secrecy and loneliness in the conduct of our major international affairs. . . . An important element in the agenda of the nation could be a careful review of the real importance or lack of importance of the attitudes toward secrecy which developed in the generation marked by the opening of the nuclear age and the fears of the Cold War. . . . My own strongly held belief is that such a study would demonstrate the number of matters which need to remain secret over anything but a short space of time is exceedingly small, and that the balance of national advantage both at home and abroad, rests with a presumption in favor of openness.[5]

The world is changing rapidly, with electronic communication and jet planes bringing people everywhere closer together. The era when it was possible for a few chiefs of state to run the world through secret diplomacy is about over.

Secret Intelligence

The second major type of information requiring security protection is secret intelligence. The relative importance of secret intelligence is in direct proportion to the danger of war and subversive action. If we have enemies who are threatening us we need to know as much as possible about their intentions so we can protect ourselves from surprise attack, or from various forms of political and economic warfare which could harm our security. In terms of priority this means that the number-one danger is the Soviet nuclear arsenal — their strategic weapons system.

Other threats, though considerably smaller, include Soviet conventional arms and Soviet clandestine attempts to overthrow or gain control of other governments. As the Cold War has abated, the covert political operations of the KGB have declined. Another high priority for current U.S. intelligence is knowledge of developments in the Middle East, especially Soviet activities with respect to Arab-Israeli hostilities and Arab oil. An important, but lower, priority relates to Chinese military intentions and the communist governments of Eastern Europe, especially East Germany.

Obviously as the Cold War declines and detente increases the requirements for secret intelligence will diminish. As will be discussed in detail in the chapter on the CIA, modern technology has rapidly replaced the need for espionage. The information obtained from the cameras of satellites flying in outer space, the electronic interception of communications, and the use of radar and computers has virtually eliminated the need for human spies. One of the strongest arguments for intelligence secrecy has been the need for protecting the sources of information — the secret

agents. There are still those who argue in support of large espionage networks on the grounds that they may produce the
ultimate source of information — an agent in place in the Kremlin. Some dream even of recruiting a member of the Politburo. In
view of the danger and expense of human espionage and the
tremendous difficulty of penetration on the one hand, and the
incredible coverage provided by the technological intelligence
devices on the other, there is very little justification for continuing
espionage and the secrecy which goes with it. Espionage is a hostile act and runs counter to the goals of detente.

Of course, there are necessary secrets in space, electronic, and
communications intelligence, too. For example, the details of
how we make our reconnaissance cameras and how they work
should probably remain secret, though we know that the Soviets
have excellent cameras too. In fact, it can be argued that if the
Soviets had not developed their own space reconnaissance program it would have been to our advantage to make ours available
to them. Much of the progress achieved in the SALT agreements
has been possible because both sides are able to inspect each
other from outer space. If only one side had this capacity no
agreement would be possible. Most of Congress and the public
have come to believe that information about our strategic weapons should be the most secret of all. However, for years, we have
followed a policy based on deterring world war through our
strategic weapons system — the so-called balance of terror. In
order for deterrence to work, each side needs to know what the
other side has. Thus, it is important for the Soviets to know what
we have, and also for us to know what they have. The arguments
for secrecy in this field have been overblown, if not completely
wrong, and have usually stemmed from domestic political considerations rather than the requirements of national security.

Another part of intelligence that technology has changed dramatically is the whole field of cryptography and codes. This area
has always been considered one of the most sensitive and secret
aspects of intelligence, which is why it was given special protection under the terms of the Espionage Act of 1917. But the days

of the one-time pad, double transposition, and invisible ink codes are about over as technology overtakes espionage. As far as the United States is concerned the computer and the code machines make it virtually impossible to break our communications systems. In all history there probably will never be another story like British Group Captain Fred W. Winterbotham's *The Ultra Secret,* which tells how British intelligence broke German codes during World War II. Information obtained from the broken German code made victory possible by 1945, according to Alfred Friendly, former managing editor of the *Washington Post,* and an American member of the "Ultra" operation, who said we had:

. . . Hitler's orders to his generals, their replies and their orders to subordinates, the field commanders' orders to their units — air force, army and navy — the situation appreciations by Germans high and low, the positions of ships at sea, the moves from one airfield to another, the names of the commanders, their cries for men and equipment, their reports on status of strength and supplies.[6]

In other words we had complete military intelligence.

Security requirements for protecting this vital information were so great that some tragic decisions had to be taken. For example, when it was learned that the Germans were planning to bomb Coventry, the city was not evacuated because that might have revealed that the code was broken. There has been no adequate explanation of why the British waited more than thirty years before revealing their secret. One theory is that the revelation might have been used to increase tensions in the Cold War since the British withheld their precious information from their wartime Soviet ally. Britain was fighting for survival and could not risk letting the Germans know their code was broken. If the Soviets had been given full details, they might have taken defensive measures against a planned German attack, thereby letting the cat out of the bag. Under the circumstances a strong case can be made for the extraordinary secrecy that was maintained. Undoubtedly the techniques of communicating secret information will continue to be secret for years to come, but the technology has changed so much and the circumstances are so different that there probably will not be another intelligence coup like "Ultra."

In addition to methods and sources, the product of intelligence is usually classified "Secret" or higher, because the processed intelligence often contains information whose disclosure might reveal a secret method or source. The most important intelligence is the final estimate that goes to the President and the members of the National Security Council. Sometimes even the national intelligence estimates contain information that could reveal the source if disclosed to a hostile intelligence organization. However, a technique known in the intelligence community as "sanitizing" allows for reports to be paraphrased in such a way as to eliminate sensitive source information but at the same time keep the sense of the intelligence. As will be discussed in the concluding chapter there is a strong case for making "sanitized" intelligence estimates available to appropriate members of Congress and, in due time, to the public.

Weapons Systems, Secret Technology, Research, and Development

The most elaborate security precautions were taken, at least in the early stages, to protect the secrets of the atomic bomb and then the hydrogen bomb. Even after the Russians and Chinese successfully developed nuclear weapons, the United States maintained secrecy in this field to avoid the proliferation of these weapons to other nations. Most Americans have assumed that because nuclear weapons are the greatest threat to our survival all security measures necessary to maintain nuclear secrets are justified.

Edward Teller, the man generally credited as contributing most to the development of our nuclear weapons, has vigorously challenged the conventional wisdom. He says:

Our policy of secrecy in science and technology has created the illusion that we are in possession of valuable information which is not available to other nations, and in particular, not available to our chief competitor, the Soviet Union. In the field of nuclear explosives where we used to have a great advantage, secrecy did not perpetuate this advantage. In the field of electronics and the art of high-speed computers a great national advantage was brought about without the aid of secrecy. That technological secrecy amounts to security is, in my opinion, indeed an illusion. . . . In 1955 the research was opened up at the first "Atoms for Peace" conference. Hopes for immediate economic generation of electricity were, however, not realized. Openness led to the establishment of schools of nuclear engineering, to vigorous industrial participation and in a dozen years to competitive production of electricity. This was due to the accumulation of dozens of small improvements, not to any major discovery. In the secret and sheltered atmosphere of government laboratories all this would not have happened.

It is well to remember that apart from any contemporary consideration, and in problems touching on international conflict, modern science has developed in a spirit of openness and has traditionally condemned secrecy. In this respect the spirit of modern science is antithetical to the spirit of the diligent researches performed for almost 2000 years by alchemists. When the secrecy and the mutual isolation of alchemists was replaced by the novel code of openness this brought about the dawn of modern chemistry. The recent era of secrecy had its origin in the Second World War and . . . was greatly strengthened by the assumption that dangerous knowledge such as the knowledge of atomic weapons must be kept secret. But every country which managed to produce the materials needed for nuclear explosives also managed within a very short time to carry out a nuclear explosion; lack of knowledge did not prove to be an effective impediment.

Actually secrecy of nuclear weapons has not worked very well. [Six] nations are members of the Nuclear Club and the number of people to whom the main lines of relevant information about nuclear weapons is available is probably between one hundred thousand and one million. Under these conditions one must accept the conclusion that nuclear secrets, as a general rule, are secrets in name only. . . . Today secrecy does give a false feeling of safety. This false feeling permits people to avoid hard decisions which would have to be faced if all the facts were out in the open. On the other hand, secrecy in the nuclear field has also the opposite result of raising fears of the unknown. Ideas which belong in science fiction rather than in military planning, could be more easily eliminated from the discussions if secrecy barriers were broken down.[7]

Another nuclear scientist who agrees with Teller about nuclear secrecy and also believes that nuclear electric power will solve the world's energy needs is Theodore Taylor. Taylor is worried that nuclear bombs might be made in a clandestine operation by a nation, a group, or even two or three people. His book *Nuclear Theft: Risks and Safeguards* describes how this might be done. Taylor believes the only way to control nuclear proliferation and clandestine bomb building is not through secrecy, but rather by carefully developed safeguards to control the special nuclear materials required to make nuclear weapons.

Taylor was once warned by an Atomic Energy Commission official that everything he had been saying was highly classified. "Taylor replied that everything he had been saying he happened to have read the day before in the *Encyclopedia Americana*."[8] Taylor, like Teller, considers most nuclear weapons secrecy an obstacle to sound policy and essential public awareness. He says:

> The Los Alamos Primer, which contains the mathematical funda-
> mentals of fission bombs, was declassified in 1964 and is now avail-
> able from the Atomic Energy Commission for two dollars and six
> cents a copy. For four dollars a book titled *Manhattan District His-
> tory, Project Y, The Los Alamos Project* can be bought from the
> Office of Technical Services of the U.S. Department of Commerce.
> Written in 1946 and 1947, this was the supersecret technical descrip-
> tion of the problems that came up during the building of the first
> atomic bombs. . . . The release of documents containing detailed
> information on the sizes, shapes, design and construction of nuclear
> explosives — and on such topics as plutonium metallurgy and the
> chemistry of initiators — seemed to follow, over the years, a pattern
> of awareness of Russian knowledge. When it became clear that the
> Russians knew something or other what then was the point of keep-
> ing it secret.[9]

Today's big weapons secrets involve not nuclear bombs but the missiles carrying the bombs and the systems that place several independently targeted warheads on those missiles (MIRV). There are also very secret experiments with lasers and other exotic forms of warfare. And most other more conventional weapons technology for strategic bombers, submarines, fighter planes, tanks, rockets, or even a new automatic rifle is kept secret. The result is that the know-how, component parts, manufacturing techniques, and final product of thousands of different weapons become part of the secrecy system.

It might make sense not to provide a potential enemy with important information about a weapon which he doesn't have and which is better than anything similar in his arsenal, but if he already has something as good or better, it doesn't make much sense to keep ours secret. It certainly doesn't make sense to keep the specifications of our fighter plane or tank classified "Secret" when one of our planes or tanks has been captured in the Middle East, Vietnam, or elsewhere. Yet the tendency in the great bureaucratic morass of the Pentagon is to keep information classified long after such protection has become meaningless.

Actually, most of the valid weapons secrecy can be justified, if at all, only during the period of development. Sometimes security precautions taken during research and development can give us an important lead for four or five years. This has been true, for example, in our substantial MIRV lead over the Soviets, especially in submarine-launched multiple warheads. However, usually when the weapon goes into production the technology is exposed and the secrets evaporate. Even so, weapons information often remains classified secret long after it has been publicly described in the technical journals.

One reason for prolonging secrecy procedures is the tremendous mechanical and administrative problem of declassifying information about a particular weapon, involving literally thousands of documents and papers. Another is bureaucratic inertia, but also a still prevalent view that anything we let the Russians have helps them. Even if they already have it.

The following remarks before the Senate Subcommittee on Intergovernmental Relations on May 31, 1974, by David O. Cooke, the Deputy Assistant Secretary of Defense who has major responsibility in the Pentagon for security classification policy, provide another revealing view of the problem:

We have issued guidelines whose effect is to declassify the majority of the Department's official records dated prior to June 30, 1950. To provide some indication of the results achieved through the use of these guidelines, the Military Departments have reported declassification of 110,000 linear feet of classified records [that's more than 20 miles of paper]. The Archivist of the U.S., who has been authorized by the Secretary of Defense to apply these guidelines to Defense records in his custody, has reported the declassification of approximately 50 million pages.

The documents now declassified are more than 25 years old, leaving a pile three times that large still classified.

Cooke added that the Defense Department is trying to reduce documents classified "Top Secret" to the absolute minimum

> . . . consistent with national security. [He says:] 180,469 were eliminated from the Top Secret inventory . . . leaving a total of 541,539. Defense industry likewise has reduced its classified holdings from 15.4 million classified documents to 13.8 million.[10]

Progress is being made, but the residue of secrecy is gigantic. So many documents have been classified through the years that the security markings have become almost meaningless. The obvious problem with such massive secrecy is that quality has been sacrificed for quantity. As the previous discussion has demonstrated there are a few types of information that ought to be protected, at least for short periods of time. If there were a very carefully controlled small program similar to the Atomic Energy Commission's "Restricted Data" it would be more likely that genuinely secret information could be kept secret. The present gargantuan system is so out of hand that it is virtually impossible to separate the wheat from the chaff.

It is absurd that a large government staff is at work reviewing documents for declassification that are over twenty-five years old. It is even worse that after such a wasteful effort, significant numbers of the documents remain classified.

A legitimate task might be the review of classified information only a few years old. In the case of diplomatic information, declassification often would be justified after a few months. Edward Teller says,

> According to my estimate our chief competitors, the Russians, can get hold of almost any piece of information they desire in the technological field within a period of approximately one year. . . . I am suggesting that a time limit of two years should be imposed. This means that any document classified . . . will be automatically freed of any classification after a period not exceeding two years from the date of the original classification.[11]

Teller believes that Americans can progress more rapidly and effectively than the Russians through open research — scientists sharing ideas and information with each other rather than being closed off, as is often the case with Russian scientists. He says:

I think that in the research phase we should have essentially no classification. In the special case of lasers this could make a great contribution by the Edisonian method of trying many small things. Classification tends to interfere with the process that could go on in our research institutions and even our universities all over the country. . . . When something has been developed to the stage where we want to make a system that is to be deployed — then at that stage let's classify it. . . . We can get an advantage of two or three or four years. Let us essentially leave research open, but classify development. Then when the development is complete at the peak of deployment, pay serious attention to rapid declassification. Because by the time we have deployed something in a wide manner, the Russians will find out about it no matter what we do.[12]

Secrecy and the Military-Industrial Complex

One of the least-understood dangers of the huge and powerful interlocking relationship of the military and the defense industry is the impact of the secrecy system on that complex. The secrecy system provides the Pentagon with a controlling grip on those industries, which to a considerable degree makes them agencies of the U.S. government. As of July 1974 there were over 11,000 industrial facilities and research centers cleared by the Department of Defense to handle and have custody of classified information. Since Executive Order 11652, providing authority for the classification system, is for the protection of U.S. government information, the security arrangements established in private industry, universities, and research centers are, in effect, U.S. government adjuncts because they are using government-owned and -controlled information at taxpayers' expense.

All research and production carried out by U.S. private enterprise under contract with the Department of Defense if it involves, or may involve, classified information requires the signing of a Department of Defense security agreement. The private facility must adhere to all U.S. government rules for safeguarding classified information. In order to meet government security standards a very complicated and expensive series of requirements must be fulfilled. In 1951 those industries which had contracts with the Pentagon were instructed in security requirements in a 16½–page Department of Defense Industrial Security Manual. Today that same manual has 272 pages of detailed security instructions.

One of the most basic requirements called for in the Security Manual is that almost all employees having access to classified information be given a U.S. government security clearance. Employees having access only to confidential information must be cleared by the contractor, except that government clearances must be granted in certain cases. In the past twenty years more than 5 million citizens have been granted government clearances. No one knows how many millions have been granted contractor clearances. They have often waited for six months or more while the clearance investigation was being conducted by security officers. And eminent scientists and other key personnel employed by an industry have, at times, been excluded from the work.

The Defense Department now has an Information Security Management course at Richmond, Virginia, available for both government and defense industry personnel. It provides training for what the departments calls classification management responsibilities.[14] The trained industrial security officers learn how to handle and store classified documents, how to deal with personnel security issues, how to supervise visitors and persons who do not have security clearances. The Industrial Security Manual provides explicit details of requirements for physical security. Many industries have their entire physical plant under security, while others have only certain secured facilities which deal with the specific defense work under contract. A secured facility has limited and controlled entrance with armed guards. All personnel must wear special badges which are shown at all times, just as is done in government agencies dealing with sensitive information.

Some parts of defense industries are so secret that personnel, in addition to showing their badges, must sign in and sign out of those particular areas. All of the standard rules regarding safes and secure rooms with combination locks and the burning of classified waste are followed.

The cost of maintaining such security facilities is substantial, but the industries and universities that have them don't protest because the government pays for almost all such expenses. This permits a firm to bill some normal operating expenses to the security charges. For example, all industries have receptionists, guards, and janitors, but when they are given clearances and become part of a security system they are chargeable to the government. William Florence, a retired U.S. Air Force security expert, has estimated that the annual cost to the taxpayer of maintaining these security facilities is over 100 million dollars a year.[15]

For most industries, universities, and research centers the financial benefits from defense contracts far outweigh any inconvenience or administrative difficulty caused by government security arrangements. Actually a cleared defense contractor gains considerable advantage over a noncleared competitor because he can make bids for sensitive weapons contracts and also because he gets special access to classified information in his field of technology. Security has become so important for the business of some companies that they will go to extraordinary lengths to avoid violations of secrecy rules and possible blacklisting. Some U.S. firms, including some very large ones, could lose as much as 60 percent of their business if the Pentagon became dissatisfied with their security and withdrew their government clearances.

In many firms, security officers operating under the guidance of military authorities have become the key men in the personnel divisions. In theory the security chiefs are not supposed to have the authority to hire and fire, but in practice their word often is law. "If security frowns at a prospective employee, we won't touch him even if he is a Nobel Prize winner," said one company executive. Some firms are so jittery about meeting Pentagon security requirements that they have installed military-type security procedures throughout their entire operation rather than limit them to areas engaged in defense activities.[16] The Pentagon sends out teams of inspectors, usually twice a year, to ascertain that the terms of the industrial security agreement are being fulfilled. It is interesting to note that during fiscal year 1974 the Pentagon made 14,000 inspections at facilities with classified material and almost 7,000 at facilities that had no classified material.[17] The reason for this is that many businesses, once cleared, keep up their security systems, even though they don't have any defense business, in the hope that some day they will win another defense contract.

One Defense Department security expert reported that it is not only the cost of operating the security system that must be considered, but also the cost of maintaining inventories of classified documents. He said at a meeting on classification management that "one Defense Department element reports that it costs in excess of three million dollars annually to maintain its classified inventory of over one million documents. You can use your own imagination when considering the cost expended by both [the Pentagon] and the defense industry in maintaining our classified inventories on a worldwide basis."

As already reported there are almost 14 million classified documents in defense industries which would mean a cost of 42 million dollars a year just to keep up the inventory. The Pentagon expert went on to say:

It came to my attention not long ago that one of our contractor facilities, a research laboratory, had on hand some 3800 linear feet of classified holdings (documents, tapes and IBM-type cards) stored in 408 security containers. It immediately occurred to me that such holdings had to be excessive for a facility of its size with only one current classified contract, and that this classified inventory undoubtedly could be reduced.

I asked my classification management people to look into the matter. The result of this inquiry was most gratifying. Within six months the facility substantially reduced its classified holdings, primarily by destruction and declassification, thereby eliminating the need for 56 expensive security containers and reducing the costs associated with the handling and inventorying of material formerly held classified. . . . This particular facility earns a "well done."[18]

This is a sad and revealing story. It demonstrates how far a small research facility with only one defense contract will go in the direction of false secrecy to protect its government security status. After six months of undoubtedly expensive work, the reduction in unnecessarily classified information is only 56 out of 408 security containers and still earns a "well done." But worst of all is the probability that most, if not all, of the information should never have been classified in the first place. According to William Florence,

The preponderance of technological information currently being designated in Defense contracts as confidential or higher does not qualify for secrecy under the restrictive "damage" standard of Executive Order 11652. In some types of contract work the degree of *unnecessary* classification approaches 100 percent; in other types, the degree is estimated at 75 percent.

More than half of all research and development is paid for by the U.S. government. A great proportion of the work is for the Pentagon. In 1974 the military research and development budget was a whopping figure in excess of 9 billion dollars. Most of this research is conducted under the control of the secrecy system and pervades the entire American scientific community. By no means limited to the research divisions of the great corporations and government-inspired "think-tanks" such as RAND, it also reaches deep into the academic community. In 1963, after President Eisenhower's farewell warning about the military-industrial complex, twenty-six universities and colleges conducted a study of the impact of government contracts on their functions. They unanimously agreed that the federal funds were beneficial though they were aware of the dangers to academic freedom. They also noted that federal funds had created an imbalance between science and nonscience departments and within the national scientific community, that 90 percent of the money went to 5 percent of the universities while 1900 schools received almost nothing. The most powerful universities received two-thirds of all their research money from the Government. For example, MIT had 75 million dollars in defense-related money and was in twenty-first place among 388 defense contractors in research and development.[19] Much the same picture remains today except that MIT has moved up to a figure of 124 million dollars.

The Vietnam War, especially the uproar on university campuses caused by the Cambodian invasion in 1970, forced the academic community to reassess their contracts with the Defense Department. Many university presidents and some trustees were opposed to U.S. involvement in Indochina and agreed with the majority of students that they should not be supporting that war effort — even indirectly. The considerations of academic freedom grew larger and the financial benefits of government largesse smaller, at least for a while. Now that the war is over however, most of the universities are back feeding in the Pentagon trough. And most of those who do take on defense contracts bow to the security requirements already described. If a professor is dealing with classified documents he too walks past the armed guard displaying his security badge as he enters the secret laboratory.

The Secrecy System: Threat to Democracy and National Security

The implications of all this are dangerous and destructive for our democracy and also for our national security. The main problem is not that we have a system of wasteful and grossly excessive secrecy (which we do), but rather that under the cloak of secrecy we run the risk of a growing totalitarianism and a defense-oriented economy.

It goes something like this: The military men are trained to defend the country. Quite understandably they want the best weapons possible, and they hire the best brains to research and create those weapons. In order to spend the taxpayers' money to research, develop, and produce those weapons they see the need to educate the taxpayers concerning the dangers threatening our security. Sometimes, because they know more than civilians do about those dangers and because civilians may be apathetic, they decide to use shock treatment — especially at budget time. This is useful too in influencing their friends in Congress.

Since the United States has a free-enterprise system based on the principles of capitalism the government doesn't build the weapons, but contracts with private industry to build them. Despite the red tape and bureaucratic nuisance industries are eager to have defense contracts because their profits, often huge profits, are guaranteed by the U.S. Treasury — the American taxpayer. The contracts contain protective clauses providing for inflation, cost overruns, and very substantial overhead. Through the years of the Cold War, defense industries, shipyards, military airfields, and research centers have burgeoned, reaching into all fifty states of the Union. They all produce jobs and income to the states. As a result, there are very few congressmen who can champion significant defense cuts without some risk to their jobs. Obviously the strongest supporters of defense spending are those whose states have the largest share of defense industry.

Quite naturally, when generals, admirals, and high-ranking CIA officials retire from government many of them find well-paid positions in defense industries and research centers. In fact, the chief executives or vice presidents of a large number of defense industries are former generals or admirals. This can be very advantageous to the business because the former generals and admirals have excellent contacts in the Pentagon and know their way around with key members of Congress. When bids are made for defense contracts those businesses with capable admirals and generals in their management are likely to do better than those who don't have such military representation. This fact gives the industries and research centers aspiring for defense contracts a powerful incentive to hire generals and admirals.

So the Pentagon controls the defense industries by controlling who gets the contracts. The Pentagon also controls defense industry by an unplanned but very real assimilation of military men into the ranks of defense-industry management. Finally, the Pentagon controls defense industry through the secrecy system. Unless an industry or research center has security clearance it cannot have a defense contract. As we have seen, this means control over information and personnel — and that is power. The competition for defense money is so great that some corporations employ their own intelligence services and mini-foreign offices. They want to know as much about the national security situation in a particular area as the generals in the Pentagon. This can strengthen their bargaining position both at the Defense Department and in Congress. Some of the huge conglomerates such as ITT, as we saw in Chile, even arrange for joint operations with CIA and Defense.

It has long been a policy of the U.S. government that most arms sales abroad are handled by private industry. In 1974 these sales amounted to almost 10 billion dollars, often at profits of from 100 to more than 200 percent. The great surplus of Arab oil money will undoubtedly make it possible for the profits, in some deals, to rise to astronomical proportions. One of the consequences of this enormous, so-called "private" arms traffic is that most of the small wars and insurrections are fought with U.S. weapons. Ironically there are frequent cases where a government is fighting with expensive equipment provided by the official U.S. military-aid program against an enemy equipped with American arms acquired through private sales. All sales by private industry abroad are approved in the Pentagon and the State Department where a license has to be obtained from the Office of Munitions Control. This is another illustration of how misguided policy and profit walk hand in hand.

Very often the weapons or the information sold by private industry abroad are classified. Explaining this to a congressional committee, a representative of the Secretary of Defense said:

A great many U.S. firms producing military equipment for the U.S. also sell to foreign countries. It is quite normal for such equipment or technical data related to it to embody official classified information. When selling this equipment abroad, U.S. firms must obtain a Munitions License from the Department of State. These licenses are granted when the Government has determined that the sale is in the interest of *world peace,* national security and *U.S. foreign policy* [emphasis added].

Under these controlled circumstances the Department of Defense supports private firms selling certain goods and services embodying official classified information. The fact that commercial gain to a

U.S. company is also involved can be regarded as an added advantage particularly since the Congress has stipulated that arms sales, to the maximum extent practicable, be made through commercial rather than Government channels.[20]

In other words, the fact that a private firm uses government-owned national security information and know-how for commercial profit is a good thing. How many taxpayers would agree?

One of the difficulties that has emerged out of the secrecy system is that some industries have begun to classify their private information with U.S. government security markings, sometimes for reasons of legitimate concern, but sometimes merely to keep information from competitors or to add prestige to information being sold to foreign defense industries. This has happened, in part, because the Pentagon has encouraged it. In a series of questions to the Department of Defense, Congressman Moorhead asked,

> On what authority does the Department of Defense provide for classifying, even with a "tentative classification" any privately owned information? Answer: The Department of Defense provides for classifying official information under the provisions of Executive Order 11652. A "tentative classification" is a marking applied to official or *privately* owned information merely to afford a degree of protection to that information on an interim basis pending review for classification purposes by an authorized classifier. . . . It is the policy of the Department of Defense that only official information may be classified. Official information is defined as that information which is owned by, produced for or by, or is subject to the control of the U.S. Government.[21]

This system of "tentative classification has led to considerable abuse resulting in the classification of private information.

Another very major problem with the secrecy system is that it is not only in conflict with the principles of democracy but runs counter to sound business practice. The secrecy system stifles competition. Only those firms with security clearances are eligible for defense contracts, which restricts competitive bidding at the outset and also tends to allow those firms with access to information special advantages for future contracts. When speed and accommodation with Pentagon regulations are required, there is a tendency to limit the number of so-called reliable potential bidders. Sometimes contracts are let on a sole-source basis. This inadequate competition with virtually guaranteed profits runs in the face of the principles of free enterprise. Since it is so advantageous to be eligible for defense contracts it is not surprising that very few defense industries criticize the secrecy system, even though they are aware of the waste and administrative handicaps the program causes.

It is impossible to measure how much money the American taxpayer loses as a result of the secrecy system, but the figure is massive. Partly as a result of secrecy huge cost overruns occur. Some of this extravagance could be avoided if members of Congress and their staffs were provided with more detailed and precise information. Congressional oversight of the Pentagon has always been most inadequate, and one of the reasons given for the lack of military accountability has been the requirement to keep information classified. We have seen cost overruns on some defense contracts amounting to as much as two billion dollars. Overruns are always attributed to inflation and unexpected hardware shortages, but some of them must be linked to the poor management, inefficiency, and waste that result from the secrecy system.

Another destructive aspect of the secrecy system is, as Edward Teller so ably explains, that it inhibits research and development. Openness in science is dynamic and produces much more effective research. Just as competition is good for business, so shared information is good for science. Secrecy stultifies free enterprise and inventiveness. As Teller and other scientists have pointed out, our space venture to the moon was open, the Soviets' was secret. We landed men on the moon; they have not. In other words, in the field of science and research our national security is enhanced by openness. The Soviets may try to imitate and utilize our inventiveness, but they will never catch up if we are open and they remain closed. The danger comes when we adopt, as we have done so extensively in the defense field, their totalitarian techniques of secrecy.

The military-industrial complex is an aberration emerging from the Cold War. It runs in the face of all the basic political and economic principles of our society. But it is powerful and dynamic because it links security policy with profit. As long as our military men can persuade the public that our national security requires a military-industrial complex there will be no change, unless the civilian leadership directs such a change. In our democracy the President is the commander-in-chief and civilians are supposed to run the defense program. Unfortunately, the only recent President who warned of the military-industrial complex because he understood its dangers was a former general — Eisenhower. For a while President Kennedy and his Secretary of Defense, Robert McNamara, asserted strong civilian authority, dealing effectively with some of the problems discussed here. However, McNamara was soon totally bogged down in the Vietnam disaster. Presidents Johnson, Nixon, and Ford have done nothing about the military-industrial complex because all three have endorsed the national security policy assumptions upon which it is based. Thus, policy, politics, and profits have been thoroughly blended.

One of the difficulties is that public education on the subject has been inadequate, partly because of the secrecy system, partly because there are so many contented beneficiaries of the military-industrial complex, and partly because the average citizen has been so poorly represented. In the military-industrial complex, as we have seen, the classic distinctions between private and public have become blurred. The government (i.e., the Defense Department) has the control, but industry has the profit — a profit completely subsidized by the American taxpayer. When the taxpayer understands this, there may be an explosive reaction, especially when the taxpayer links the waste and extravagance of the military-industrial complex with the present recession and looming depression which is affecting his personal life. It may be, though, that change will come at the ballot box through the election of a new President and members of Congress seeking change.

One of the truisms about military production is that most of its end result is useful only in war. The fact that a large segment of our industry is tied up in military production for a possible war which is progressively less probable is a luxury we can no longer afford. A depression would threaten our national security much more seriously than Russia could, with its own deep economic problems. If the U.S. economy should collapse there should be no illusions, however, about the Soviets' not exploiting such an opportunity. There will be much less possibility of collapse if we seek to reform the disastrous practices of the military-industrial complex.

4

CIA and the Intelligence Community

The most controversial, least understood, and recently most criticized part of the national security establishment has been the Central Intelligence Agency (CIA). For the past decade CIA has been referred to as the very heart of "The Invisible Government" — a vast network of secret plans and operations for which there is little or no public accountability. There is a growing demand for better control and oversight if not outright elimination of CIA's covert operations (the so-called "department of dirty tricks"). The furor over CIA has been fueled by the linking of the agency with the "plumbers" and Watergate as well as the revelations about CIA involvement in Chile and domestic operations against U.S. citizens. A reassessment of the role and functions of CIA is long overdue, not only from the standpoint of phasing out archaic programs, but also for the purpose of revitalizing essential intelligence missions which have sunk to a low ebb.

As we have seen in the history of the secrecy system, there has been the strange phenomenon of a steady increase in secret government at a time when the Cold War was abating. Bureaucracies, once in operation and following a system, have a way of doing more of the same. They usually don't stop until their funds are cut off. In the case of CIA, created to fight the Cold War, there has clearly been inadequate adjustment to the emerging detente with the communist powers. Since clandestine operations, on both sides, are an obvious impediment to the process of detente a strong case can be made for phasing them out by both the U.S. and U.S.S.R.

In addition to clandestine political, paramilitary, and espionage operations, CIA has two other extremely important functions. The first is to provide the President and the National Security Council with intelligence estimates about major foreign developments relating to national security. Major changes in the organization and approach to the estimating process since 1973 indicate a decline in the prestige and effectiveness of that role. The second is to coordinate the intelligence effort of all the agencies involved. This responsibility is especially important in connection with intelligence obtained through technology — satellite reconnaissance, radar, code breaking, electronic intercepts and eavesdropping, and computers. This crucial function has apparently been increasingly strengthened by improved management and better cooperation among participating agencies. It continues to be important to have CIA in a coordinating role independent of the Defense and State departments. The questions for the future are what intelligence functions remain essential to the U.S. government, how best to organize them, and how to insure better accountability.

The Origins of CIA

It is not possible to understand CIA without looking at its roots, its reason for being. When World War II ended Americans were jubilant — peace had come, the armed forces could be demobilized, and OSS could be phased out. It was with considerable shock, therefore, that the public began to learn that Stalin and the Russians were not our friends and allies, but implacable enemies. More disturbing was the gradual realization that this was much more than a struggle between nations — it was a struggle of ideology. The dogma of Marxism-Leninism pursued by Moscow-led international communism called for a struggle which they claimed would inevitably lead to world domination by communism. Communist leaders asserted that Marxism-Leninism was infallible, and that fatal flaws within the "imperialistic-capitalistic" governments would lead to their decay and collapse in the face of competition from the communist world.

Only a handful of Americans had sufficient experience and

knowledge of Soviet affairs to comprehend the mysterious ideology. So the "Mr. X" article of George Kennan in *Foreign Affairs,* July 1947, entitled "The Sources of Soviet Conduct," had a special and lasting impact. Speaking of the ideology, Kennan said:

> The first of these concepts is that of the innate antagonism between Capitalism and Socialism (communism). . . . It means that there can never be on Moscow's side any sincere assumption of a community of aims between the Soviet Union and powers which are regarded as capitalist. . . . If the Soviet Government occasionally sets its signature to documents which would indicate the contrary, this is to be regarded as a tactical manoeuvre permissible in dealing with the enemy (who is without honor). . . . And from it flow many of the phenomena which we find disturbing in the Kremlin's conduct of foreign policy: the secretiveness, the lack of frankness, the dupose. . . . This brings us to the second of the concepts important to contemporary Soviet outlook. That is the infallibility of the Kremlin. The Soviet concept of power, which permits no focal points of organization outside the party itself, requires that the party leaderplicity, the wary suspiciousness, and the basic unfriendliness of purship remain in theory the sole repository of truth. For if truth were to be found elsewhere, there would be justification for its expression in organized activity. But it is precisely that which the Kremlin cannot and will not permit. . . . On the principle of infallibility there rests the iron discipline of the Communist Party. . . . But their [the two concepts'] effect cannot be understood unless a third factor be taken into account: namely, the fact that the leadership is at liberty to put forward for tactical purposes any particular thesis which it finds useful to the cause at any particular moment and to require the faithful and unquestioning acceptance of that thesis by the members of the movement as a whole. That means that the truth is not constant but is actually created, for all intents and purposes, by the Soviet leaders themselves. It may vary from week to week, from month to month. It is nothing absolute and immutable — nothing which flows from objective reality. It is only the most recent manifestation of the wisdom of those in whom the ultimate wisdom is supposed to reside, because they represent the logic of history. . . . But we have seen that the Kremlin is under no ideological compulsion to accomplish its purpose in a hurry. . . . Its main concern is to make sure that it has filled every nook and cranny available to it in the basin of world power. But if it finds unassailable barriers in its path, it accepts these philosophically and accommodates itself to them. The main thing is that there should always be pressure, unceasing constant pressure, toward the desired goal. There is no trace

of any given time. . . . In these circumstances it is clear that the main element of any United States policy toward the Soviet Union must be that of a long term, patient but firm and vigilant containment of Russian expansive tendencies.[1]

So we were confronted with an enemy with iron discipline and patience, ready to lie and manipulate the truth for tactical purpose, confronting us with constant, unceasing pressure, always with an eye to the ultimate goal of our collapse and communist control of the world. The more we studied the ideology and its operational application the clearer it became that we were up against something new. The Red Army and the Soviet military establishment were always referred to as purely defensive forces. (In fact, the Red Army has not once fought anywhere in the world outside of the so-called Communist Bloc, which includes the countries of Eastern Europe.) We soon discovered that the main weapon of Soviet pressure was to be clandestine political and psychological warfare.

All communists were trained in the operational principles of political warfare, what they called "agitprop" (agitation and propaganda). Young communists were indoctrinated to hate imperialism, especially the United States, and to understand the world view of what Stalin called the "two camps" (the good camp of communism and the bad camp of capitalism). Moscow had a great advantage, temporarily at least, in the fact that all communists were loyal to Soviet hegemony and were therefore proxy agents of Soviet power. Thus it was possible for Soviets to train and finance Italian or French communists, for example, so that they could gain power and influence on behalf of Moscow in the affairs of Italy or France.

Soon it became apparent that local communists were operating as agents of the Kremlin not only in national affairs, but in international organizations as well. The communists penetrated international labor organizations, youth movements, peace groups, intellectual and writers' organizations, as well as the media and all other useful outlets for political action and propaganda. Most Soviet diplomats at the UN and embassies abroad were members of the secret police apparatus (now know as the KGB). Just as

Soviet society in the U.S.S.R. was totalitarian, secret, and conspiratorial, so was the foreign operation of international communism run by and for Moscow.

George Kennan had called for containment of these Soviet "expansive tendencies," but the United States had no counterpart to the Communist party, nor did it have any mechanism for checking Soviet clandestine warfare. So in 1948 the NSC created an organization to run covert operations led by Frank Wisner, a former senior OSS officer. The organization, with the cover name of Office of Policy Coordination, operated within CIA but was also under the joint authority of State and Defense. At about the same time, an Office of Special Operations was created to handle covert intelligence and counterintelligence. It soon became apparent that the two organizations were creating administrative chaos and operational conflict, especially overseas, so in January 1951 they were merged into the "Directorate of Plans" as a single organization of clandestine services completely within CIA, which was then under the direction of General Walter Bedell Smith.

President Truman, concerned about the expanding covert political operations run from Moscow through international communism, created the Psychological Strategy Board (PSB) in 1951. The PSB director was Gordon Gray and the deputy director was Robert Cutler (later to become NSC staff chief for President Eisenhower), the other members were Undersecretary of State James Webb, Deputy Secretary of Defense William Foster, and Deputy Director of CIA Allen Dulles. The purpose of the PSB was to establish policy and coordinate operations in the entire field of psychological strategy, including covert operations. One of the assignments was to prepare a "strategic concept" for waging the Cold War. Among the members of the "strategic concept" committee were George Kennan, Charles Bohlen, and Frank Wisner.

They planned the creation of Radio Free Europe, Radio Liberty, and various organizations made up of exiles from the Baltic States and Eastern Europe who could represent an oppo-

sition political voice for the captive peoples of Eastern Europe.
The PSB also planned and obtained authority and funding for the
"Escapee Program," which provided care, resettlement, and encouragement for thousands of escapees and defectors from the
captive countries of Eastern Europe. As Kennan said in his "X"
article,

> The United States has it in its power to increase enormously the
> strains under which Soviet policy must operate, to force upon the
> Kremlin a far greater degree of moderation and circumspection
> than it has had to observe in recent years, and in this way to promote
> tendencies which must eventually find their outlet in either the break
> up or the gradual mellowing of Soviet power.

The PSB plans and the CIA operations were calculated to create
such strains.

General Reinhard Gehlen: Our Man in Germany

During this early phase of Cold War covert operations an
extraordinary twist of fate which was to have far-reaching implications was developing. Reinhard Gehlen, a Nazi general who
had been Hitler's chief of intelligence for the U.S.S.R. and Eastern
Europe from 1941 to the end of the war, had arranged to have
himself captured by American forces. He had also arranged to
have all of his intelligence files on the Soviet Union packed in
fifty steel cases and hidden underground.[2] Since the United States
had so little knowledge and so few Soviet intelligence specialists
there was considerable interest among U.S. military chiefs in
Germany and Washington when Gehlen offered his services.
Soon a deal had been made and the Gehlen organization went to
work for General Sibert, the head of Army G-2 in Germany in
1946. By the end of 1947 Gehlen and his organization had been
installed in the pretty village of Pullach, eight miles from Munich,
in a housing development built for SS officers. By then Gehlen
was working exclusively for CIA, with a charter granting great
independence and an all-German staff which soon amounted to
400 at the headquarters. During the next ten years CIA reportedly
subsidized the Gehlen organization with 200 million dollars,

partly from agency funds and partly by inducing the American business world to contribute large sums of money.[3]

General Gehlen had been one of the planners of "Operation Barbarossa," which was the German attack on the Soviet Union in 1941, sending Nazi divisions six hundred miles into the U.S.S.R. and forcing fifty million Russians under Hitler's rule. When Gehlen became chief of intelligence for the Eastern Front he began organizing a Russian Army of Liberation formed of anti-communist prisoners of war and partisans. By the spring of 1943 the liberation army under the command of defected Soviet General Andrei Vlassov was ready to move. Vlassov and Gehlen estimated that there were hundreds of thousands of anti-communist Russians prepared to join with the Germans in the overthrow of Stalin. At first Vlassov's propaganda leaflets promising good treatment to deserters and employment in the Vlassov movement produced massive defections. But Hitler did not agree with the terms and ordered mass executions and brutal treatment for the Russian deserters and prisoners. Had Hitler not been a maniac, Gehlen's plans might have produced a German victory in the East, certainly a substantial prolongation of the war.[4]

It is not surprising that the Soviets were jolted to find a Nazi general, for all practical purposes, in charge of U.S. intelligence operations directed against the U.S.S.R. Moscow described Gehlen as a "fascist criminal," a "revanchist," and a "warmonger." He was also named "as the biggest single factor in the prevention of a possible East-West detente."[5] There can be little doubt that the Soviets, fearing the Germans more than any other people, were greatly influenced in their assessment of U.S. intentions by the fact that the United States selected Gehlen for this role. But there can be little doubt, too, that given Stalin's aggressive moves at the time the United States would take advantage of every useful source of intelligence on the U.S.S.R.

The investment in Gehlen soon paid off for CIA. By 1950 seventy percent of all the U.S. government's information on Soviet forces and armaments came from the Gehlen organization.[6] The CIA was alerted by Gehlen in advance of the Pilsen uprising in East Germany in 1953, the Hungarian revolt in 1956, and the Soviet invasion in Czechoslovakia in 1968. Gehlen claims to have been first to have obtained a copy of Krushchev's secret speech denouncing Stalin. His intelligence operations exposed some of the most successful Soviet secret agents, and his plans led to the six hundred–yard tunnel CIA dug under East Berlin where the main telephone trunk lines leading to Moscow and other capitals in Eastern Europe were tapped and conversations tape recorded for nine months, until the operation was discovered. In June 1967 CIA Director Richard Helms was able to predict the exact date of the six-day Israeli attack in the Middle East. His source? General Gehlen.

CIA and the Dulles Brothers

To get back to the earlier days of the Cold War, CIA reached the pinnacle of its power and influence during the Eisenhower years. In January 1953 John Foster Dulles became Secretary of State and his brother Allen was Director of Central Intelligence. Foster Dulles was soon enunciating the policy of "massive retaliation" and a policy of "liberation" for Eastern Europe. Highly moralistic in his rhetoric, but unwilling to face the challenge of Joseph McCarthy, Dulles allowed morale in the State Department to drop to the lowest point in history. Partly because of the low esprit in the Department but also because he had an essential mistrust of the Foreign Service, Foster Dulles looked to Allen to take on the operational responsibilities of the Cold War. He would set the policy and Allen would carry it out.

Since CIA had already been granted the major role of covert political operations, this broader responsibility for Cold War operations was not too surprising. But it did have a fundamental and remarkable impact on the conduct of U.S. foreign policy. Allen Dulles was a doer, with a warm and friendly personality. Like General Donovan of OSS, Dulles attracted highly intelligent, highly motivated people who believed that the struggle against Stalin and international communism was similar in importance to the war against Hitler and Japan. Most of the top positions in

CIA, in those early days, were filled by liberals and original thinkers. Morale was very high.

The CIA station chiefs abroad, though they only carried the rank of first secretary or counselor in the diplomatic lists, were often more powerful than the ambassadors. Soon the word got around that the best way to communicate with the Secretary of State was through his brother. So, very important communications were often passed through the CIA chief to Washington. Another factor adding to the power of the CIA station chiefs was that they were responsible for handing out the money for anti-communist activities or for political parties struggling to win elections against communist parties, as in France and Italy. During the fifties CIA was undoubtedly more influential abroad than the Foreign Service of the State Department.

It was during this period that CIA leaders discovered that anti-communists of the left, especially socialists, were politically more effective than conservatives. This was so because socialism like the ideology of communism, Marxism-Leninism, was calculated to appeal to the workers, the proletariat, the have-nots. Socialists were some of the toughest fighters against communism. So CIA moved extensively into the anti-communist left. Labor leaders, writers and other intellectuals, socialist politicians, and student leaders were given financial support and were provided with information exposing communist subversion and political action.

The CIA arranged to finance and brief American leaders of the AFL-CIO and the National Student Association who participated in international labor and student organizations and meetings. The CIA supported anti-communist book publishing, magazines, cultural organizations, and veterans groups. During the early years of the Cold War the priority was given to fomenting resistance and unrest in captive Eastern Europe and blocking communist operations in Western Europe. With the help of the Marshall Plan and subsequent economic aid and the military alliance of NATO, Western Europe became secure, but CIA can be credited with much of the success in defeating communist attempts at subversion.

During the height of the Stalin era the decision was made to fight fire with fire. It was agreed that the end of defeating communism justified using subversive means. Since the communists were operating secretly, using covert political and psychological techniques, it was generally accepted within the U.S. government that we had to use the same methods. The Cold War had already produced a hot war in Korea and Americans were dying. Since the very nature of espionage and secret operations is to appear as something you are not, CIA officers were trained to deceive, to lie. If asked a direct question about their work CIA personnel were expected not to say "no comment" because that meant the same as "yes," but to answer with a cover story, a deception. In the same manner, questions from the press about U.S. covert activities were to be denied or handled with a cover story. Such deception of the American public was rationalized on grounds that it was better to deceive our own people than to give vital information to our enemies, the communists.

The communists, for their part, were never embarrassed by questions from their press because that press was completely controlled. Secret operations were totally secret and there was no such thing as a leak. This was true then, as it is today. As George Kennan pointed out in his "X" article, it was commonplace for the people of the U.S.S.R. to be lied to by their government if that were tactically useful to the men in the Kremlin, for either internal or external reasons. The American explanation for deceiving the public was to prevent the enemy from getting the information. This was the reason until the Vietnam War, when Americans were lied to because the people opposed the war and because Johnson and Nixon feared the political consquences of public reaction.

The "Gray Operations"

During the early fifties, the NSC established guidelines for what were known as "gray operations," operations which could involve Americans and/or American money, but should not be attributable to the U.S. government. If the U.S. government were known to be directly involved, it could be embarrassing to the United

States and might be the subject of diplomatic protest or more serious action. Direct U.S. involvement, if known, might also make the operation less effective. Thus, such operations were supposed to be plausibly deniable. A classic illustration of a now highly publicized gray operation was Radio Free Europe. Located in Munich, RFE was clearly an American instrument of the Cold War. But it was believed important that this appear to be a private radio venture. So the "Crusade for Freedom" was created, and every year the Advertising Council helped to raise money so that East Europeans could communicate with their people behind the Iron Curtain. If it had been acknowledged that RFE was a U.S. government propaganda asset it was felt that the legitimacy of the radio broadcasts as voices of Eastern Europe would decline. It would be the same as the "Voice of America," it was said. It was also felt that open U.S. government sponsorship and funding might make the German government vulnerable to diplomatic protest or to domestic political attack. Apparently none of the theories amounted to much, because RFE still broadcasts from Munich today as a fully acknowledged asset of the U.S. government.

After Stalin's death, the Korean War settlement, the recovery of Western Europe, the Geneva summit, the policy of liberalization in Eastern Europe, and the publication in 1956 of Krushchev's secret speech attacking Stalin and the "Cult of Personality," the intensity of the Cold War began to decline. When the "thaw" got out of hand in Hungary, with freedom fighters winning a temporary victory but soon crushed by Soviet tanks, the CIA gave up any illusions of liberating Eastern Europe. By 1957 the pace of covert operations in Europe, on both sides, had slowed dramatically, except for Berlin, where hundreds of spies and counterspies were constantly peddling their wares.

The action was gradually shifting from Europe to the Middle East, Asia, Africa, and Latin America. The end of the colonial empires of Britain, France, Belgium, and the Netherlands left a power vacuum which both the U.S. and the U.S.S.R. were determined to fill. In this connection a most unfortunate policy directive was issued by Secretary of State Dulles. He held "neutralism" to be almost as dangerous as communism. It was essential, he said, that political leaders be in the anti-communist camp of the "Free World." A neutralist was not likely to be neutral for long, he believed, because a neutral government would soon be taken over by the communists. Thus, instead of following the sensible policy of working with the dynamic left, as was done in Europe, CIA was instructed to support anti-communists who would "stand up and be counted."

While it is true that there were not many sophisticated politicians (such as the European socialists) to be found in Asia, the Middle East, Africa, or Latin America, there were many strong nationalists, as there are today, who wanted to be independent of both Washington and Moscow. Instead of pursuing an enlightened policy of encouraging and strengthening these nationalist tendencies, Dulles felt there was too much danger of communist subversion and overthrow. Thus CIA supported only those who were willing to assert their strong anti-communism and to accept U.S. political support and guidance. Such leaders were invariably rightist reactionaries with a narrow popular base — military dictators, more often than not.

This Dulles policy probably had more to do with many subsequent U.S. foreign policy failures than any other single factor in world affairs and undoubtedly extended the Cold War for at least ten years beyond the time when it should have lost its momentum. This was true because right-wing dictatorships are most vulnerable to resistance movements, and resistance movements have a tendency to accept communist support, especially if they can't get it elsewhere.

So, CIA began fighting communism all over the world, usually by supporting surrogate right-wing dictators. There were some so-called successes, such as the campaign to defeat the Huk guerrillas in the Philippines in 1950/53; the overthrow of Mossadegh in Iran which restored the Shah to full power in 1953; the overthrow of the pro-communist Arbenz government in Guatemala in 1954; the defeat of Allende in the Chilean election of

1958; the defeat of Soviet moves in the Congo and the successful support of Adoula and Mobutu in 1961; and the secret war in Laos 1962/73 which CIA Director William Colby said was a successful covert action.[7] There have also been highly publicized failures, such as the attempt to overthrow the government of President Sukarno of Indonesia in 1958; the Bay of Pigs invasion to oust Castro in Cuba in 1961; and numerous operations and programs to defeat the Vietcong in South Vietnam running through the entire Vietnam War.[8]

Through the fifties CIA was at its peak as a powerful instrument of U.S. Cold War operations. There were almost no public relations problems, and those few members of Congress who had some superficial knowledge of the Agency's clandestine operations were content that it was performing an important role in containing communism. The CIA was accepted as an essential part of the struggle, as was the secrecy about its activities. The objective of stopping the spread of communism was endorsed by an overwhelming consensus of the American public, including leaders from labor, business, the press, universities, both political parties, and even the churches. The Cold War constituency was so broad that it was not surprising to find members of Congress supinely accepting the fact that the CIA budget was completely hidden, without any public accountability.

It was not until the U-2 incident wrecked the Eisenhower-Krushchev summit of 1960 that CIA received its first bad press. Even then, when the mysterious U-2 operations were explained to the public there was broad acceptance of the strategic goal of acquiring information about the Soviet weapons system. Unfortunately, however, there was inadequate understanding of the damage done to the very real potential for a relaxation of tensions between the U.S. and the U.S.S.R. The detente that Nixon and Kissinger initiated with Brezhnev in 1972 might have come twelve years earlier, with a saving of hundreds of thousands of lives and billions of dollars.

CIA Becomes Controversial

The beginning of serious public mistrust and questioning of

the covert role of CIA came with the Bay of Pigs fiasco of 1961. Here again, there was less questioning of the objective than of the poor planning and performance. Most Americans had accepted U.S. policy concern about the growing influence of Castro in parts of Latin America. He was a communist and his government was dependent on Moscow. There had been a break in the wall of containment and a hostile communist government had emerged in the Western Hemisphere. So the issue was not whether it was appropriate to try to overthrow Premier Castro, but that the U.S. government had been involved in a disastrous, bloody failure which exposed very bad judgment on the part of the President and his principal advisors. Despite the serious doubts raised in some circles by the Bay of Pigs, CIA paramilitary operations continued through both the Johnson and Nixon administrations in both Vietnam and Laos.

In 1967 *Ramparts* magazine exposed the CIA funding and influence over the National Student Association, U.S. international labor activities, and many other activities such as Radio Free Europe and Radio Liberty. An immediate flurry of news stories and articles appeared, detailing other CIA subsidies to the Congress of Cultural Freedom, *Encounter* magazine, and other cultural and educational organizations. It was remarkable that CIA's support of these activities had not been exposed years before, but what was even more remarkable was that CIA was still funding such activities years after the battle for Western Europe had been won and the policy of liberation for Eastern Europe had been dropped.

As a result of the furor caused by the press exposé, President Johnson appointed a special committee, consisting of Undersecretary of State Nicholas Katzenbach as chairman, HEW Secretary John Gardner, and CIA Director Richard Helms to study CIA relations with private organizations. The committee unanimously recommended that: "No federal agency shall provide any covert financial assistance or support, direct or indirect, to any of the nation's educational or private voluntary organizations." President Johnson accepted the recommendation, which became national policy. After new mechanisms for funding were arranged for some of the programs considered to merit continuity, such as RFE and Radio Liberty, CIA phased out the rest of such operations — at least those involving U.S. organizations.[9]

Profound changes in world affairs have occurred since CIA was given the mission of waging the clandestine side of the Cold War, yet neither the CIA nor the KGB have significantly modified their activities to reflect the new reality. As noted before, polycentrism is rampant — Moscow no longer controls international communism. In fact, Moscow doesn't control the communist parties of Eastern Europe: Rumania pursues many independent policies; Albania is closer to China than to Russia; Yugoslavia remains completely independent, having recently broken up an anti-Tito spy ring run by the KGB. Even more important than the erosion of Kremlin control in Eastern Europe is the enmity of China. Soviet leaders now openly assert that China is the greatest threat to Soviet security in the world. Hanoi has long been independent of Moscow domination. Castro's Cuba has been recognized by most Latin American governments. The communist party of Italy has become so independent of Moscow that it publicly endorses anti-Soviet positions and it gives every appearance of intending to become a legitimate Italian nationalist political party. All of these developments, combined with the United States opening to China and the growing detente with Russia, make it clear that the original rationale for CIA covert operations has been overtaken by events.

Most critics of CIA have concentrated their attack on the covert political, psychological, and paramilitary operations, but not espionage. In fact, there seems to be a general belief that espionage is here to stay. It is true that there are large spy networks all over the world, especially in such places as Berlin and Hong Kong, but the days of Mata Hari and *The Spy Who Came in from the Cold* are numbered. The spy business is very seldom worth the risk or the money any longer. It has been overtaken by the techniques of counterintelligence and most especially by technology.

As in many other things, the machine is replacing the human being in the business of intelligence gathering.

The Decline of Espionage

It was generally conceded during World War II that the finest intelligence service in the world was the British. In fact, much of OSS and the early CIA was modeled after the British. But in 1951 Guy Burgess and Donald MacLean, who were British foreign service officers, escaped to Moscow. They had been under intensive investigation by British counterintelligence because, as it turned out, they were both communist spies. They were able to avoid arrest and disappear behind the Iron Curtain because Burgess had advance warning from Kim Philby, with whom they had worked closely in Washington, where he was in charge of British Intelligence (SIS) and liaison with CIA.

As we now know, Kim Philby's career was a disaster for British SIS, one of the greatest disasters in the history of espionage. A graduate of England's "best schools," Philby lived the life of a double agent for thirty years. He became a Soviet agent in 1933 with instructions to penetrate British intelligence.[10] He carried out those instructions with phenomenal success. By the end of the war he had become Chief of Section IX of SIS, in charge of all anti-communist and anti-Soviet counterintelligence.[11] In other words, a Soviet agent was in charge of protecting Britain and British intelligence from communist penetration. From this powerful vantage point he could help to promote the success of Soviet espionage.

Later, when he was the liaison with CIA, he was able to feed the Soviets details of the most sensitive covert operations. For example, in 1950 there appeared to be a possibility of a revolt in Albania against Soviet domination. The CIA and SIS had organized well-armed bands of resistance fighters and secret agents who were infiltrated into Albania, where more than half were killed in a well-prepared ambush. We know now that Philby had betrayed the operation, in advance, to his bosses in the Kremlin. When the Burgess-MacLean escape occurred the British in Washington were under a cloud of suspicion, especially in the midst of the uproar caused by the communist spy charges of Joseph McCarthy, which were at their height. Both CIA and M15 (British counterintelligence) had doubts, at that time, about the loyalty of Kim Philby, but SIS obstinately continued to insist that he was above suspicion.[12] Philby was finally taken out of executive responsibility, but incredibly he was allowed to remain in British intelligence until he fled from Beirut to Moscow in 1963, where he became a Soviet citizen and proceeded to publish much of the story of his thirty years of service to the Kremlin.[13]

Philby was far and away the biggest fish in the Soviet pond, but there were other penetrations of the SIS, one of the most important of whom was George Blake. Blake started his career in the Foreign Office and was sent to Korea, where he was captured by the communists and suffered hardships in Korean prison camps. After his return to London he was taken into the SIS and trained before being sent to Berlin, where he was assigned to infiltrate the Soviet espionage network. Unbeknownst to his employers he was already an agent of the KGB.[14] He worked in this sensitive position, without discovery, for more than eight years, during which time he told the Soviets about the CIA tunnel under Berlin. He had also betrayed many other Western intelligence operations to the KGB including more than fifty SIS, CIA, and Gehlen secret agents. In 1961 he was apprehended, tried at Old Bailey, and sentenced to forty-two years in prison. Shortly thereafter he mysteriously escaped from Wormwood Scrubs (the security prison) and vanished. In 1970 he finally surfaced in Moscow, having been awarded the Order of Lenin. The citation read:

Comrade Blake had rendered eminent services over a long period of years and under perilous conditions, and had foiled the operations of the British Secret Service and other hostile organizations which were directed against the Soviet Union and other socialist countries.[15]

Even more closely linked with CIA than British SIS was the West German intelligence organization of General Reinhard Gehlen. In 1955, with the establishment of the German Federal Republic under Chancellor Konrad Adenauer, it was not surprising that the Gehlen organization became the intelligence service of West Germany. But CIA continued to subsidize part of the cost of the organization and maintained extremely close liaison with it. So there was considerable shock when it was discovered in 1961 that the KGB had penetrated the Gehlen organization for ten years in a manner very similar to that of Philby and the SIS. The German Philby was Heinz Felfe, who also had become chief of counterespionage against the Soviet Union. Felfe was an opportunist who had been an active Nazi during the war; later he worked for British SIS but was considered a dubious risk; soon he was working for CIA and Gehlen, but eventually decided that he could make more money from the KGB.[16]

During the ten-year period he served the Soviets, Felfe exposed all of the Gehlen bases in the Soviet-controlled territory. Ninety-four agents and informers had been betrayed, along with codes, communication outlets, and courier channels, all carefully recorded on 300 Minox films totaling over 15,000 photographs, 20 tapes, and numerous radio messages. All Gehlen agents in Eastern Europe and the U.S.S.R. were affected because nobody knew the extent of the betrayal or whether they could still trust their contacts.[17] The Felfe affair, combined with changes in German political leadership and the new intelligence technology, contributed to the fading impact of Gehlen, who retired in 1968. The KGB had extensively penetrated, over a long period of time, the two Western intelligence organizations linked most closely to CIA. Their decline marked the end of an era. Human espionage was becoming insignificant to the business of national security decision making.

The Era of Technical Intelligence

Today very little intelligence comes from clandestine sources — perhaps five percent. The rest comes from the new technology or from open sources such as official reports, the news media, and scholarly journals. A considerable amount of useful information comes from research analysts using the same scholarly methods as university social scientists. As the usefulness of spies for intelligence collection has decreased, the science of technical intelligence has burgeoned. Code-breaking and cryptography are among the oldest forms of technical intelligence. One of the most publicized successes was the breaking of the Japanese code before World War II, but unfortunately it didn't avert Pearl Harbor.

In 1974 we also learned the incredible fact that the British had broken the German code during most of World War II. Today, because of electronic scrambling and computers, it is almost impossible to break codes of advanced nations; nevertheless, communications intercepts of less closely protected information can provide valuable intelligence.

During periods of warfare or even peacetime maneuvers valuable intelligence can be obtained by intercepting messages between tank commanders, for example, or between military aircraft and the ground. Communications between headquarters laboratories and instrumentation stations at weapons test sites, especially missile test ranges, can provide invaluable intelligence. Much of the interception can be accomplished from international waters or from friendly countries bordering the target area. However, the United States has found that depending on our friends to provide eavesdropping stations can create difficult problems of political indebtedness, according to Herbert Scoville, former Assistant Director of CIA in charge of scientific intelligence.

One of the more dangerous types of intercept operations occurs when there is an attempt to obtain air defense communications by flying very close to the target country's borders. There is always the danger that the plane may be shot down or that the target country may consider the flight a provocation. Related to communications intelligence (COMINT) is the interception of radio waves not used for communications, particularly radar, a kind of intelligence known as ELINT. Radar is used for tracking and detecting missiles and aircraft. In fact, most military operations (including naval) use radar, so ELINT is an important part of military intelligence.

As in the case of COMINT there are certain ELINT collecting operations that are provocative, especially attempts to detect anti-aircraft radar by flying aircraft or sailing ships close to the border with intercept equipment. Publicized examples are the 1960 incident off the Arctic Coast of the U.S.S.R., when a U.S. RB-47 was shot down and the crew captured by the Soviets; and the seizure of the *Pueblo* off the coast of Korea in 1968. The U.S. Navy operates at least a dozen ships like the *Pueblo*. The Soviets have a much larger fleet of such spy ships, often disguised as fishing trawlers supposedly limiting their operations to international waters. These ELINT ships are not only for coastal radar intercepts, but also to pick up the noises of submarines.

Another type of ELINT is the interception of telemetry signals sent at weapons-testing sites. Most data of this sort can be obtained at long distance, but some may be obtained from closer sites. For example, it is known that the United States has several stations in Turkey located on the southern border of the U.S.S.R., where much of Soviet weapons testing and missile launching is conducted. Since intelligence obtained from these sources is important, the United States is embarrassed when Congress wishes to cut off aid to Turkey for continuing to grow poppies for the heroin market in the United States.[18] More recently Congress moved to cut off aid to Turkey because of its invasion of Cyprus. The ensuing dispute between Ford and Kissinger, on one side, and a majority of Congress on the other was undoubtedly intensified by U.S. intelligence considerations.

The use of active radars to observe missiles in flight is known as RADINT. This type of electronic intelligence collection permitted the United States to spot the first Soviet ICBM test flight in 1957 and to monitor virtually all long-range-missile launches since that date. In order to observe medium and intermediate intercontinental missile tests the United States has had to maintain a base in Turkey. It was a very large installation, transmitting very powerful radio waves, so it was impossible to keep its presence secret from the Soviets. Apparently, however, no official protest was ever made to Turkey by the Soviet Foreign Office.[20]

Various methods are used to detect nuclear tests from long distances, including the use of acoustic and seismic receivers to pick up the shock waves a nuclear explosion transmits through the air and the earth. These measurements provide information about the size and location of the nuclear test. Tests in the atmosphere are precisely detected by examining smaller amounts of radioactive debris, studied by radio chemical analysis. Aircraft flying over international waters thousands of miles away from an atmospheric test can obtain adequate samples of radioactive debris from clouds. No provocative action is involved in acquiring the necessary information to detect nuclear tests.

By far the most important technological advance in intelligence collection is photoreconnaissance. Now, the entire Soviet Union can be photographed in a few days. In time, any target in the world can be observed by photo, the only limitation being cloud cover; and there are few places on earth that are continuously covered by clouds.[21]

According to Scoville, the U-2 which was developed by CIA could take pictures during a single flight covering territory 100 miles wide and 300 miles long. From 1956 to 1959 the main source of information about the Soviet ballistic missile program was the U-2. In fact, when U.S. officials ascertained that the Soviets had fully tested an operational ICBM there was fear that the Soviets might move into a lead over the United States — the so-called "missile gap." The desire to obtain more information about this possible gap was reportedly the main reason for risking Gary Powers's U-2 flight in 1960. The U-2 was also used over China to obtain information not available through any other technique, and the U-2 detected the Soviet missiles in Cuba in 1962.

During the early sixties both Moscow and Washington developed the capacity to use satellites to photograph each other's territory so accurately that missile silos could be identified. The strategic power of both sides could be measured from the sky — the most critical intelligence available. The satellites are able to photograph such wide swaths of territory that the entire Soviet Union can be covered in three or four days with one satellite. The satellites can be programmed to photograph very large areas or small specific areas requiring more precise detail. The cameras are capable of such accurate resolution that objects measuring a few feet or less can be observed. The information obtained by the satellites is transmitted back to earth by TV, or by returning the film in capsules which are recovered. The TV transmissions to ground take only an hour or two, but the pictures do not usually have the best quality and resolution. Film returned by recoverable capsule insures better pictures, but the return to earth and the subsequent development may result in a delay of several days, even a week or more.[22]

For years neither the Soviets nor the United States admitted their comprehensive information-gathering activities conducted from outer space. There may have been concern about the legality of such operations, but since they were both doing it there is a certain absurdity in the high secrecy that was maintained. In fact, the awareness by each side of the details of the strategic capability of the other was a stabilizing influence. Both sides became certain of their mutual ability to destroy each other. In 1967 a UN Treaty on Outer Space was adopted which banned the placing of weapons of mass destruction in space. It did not ban space reconnaissance, though there were no specific agreements endorsing spies in the sky either.

The first formal approval of space reconnaissance came in the interim SALT agreement signed in Moscow in 1972. The United States and the Soviets agreed that national technical means should be used to verify the provisions of the arms control agreements. They also agreed that the information-collection methods should not be interfered with and that there should be no deliberate attempts to conceal collection methods. Since no other country has ever objected to space reconnaissance, it may be assumed that this vital form of information gathering is now openly accepted.

Technical intelligence now produces comprehensive and reliable information never approached in volume or accuracy by other methods. The hard facts obtained from technical intelligence, without any international provocation, challenge the continuing validity of the more risky, politically sensitive techniques of human espionage. The U.S. defenders of espionage maintain, however, that technology while extremely valuable does not provide us with the information about the plans and intentions of our adversaries. They claim that a single high-ranking agent in the Kremlin can provide us with such vital information about Soviet intentions that it is still worth the investment of thousands of manhours and millions of dollars to acquire such a source of information. In view of the record, this classical position of espionage advocates is highly debatable and will be discussed in detail in the concluding chapter.

The Dubious Role of the KGB

As we have seen, the Soviets too have mastered most of the technology of information gathering. They can feel secure in the knowledge that they have precise information about what were once considered U.S. strategic secrets. In an era when Chairman Brezhnev says that "detente is irreversible" how can the continuing foreign covert political and espionage operations of the KGB be justified? Quite clearly, most KGB operations today are not essential to Soviet security needs in the intelligence field and often run counter to Soviet policy objectives in the political field.

Undoubtedly there is even greater bureaucratic resistance to change in the KGB than in the CIA. In fact, the entire Soviet system has very little flexibility when it comes to adjustments to realities which have changed the entire function and operation of secret services. Soviet society is still essentially closed, still pursuing a conspiratorial form of government which operates in secret and breeds paranoia — a constant fear of attack from without and within. In order to wage its struggle to control and expand its power, the Kremlin has always relied on a huge secret police apparatus. Today the KGB reportedly numbers 90,000 staff officers, most of whom serve in the U.S.S.R. insuring political and security control over the people and protecting the state from any external subversion.[23] Though there has been a decline in KGB activities abroad, Soviet foreign policy is still conducted extensively through clandestine operations, and a significant segment of all Soviet diplomats abroad are KGB officers. But KGB covert operations, like most CIA covert operations, are archaic and obsolete vestiges of the Cold War.

The leaders in Moscow can't help being aware that some of their major foreign policy setbacks have occurred as a result of KGB operations. The following are three recent illustrations:

In August and September of 1969 the KGB mounted a major deception campaign which was orchestrated in several world capitals over a period of six months. In Washington a so-called Second Secretary of the Soviet Embassy had lunch with a U.S. expert in Sino-Soviet affairs. The Soviet official was Boris Davidov, a senior KGB officer. Referring to armed clashes with the Chinese on the eastern border of the U.S.S.R., Davidov said, "The situation is very serious. In fact, it is so serious that my government may be forced to take much stronger action." "What kind of action do you envisage?" asked the American. "A preemptive strike?" Davidov replied, "Yes. A preemptive strike is being contemplated, and the use of nuclear weapons is not being excluded. What would be the attitude of the U.S. government if we made such a strike?" The American immediately reported the conversation which was relayed to the White House. President Nixon ordered that no response be made to this or any similar Soviet inquiry.[24]

In London, meanwhile, Victor Louis, undoubtedly the most publicized of all KGB operatives, wrote an article for the *London Evening News* which indicated that the Soviet Union was considering a preemptive nuclear strike against China. During the next several months there was a flurry of news items about aggressive Soviet intentions. In December, writing under a headline saying, "Chinese Communists Appear to Expect a Russian Attack," Joseph Alsop reported that long stalled talks dealing with border incidents were proceeding between the Soviets and Chinese. He said:

It is perfectly clear that the Chinese only consented to talk at all because of Soviet threats. . . . The language of the Chinese announcement of the talks quite openly implied that there had been Soviet threats of an extremely crude and brutal kind.[25]

So the KGB operation succeeded in pressuring the Chinese to resume the talks, but it also so alarmed the Chinese leaders that they put out feelers for secret negotiations with the United States. Shortly thereafter Henry Kissinger began his secret contacts which led to President Nixon's visit to China and the ensuing breakthrough toward more friendly U.S.–Chinese relations and membership for China in the United Nations. Surely no development has provided a greater setback to Soviet foreign policy, and the extent to which the KGB contributed to this must be considered part of an incredible blunder.

In 1955 the KGB began cultivating Sami Sharaf. By 1959 Sharaf emerged as the de facto chief of Egyptian intelligence. He arranged for joint Egyptian–KGB operations and Soviet training of Egyptian spies. By 1967 he had become Nasser's most trusted advisor and had more influence than such pro-Soviet leaders as Vice President Ali Sabry, Interior Minister Sharawi Gomaa, and War Minister Mohammed Fawzi. When Nasser made his decision to attack Israel, Sharaf was in the wings.

Nasser died in 1970 and was succeeded by Anwar Sadat. Sadat was neither pro-Soviet nor anti-Western, but he was very pro-Egyptian. He showed such independence that the Soviets began to worry about whether they would have sufficient political control to protect their substantial investment in Egypt. By the spring of 1971 Soviet leaders instructed the KGB to work out plans with Sharaf for a coup to replace Sadat. But Sadat was tipped off about the plot and the fact that he had inherited from Nasser both a chief of intelligence who was a KGB agent and senior ministers who were pro-Soviet conspirators. Sadat moved swiftly and had them all arrested, including ninety other plotters. Many Soviet military and diplomatic personnel were declared *persona non grata*. It looked as though the entire Soviet Middle East strategy would be a total loss.[26]

But Sadat was an Egyptian nationalist. He needed arms. He continued to accept the most modern of Soviet planes, tanks, and ground-to-air missiles. He accepted anything he could get from the Soviets until he had achieved his purpose in the "Yom Kippur" war of 1973. However, he did not forget how close the KGB had come to ending his career. There followed the extraordinary series of talks with Henry Kissinger ending in the tumultuous welcome to President Nixon, the restoration of diplomatic relations, and the beginning of a substantial American aid program for Egypt. Again KGB operations had set back Soviet foreign policy objectives.

In 1956 the East German intelligence services, which for years have been directed by the KGB, sent Gunther Guillaume, as an escapee from communism, to build a new life in West Germany. He did extraordinarily well. In seventeen years he moved from running a wurst and flower stand to becoming Chancellor Willy Brandt's personal assistant, one of three key aides. As one West German official described it, "It was as if John Ehrlichman turned out to be a Soviet agent." When it was uncovered, in the spring of 1974, that Guillaume was a spy, Brandt decided that it was in the best interest of the Federal Republic for him to resign.[27]

Brandt's resignation could have been a crushing blow to Soviet foreign policy. As it turned out, his successor, Helmut Schmidt, has continued most of Brandt's policies in external affairs. Brandt was the originator of the so-called "Ost policy" leading to a thaw in West Germany's relations with the Soviets and other East European governments, especially the recognition of East Germany as a separate, independent nation. Brandt's policies accomplished as much as did those of Kissinger and Nixon to promote detente. Chairman Brezhnev has been a fully committed advocate of relaxing tensions with West Germany and has been especially concerned that the recognition of East Germany should be consummated. Imagine what would have happened if Guillaume's arrest, and Brandt's resignation had led to the collapse of the "Ost policy." Here is an example of a situation where Guillaume should have been recalled before any political breakdown could occur, but the KGB left him in place, at incredible risk.

Thus, in the three most important areas of Soviet foreign policy, other than the United States, there have been serious consequences directly attributable to KGB operations. In China and the Middle East there have been major defeats; in West Germany there was a potential disaster that, fortunately for the KGB, probably won't materialize. Brezhnev must be wondering whether such operations should continue.

National Intelligence Estimates

The most important function of CIA and its Director is to provide the national intelligence estimates which assist the President and the National Security Council in making decisions about U.S. foreign and defense policy. These estimates are the ultimate distillation of all of the intelligence available whether obtained from space reconnaissance, espionage, electronic intercepts, or scholarly research. The CIA as coordinator of all U.S. intelligence has access to the information of all U.S. agencies responsible for intelligence collection. The Director of Central Intelligence (DCI) is chairman of the U.S. Intelligence Board (USIB), which includes the Defense Intelligence Agency (DIA), the National Security Agency (NSA) specializing in electronic intelligence, the State Department's Bureau of Intelligence and Research (INR), and representatives of the FBI, Atomic Energy Commission, and Treasury. The USIB reviews and comments on all national intelligence estimates before they are transmitted by DCI.

The man who had the greatest influence on the theory and practice of intelligence estimating was Sherman Kent, who was a senior research analyst in OSS and then, for more than twenty years, Chairman of CIA's Board of National Estimates. Kent believed that intelligence estimating should not become involved in recommending policy. The estimator should analyze the alternative courses without indicating choice. He considered intelligence to be knowledge for the practical matter of taking action, but he believed that decisions should be reached by the policy makers — the President and the secretaries of State and Defense. He believed that "intelligence should be close to policy, plans and operations for guidance, but not so close that it loses objectivity and integrity of judgment."[28] If an estimator had a personal stake in the outcome of a particular policy or operation his impartiality would be lost.

For the same reason Kent believed that estimators should be organizationally independent of the Defense and State departments. It was important that the DCI report directly to the President. Long before the creation of CIA, Walter Lippmann writing in *Public Opinion* (1922) said, "The only institutional safeguard [for impartial and objective analysis] is to separate as absolutely as it is possible to do so the staff which executes from the staff which investigates.

Until recently the theory of keeping intelligence estimating out of policy making has been practiced. But the theory of organizational separation has never been achieved. From the outset the Director of Central Intelligence has been responsible for all covert operations. Obviously a man who is responsible, for example, for an operation calling for the overthrow of the government of Iran will not be dispassionate in estimating the future of that country. The most unfortunate illustration of the consequences of having the DCI responsible for both estimates and operations was the Bay of Pigs disaster.

The other serious breakdown in the theory of separating estimators from operators is that all estimates before transmittal to the NSC must be approved by USIB. In other words, the operating agencies are participants in the estimating process. Furthermore, if a member agency does not agree with the final estimate as approved by DCI they have a right to file a dissent, and often do. This has been especially true of estimates about Soviet intentions. Since the Director of Defense Intelligence reports to the Secretary of Defense and the Joint Chiefs of Staff, it is not surprising that his estimates are often colored by policy positions of the Department of Defense. For example, from 1963 to 1965, when the Defense Department was pressing for a U.S. anti-ballistic missile (ABM) system, the DIA representative entered one dissenting footnote after another to NIE's dealing with the Soviet ABM plans which claimed that they were establishing ABM's around Leningrad. This did not prove to be true, but President Johnson granted hundreds of millions in development funds for an American ABM, just in case.[29]. Another danger in having the operating agencies participate in the estimating process is that there is a tendency to reach for the least common denominator.

The Board of National Estimates consisted of twelve to fifteen men and women from various backgrounds of law, business, university, military, or career intelligence, but in all cases with long experience in national security affairs and some specialized knowledge. An estimate may deal with a long-term prognosis such as the probable status of Soviet relations with China in five years, or it may deal with the most likely alternative courses of action in a crisis looming a week or two away. The most difficult aspect of estimating is political — the human element. Weapons systems, levels of military production, or the relative success of agricultural programs can be estimated with considerable precision; but when it comes to estimating the intentions of political leaders, or what will happen after the death of Mao or Tito the speculative element of educated guessing becomes more pronounced.

The estimator is not a collector, collator, or researcher; he is what Kent calls a "speculative evaluator."[30] After all the available data are gathered and sifted relating to a particular problem the estimator examines it and then makes an educated guess about what is going to happen. According to Kent such informed guessing, subject to error as it has to be, is far preferable to the alternative — "the crystal ball." One of the major criticisms of the use of national estimates as a guide for policy is that they are limited to information from abroad while foreign and defense policy is inextricably linked with domestic affairs. The policy maker must always be weighing the domestic political implications of any decision he makes. American policy in the Middle East provides an important illustration of this point. Even so, the policy maker while weighing all the aspects of a decision is certainly assisted if he has the best possible estimate of the situation abroad.

Related to the foregoing is the fact than an experienced policy maker with his sense of politics both national and international can sometimes make a shrewder guess than any intelligence estimator can. But that is not often the case. Unfortunately, a much more common occurrence is that an estimate is ignored because the emotional conviction and wishful thinking of the policy maker is controlling. The most tragic illustration of this happening time after time was the Vietnam War. The Pentagon Papers are full of illustrations of sound estimates being ignored in favor of disastrous policy decisions based on wishful, unwarranted optimism. For example, just before President Johnson ordered the massive intervention of U.S. troops the CIA estimate warned: "We will find ourselves mired down in combat in the jungle in a military effort that we cannot win and from which we will have extreme difficulty extracting ourselves." It should be pointed out that the only consistently skeptical member of the intelligence community challenging the optimism of U.S. Vietnam policy makers was INR in the State Department. According to Thomas Hughes, Director of INR at the time, there were hundreds of critical INR briefing items that were not mentioned in the Pentagon Papers at all. Hughes says, "The power not to listen may extend, it seems, to some of the authors of the Pentagon Papers."[31] Usually the Defense Department intelligence experts were very wrong on Vietnam.

As has been noted, the participation of intelligence representatives from the operating agencies, especially Defense, has tended to dilute the independence and objectivity of the estimating process. Given the flaws in the system, however, the CIA estimates have probably had more successes than failures. But that does not say much for the utility of the most important part of the intelligence business especially in those instances when the estimators have been correct and have been ignored, as was the case of Vietnam and the 1973 "Yom Kippur" war in the Middle East.

There have been national estimates which reached conclusions based on very bad guesses. In 1962, prior to the Cuban missile crisis, the NIE predicted that the Soviet Union would not take the enormous risk of placing nuclear-tipped missiles in Cuba. That estimate was accepted by the policy makers with extremely serious consequences. During the height of the crisis an estimate was produced warning that, rather than accept President Kennedy's ultimatum calling for the removal of the Soviet missiles, Kruschchev might risk nuclear war.[32] Fortunately that estimate was rejected by the policy makers.

Recently there have been complaints, especially from Henry Kissinger, that the estimating process has been insufficiently responsive to the needs of policy makers. Kissinger reportedly complained that the estimate had become "homogenized" and that basic objections to certain findings were submerged in fuzzy prose.[33] So, in the summer of 1973 William Colby abolished the Office of National Estimates and established a corps of National Intelligence Officers (NIO's). Each NIO would be responsible for a major geographic or functional subject and would be the intelligence specialist at the highest level in the government for that one subject. Thus there is an NIO for the U.S.S.R., China, Middle East, etc., and one for arms control, energy, and strategic weapons, etc. The studies prepared by the NIO's are reviewed by the U.S. Intelligence Board. Under this program the estimates will be produced by individual experts and will not go through the more rigorous staffing and discussion which was part of the process in the Board of National Estimates.

One former member of the Board said: "They're selling out to the Pentagon and the Defense Intelligence Agency. If the CIA made any contribution to the intelligence community it was that its analysts had no axes to grind, no military hardware programs and no policies to defend."[34] Officials of the CIA are concerned that Kissinger is not very interested in having an objective estimate which may challenge his policy conclusions.

When CIA and the military intelligence people have differed, Kissinger has tended to accept the military views. In 1969 the Pentagon asserted that the Russians had tested MIRV; CIA said no. Kissinger accepted the Defense view, but CIA was right. Kissinger

. . . minimized CIA warnings that the Viet Cong was still much
strong than the U.S. Command in Saigon claimed and that
pacification was far from successful. Kissinger, CIA people say,
never requested the Agency's opinion on the DIA plan to snatch
American war prisoners from the Sontay camp in North Vietnam
(the camp was empty when the raiders landed). No questions, they
say, were put to the intelligence community when the Administration decided on the Cambodian invasion in 1970, nor when the
White House decided to support the South Vietnamese thrust into
Laos in 1971 to sever the Ho Chi Minh Trail (the operation failed)
[according to investigative reporter, Tad Szulc]. CIA people wonder
why Kissinger never ordered the intelligence community to prepare
studies on all these plans before deciding to carry them out. . . .
To put it simply Kissinger devised a series of sophisticated moves
to weaken the intelligence apparatus so that he could become the
chief interpreter and arbiter of the intelligence product emanating
from each agency.[35]

The NIO's work closely with the staff of the NSC, which still is
directed by Henry Kissinger. Thus, Kissinger wearing his two
hats as Secretary of State and Presidential Assistant for National
Security Affairs is both producer and consumer of intelligence
estimates. He is also Chairman of the "40 Committee," which
has responsibility for approving all CIA covert operations. In
effect, Kissinger now stands between the Director of CIA and the
President in all its aspects. The independence and objectivity
originally contemplated in the National Security Act has been
seriously eroded. What to do about this will be the subject of a
concluding chapter.

5

Secrecy and the Media

In the First Amendment, the Founding Fathers gave the free press the protection it must have to fulfill its essential role in our democracy. The press was to serve the governed, not the governors. The Government's power to censor the press was abolished so that the press would remain forever free to censure the Government. The press was protected so that it could bare the secrets of government and inform the people. Only a free and unrestrained press can effectively expose deception in Government.[1]

So spoke Justice Hugo Black in the Pentagon Papers case. But until the Pentagon Papers were published by the *New York Times* and the *Washington Post* in 1971 the press did not have a reputation of exposing "top secrets" in matters of national security.

During the Cold War there was a vast consensus, including the press, which held that secrecy was an essential part of our stuggle with the communists, and no secrets should be published which would aid the communists. In matters of foreign policy and defense it was generally accepted that the people should delegate this authority to the President and he and his staff should be entrusted with making national security decisions in secret. The Cold War was considered by most to have essentially the same ground rules as a hot war.

The Korean War was very hot and was declared a national emergency. The Vietnam War, though undeclared, was even hotter and longer, with almost 50,000 Americans dead and hundreds of thousands wounded. These wars along with others in the Middle East, Africa, Asia, and Latin America involving U.S. supplies, equipment, and advisors and the ever-present balance of nuclear terror gave strong impetus for cooperation by the press with executive secrecy. In matters of national security most of the press felt they were serving the governed by not revealing the secrets of the governors. Most of the public would have been highly critical of any intentional exposure of national security secrets.

Under these circumstances it is probably not surprising that the press showed great discipline and restraint about exposing government secrets. As the noted columnist Stewart Alsop remarked:

> The Government has authentic secrets, and the right to protect them. The press has no God-given right to nose around such subjects as technical defense information which might be useful to a potential enemy, or order-of-battle information in wartime, or secret diplomatic negotiations to end a war, or a number of other categories of secrets.[2]

There have been numerous instances of members of the press voluntarily withholding extremely sensitive information. Chalmers Roberts, former diplomatic editor of the *Washington Post,* discovered the secret of the U-2 a year before Gary Powers was shot down in Russia. He said:

> I discussed whether it should be written about, but we decided against it. It turned out that some other newsmen also had discovered the secret, but they too remained silent. . . . We took the position that the national interest came before the story because we knew the U.S. very much needed to discover the secrets of Soviet missilery.[3]

The habit of thinking about the national interest was not uncommon among members of the press.

In early 1961 as the Bay of Pigs invasion plans ripened Gilbert Harrison, editor-in-chief of the *New Republic,* received a very full account of what was about to happen. Worried about the security implications of the story, he queried his friend President John Kennedy, who asked him not to print. He did not. Tad Szulc of the *New York Times* also got the story, but his bosses Orvil Dryfoos, the *Times* publisher, and James "Scotty" Reston were concerned about the national security implications and decided to play down the sensational aspects with no mention of

CIA. Dryfoos was especially concerned about the safety of the Cuban refugees who were about to risk their lives.[4] Ironically, shortly after the Bay of Pigs, Kennedy told Turner Catledge of the *New York Times,* "If you had printed more about the operation you would have saved us from a colossal mistake.[5]

Also in 1961, the *New York Times* unearthed the details of a secret base in the Rocky Mountains of Colorado where CIA was training Tibetans in guerrilla warfare, preparing them to return to Tibet to harass their Chinese occupiers. The story was never printed because the Defense Department learned that the *Times* had the story and asked that it not be revealed.[6] A day before the Cuban missile crisis was revealed to the American public by President Kennedy the *New York Times* learned most of the details. Again they were persuaded by the White House not to publish on grounds of national security.[7] The restraint of papers like the *Times* and the *Washington Post* was characteristic of the press throughout the fifties and early sixties; in fact, well into the U.S. involvement in the Vietnam War.

Government and the Press: The Cold War Cozy Relationship

Instead of assuming the role of public watchdog on matters of national security, most of the press developed a cozy working relationship with the government. In return for maintaining essential security and trust, the press was given important information through background briefings and tips. The most trusted columnists, editorial writers, and newsmen were often sought out to receive special briefings from the President and his top aides. Writers and their editors were not only willing but eager to assist in advancing U.S. Cold War objectives so long as the public was not being deceived in the process.

President Kennedy was a master of creative communication with the press — sometimes called "news management." He thoroughly enjoyed contact with the press and it was reciprocated to mutual advantage. In 1961, after his trip to Vienna to talk with Krushchev, Kennedy came back with foreboding about Soviet intentions in Berlin. He decided to sound the alarm at home. He had a very full discussion with "Scotty"Reston of the *New York Times* and confided some of his deep fears also to Phil Graham, editor of the *Washington Post.* Graham immediately called in his top foreign affairs writers Chalmers Roberts and Murray Marder, who wrote a series of articles about West Berlin called "The Beleaguered Bastion."[8]

There were occasionally newsbreaks that didn't reflect such happy cooperation with the White House. Stewart Alsop tells a wonderful story of the ingenuity of Chalmers Roberts and Murray Marder in digging for a story:

A good deal of Washington reporting has much in common with paleontology. A paleontologist will dig up a couple of square inches of skull, a wrist bone, and a rib, and from the morsels he will confidently reconstruct the entire skeleton of some prehistoric animal. In the same way, a reporter may come upon a few seemingly unrelated facts, and be able, from his knowledge of the whole situation, to construct a hypothesis which he can confirm with a few interviews or telephone calls. . . .

Marder and Frankel [*New York Times*] stopped to chat with McGeorge Bundy in the hall. Bundy fell to complaining about the eternal nosiness of the Washington press which made it almost impossible to carry on delicate and secret negotiations. As a matter of fact, he remarked, he was sitting at that very moment on a red-hot secret, which ought to remain secret, and he gave it a half-life of about forty-eight hours. Marder asked Bundy jokingly whether he'd take even odds against the story being in the next morning's *Post,* and Bundy smilingly agreed to the bet.

At this point Marder and Frankel already had their square inch of skull — they knew there was a story, and although they did not know what the story was, they were pretty sure that it had to do with the Cuban crisis. On their way out of the White House, they ran into George Ball, then Under Secretary of State, who was wearing a small grin.

Marder asked Ball what he was looking so cheerful about, and Ball replied airily that things weren't going too badly. Ball's grin was the wrist bone. Marder and Frankel knew that Ball was deeply involved in the effort to have the IL-28 bombers removed. [The United States had insisted that the Soviets remove not only their missiles but also their bombers from Cuba.] They both instantly constructed the same hypothesis — that some message had been received from the Soviet side promising to remove the bombers.

Both returned to their respective offices and began trying to confirm the hypothesis.

The vast *Times* staff got on the telephone to ask all sources whether it was true that Kennedy had received a message from Khrushchev promising to remove the bombers. Marder back at the *Post* recruited the help of Chalmers Roberts, the able *Post* foreign affairs specialist, and they decided to try a different tack. Their question was: "What was in the message from Khrushchev to Kennedy about the IL-28's?"

On about his fifth call Roberts hit pay dirt: "For Crissakes, how did you know about that? I can't tell you what was in the message." That was the rib — now Marder and Roberts knew their hypothesis was essentially correct. A little more checking, and Roberts was able to write a hard story, carried in the bulldog edition of the *Washington Post,* to the effect that Khrushchev had sent a message to Kennedy agreeing to remove the planes. Within minutes after the paper hit the streets, Roberts got an angry call from Bundy, who was in a considerable state of perturbation.

The *Post* story, Bundy said, was all wrong. Did Bundy mean to deny that there had been a message from Khrushchev, or that Khrushchev had agreed to remove the bombers? No, but there were qualifications. What qualifications? Well, for one thing Krushchev was demanding a public promise that the U.S. would not invade Cuba. After a few further exchanges, Roberts was able to write a story for the later editions of the Post describing the Krushchev offer in some detail, and beating the *Times* all hollow.[9]

There was always a certain amount of combat between the press and the government, but for the most part there was cooperation on matters related to winning the Cold War. Chalmers Roberts had this to say after a career spanning six presidents:

> While the press generally takes the position that any administration in power in Washington is trying either to "manage" or to "suppress" the news, often both at the same time, I think it is a fact that the U.S. Government, its executive and legislative branches taken as a whole remains remarkably open — even sievelike.[10]

There was an openness even in matters of national security so long as there was trust. The trust did not break down until the U.S. involvement in the Vietnam War.

Even after Vietnam and Watergate there have been instances of the press not publishing a story on grounds of national security. The most sensational example was the March 1975 story of the huge 350 million dollar ship Howard Hughes built for CIA for the purpose of dredging up parts of a sunken Soviet submarine to recover its nuclear-tipped missiles and code machine for intelligence purposes. The CIA used the gigantic ship in the summer of 1974 to carry out the top secret operation, but reportedly could not get up the code machine which, though out of date, might have enabled the code breakers to obtain valuable information about past Soviet policies and communications systems.

Some members of the press finally got on to the story, but because CIA was considering another try and because the operation might embarrass U.S.–Soviet detente negotiations CIA Director William E. Colby asked them not to publish. Among those who cooperated were *the New York Times, the Washington Post, the Los Angeles Times, Time, Newsweek, Parade* magazine, CBS, NBC, and National Public Radio. The story was finally broken by columnist Jack Anderson on his radio show. Anderson said that some of the press had become shaken by the power of the Watergate revelations to topple a president. Because of that he said:

> A lot of editors and reporters are wearing a hair shirt — sackcloth and ashes and lace and they're overdoing it a little bit, trying to prove too hard how patriotic and responsible we are. . . . The country was better served by a watchful press. . . . I don't think the government has a right to cover up a boondoggle. . . . $350 million literally went down the drain.

Benjamin Bradlee, executive editor of the *Washington Post,* said:

> This happens more often than the public might think, and when you have these decisions you have a balance. On the one side there's a claim by a government official of some standing that what you're about to print will harm the country's national security. But on the other side you have the conviction that you're being conned, that what is at stake is not any national security, but just plain embarrassment.[11]

The doubts expressed by Bradlee are the sad result of too much executive lying, too much "wolf-calling."

As we have seen, there were some lies along the way during the Cold War, but unfortunately not enough to arouse the anger of the American people and their press. President Eisenhower did lie about the U-2 incident, which he later assessed as the greatest mistake of his life. President Kennedy certainly dissembled about the Bay of Pigs and U.S. involvement in the plans for the overthrow of Diem. During the Cuban missile crisis Arthur Sylvester, the Assistant Secretary of Defense for Public Affairs, was heavily criticized by the press for having said: "The Pentagon has no information indicating the presence of offensive weapons in Cuba." Sylvester later said that

> . . . news generated by action of the government . . . are part of the arsenal of weaponry that a President has. . . . The results in my opinion justify the methods used. [Later he went even further and said:] . . . [It's] inherent in [the] government's right if necessary, to lie to save itself when it's going up into a nuclear war. That seems to me basic-basic.[12]

Johnson, Nixon, and the "Big Lie" Technique

Such thinking reflected the beginning stages of the use of the "big lie" to deceive Americans, under the guise of national security, a practice which has eaten away at the fabric of trust in government so essential to the successful functioning of a democracy. In time the "big lie" would be used not for the purpose of preventing a nuclear war, but for deceiving the public to gain support for a President's action when such support might not be obtained if the true story were known. The "big lie" technique was first perfected by Lyndon Johnson and then totally embraced by his successor Richard Nixon. Tragically for the nation, the extent of the lying by both men was discovered late in their White House tenure. A significant share of the responsibility for this must be borne by the press.

In January 1964 President Johnson talking to several reporters on his plane expressed his philosophy of working with the press: "If you play along with me I'll play along with you. I'll make big men of you. If you want to play it the other way I know how to play it both ways, too, and I know how to cut off the flow of news. . . ."[13] Most of the press got the message — and played the game. The major game was in Vietnam. Even in the so-called rescue operation when the Marines were sent into the Dominican Republic in April 1965 there was gross deception. Explaining the action President Johnson said, ". . . some 1500 innocent people were murdered and shot, and their heads cut off. . . ."[14] Later no U.S. official including U.S. Ambassador to the Dominican Republic, Tapley Bennett, could locate or explain the 1500 headless victims discovered by the President to arouse the American public.

But the use of the "big lie" as a tool of U.S. policy making has been centered in the Vietnam War from the so-called Tonkin Gulf incident to the present. Evidence is now in that the Tonkin Gulf incident was a fraud, manipulated by the Johnson Administration to anger the U.S. public and to generate in Congress the patriotic zeal that led to the almost unanimous resolution giving the President a free hand to escalate U.S. involvement in Vietnam. During the 1964 election campaign the President, having already decided to involve a large number of U.S. forces, assured the American people that the war in Vietnam should be fought by the Vietnamese themselves.

After the election he started the process of massive U.S. troop intervention and bombing which soon resulted in a war totally run by American commanders. From the outset there was an arrogance of U.S. power and an unwarranted optimism that led us deeper and deeper into the morass. There was never any intention to seriously negotiate a compromise solution, though the public was constantly informed that a negotiated settlement was our goal. The goal was a military victory over the Vietcong and the North Vietnamese, but the longer the war lasted and the more American boys were killed the more necessary it became to deceive the people. The President and his advisors were always seeing "light at the end of the tunnel." The whole sordid story of the Johnson era has now been revealed in the Pentagon Papers and such books as *The Best and the Brightest* by David Halber-stam. Unfortunately the information in those publications was not revealed until 1971 and 1972. The press could have made the difference had it told the real story as early as 1964, and on into 1967.

Now, it can be said that the press along with the public was deceived for all of those years. Indeed it was, but the deception was possible because too much of the press was eagerly willing to be manipulated — it had accepted the Johnson Administration policy assumptions. The Cold War consensus had continued into the Vietnam War, and most of the press accepted the premise of continuing to contain communism, blocking the "wars of libera-tion" of the Chinese communists, and arresting the dangers of "falling dominoes." Had there been more common sense and less accommodation to the fascination of power there would have been less tolerance for the politics of deceit.

Writing on this subject, *Washington Post* correspondent Haynes Johnson said:

I believe these conditions are among the terrible prices of the war in Vietnam. . . . [For] years the Washington press corps was a willing accomplice of government secrecy, official trial balloons, and justifications for policy failures. To some extent, it still is. My basic criticism of the press is that it was not critical enough — and I mean intelligent, sophisticated criticism, not mere name-calling. The press allowed itself to be used by the Government. By and large, it was a staunch supporter of government policies, particularly in foreign affairs. . . . Senator Fulbright described the *Washington Post* in 1967 . . . as "a newspaper which has obsequi-ously supported the Administration's policy in Vietnam," and President Lyndon Johnson told the editor of that newspaper that his editorials were worth a division to him.[15]

During these years the editorials of the *New York Times* were also supporting the Administration commitment in Vietnam, more often than not.

It was not the press that took the lead in bringing down Presi-dent Johnson. It was the people. The credibility gap caused by the lies of the Johnson Administration was too much for the voters of New Hampshire, and it was evident that Johnson would have been even more decisively rejected by the voters of Wisconsin. So, the President decided in March 1968 not to run again. The President had operated secretly and deceptively under the cloak of national security, playing on the trust of the people, assuring them that he had secret information not available to them which made it necessary for him to do what he was doing. Well, that trust came to an end. The demise of Johnson, however, did not have any instructive impact on his successor. In fact, Richard Nixon operated even more secretively and also adopted the "big lie" tactic. In the light of the Johnson experience with credibility it is amazing to observe how close Nixon and his men came to getting away with their deception. It is amazing too how quickly the public loses sight, in the fog of Watergate, of the fact that the major roots of the Nixon conspiracy were in the Vietnam War.

One of the reasons for this public myopia has been the failure of the press. No one has produced the Pentagon Papers of the Nixon years, yet we already know that the war was needlessly extended through four more years culminating in a well-orchestrated "peace is at hand" speech by Henry Kissinger just prior to the 1972 election. The four years were required because Richard Nixon believed in the commitment in Vietnam just as much as Lyndon Johnson did. Like Johnson, Nixon believed we should not negotiate a compromise solution. He said he wanted to negotiate, but the North Vietnamese were unwilling to enter into serious talks (i.e., unwilling to allow Thieu to remain in power). So he devised the policy of "Vietnamization," allowing him to pursue the politically popular course of gradually withdrawing all U.S. troops phased over four years, and thus ensuring his reelection. As in the early years of Johnson's massive intervention most of the press was hoodwinked by the policy of "Vietnamization." Like the public, most of the press was so relieved that U.S. troops were gradually returning home that there was very little exposure of the deceptions and inconsistencies of "Vietnamization."

Inadequate attention was given to the huge increase in the

U.S. air war. More bombs were dropped during the first three Nixon years than the last three Johnson years at the height of U.S. involvement. A Cornell University study published in 1971 concluded that the United States had dropped 6,000,000 tons of bombs and other munitions in Indochina, more than three times the total in Europe and the Pacific in World War II.[16]

Thinking back, it is difficult to comprehend how the Nixon Administration, any more than the Johnson Administration, was able to get away with misrepresentation of facts especially in view of the invasions of Laos and Cambodia, the secret bombing of Cambodia, the Sontay affair, the massive Christmas bombing of Hanoi and Haiphong, and finally the "peace agreement" which provided neither peace nor agreement. Though President Nixon was notoriously poor with the press, Henry Kissinger by contrast was remarkably effective — remarkable because so many of the policies he was peddling were either bad or not very good. Yet for years Kissinger, especially through his backgrounders, succeeded in maintaining a relationship with most of the Washington press corps which was strongly supportive and admiring, often verging on outright adoration. A recent popular explanation of this phenomenon developed by pundit Joseph Kraft, has it that Nixon came to be so hated that Kissinger was able to assume the role of "secret good guy," even though he was often the architect of much of Nixon's foreign policy.

The Pentagon Papers and the Ellsberg Trial

We know now that publication of the Pentagon Papers in June 1971 sent a chill of fear through the Nixon Administration. The fact that Daniel Ellsberg had released those papers was so disturbing to Nixon and his men that the "White House plumbers" were created, a psychological profile (or two), of Ellsberg was requested from CIA, and the infamous break-in of the office of Ellsberg's psychiatrist was planned and authorized by the White House. The trauma created by one sensational revelation after another as the Watergate story unfolded has so benumbed most Americans that insufficient attention has focused on the Ellsberg story.

At the time of the publication of some of the Pentagon Papers in the *New York Times* and the *Washington Post* most readers were angered and depressed to read of the deception, lying, and fuzzy thinking characteristic of the Vietnam policy making of the Johnson years. But the Nixon Administration was in no way involved in the Pentagon Papers drama. Why should the release of those papers cause such panic for Nixon and his men? The reason was that Nixon had been employing the same kind of secret deception concerning Vietnam, under the cover of national security interests, as Lyndon Johnson. Nixon was acutely aware that Vietnam had ended Johnson's career and was determined that it would not end his own. If the exposures in the Pentagon Papers were linked to his own operations he saw that his chances in 1972 could be jeopardized.

Nixon's willingness to employ desperate and illegal measures in secrecy, justified by so-called overriding national security considerations of the Vietnam War, started in 1970 when he approved the "Huston Plan," which was produced after the Cambodia invasion when the country was in a turmoil of marches on Washington, campus disorders, and bombings. The nation was dangerously divided and the political consequences for Nixon were obvious.

A young White House staffer named Tom Charles Huston was given the assignment of preparing a coordinated plan. In addition to the FBI, the planning agencies included the intelligence agencies of CIA, the Defense Intelligence Agency, and the National Security Agency — none of which has authority to engage in domestic political affairs. The report signed by the directors of CIA, DIA, and NSA not only called for the intelligence agencies to engage in internal U.S. affairs, which is expressly prohibited by statute, but also authorized illegal measures such as burglary, surreptitious entry, opening private mail, and electronic surveillance. Huston said that

. . . the public disclosure of these techniques would result in widespread publicity and embarrassment, but operations of this type are performed by a small number of carefully trained and selected personnel under strict supervision. The technique is implemented only after full security is assured. It has been used in the past with highly successful results and without adverse effects.

J. Edgar Hoover of the FBI was the only opponent of the plan.[17] The President, weighing the risks of engaging in illegal activities, jeopardizing his intelligence agencies, and facing the opposition of his FBI Director, made the incredible decision to approve the plan. The fact that the President was prepared to take such a risk demonstrates how desperate he was. Hoover persisted in his opposition with the result that Nixon reversed himself. However, this confrontation between Nixon and the FBI soon had farreaching and devastating consequences. The CIA became actively involved in domestic operations against the anti-war groups.

In the fall of 1970 the government discovered that Ellsberg had duplicated some of the Pentagon Papers. There was an intensive security investigation at the RAND Corporation where Ellsberg had been employed. Several volumes of the "Top Secret" papers had been brought from Washington to RAND in Santa Monica, California, where Ellsberg took them out for reproduction and then returned them to the classified files of RAND. Through the next several months copies were given to several sources, including the New York Times, which began to publish daily installments on June 13, 1971. The Times published for three days and then was ordered by Federal District Court Judge Murray Gurfein to halt on grounds of "grave and immediate danger to the security of the United States."

At about the same time, the Washington Post had obtained more than half the papers that Ellsberg had originally copied. After a lengthy battle between the cautious lawyers and the enthusiastic newsmen, publisher Kay Graham decided to tell the story.[18] After two installments and two contentious hearings in the Circuit Court of Appeals, the Post too was ordered to cease publication. The courts also restrained the Boston Globe and St. Louis Post-Dispatch from publication. This was the first time in American history that the press had been restrained from publishing foreign policy material which the government claimed was a threat to national security.

While the decision of the lower courts was being appealed to the Supreme Court by the newspapers, Herbert Klein, the President's Director of Communication, held a backgrounder for the press at which he said the question of whether the *Times* had endangered the nation's security was of less concern to the Administration than permitting a precedent that would encourage future leaks.[19] This was a very revealing admission that the real concern was the political vulnerability of the Nixon regime to future Pentagon Papers–type revelations.

The government apparently did not think it had a solid case on grounds covered in the Espionage Act nor in the Executive Order establishing security classification authority as a basis for prosecution. In fact, the government's brief did not cite the espionage statutes nor did it question whether criminal laws had been violated. The government wanted a continuing injunction against publication on grounds of national security. Solicitor General Erwin Griswold, arguing the government's case, did indicate that it would be extremely difficult to obtain a jury conviction of a criminal offense for the publication of the papers if the Court ruled that the papers could be published.

The *Times* and *Post* challenged the government's position on many grounds, especially the whole interpretation of secrecy. One of the best-informed affidavits was produced by Max Frankel, the chief of the Washington Bureau of the *New York Times*. He said reporters

> . . . regularly make use of so-called classified, secret, and top secret information and documentation. . . . [Without] the use of "secrets" . . . there could be no adequate diplomatic, military and political reporting of the kind our people take for granted, either abroad or in Washington. . . . I know how strange all this must sound. We have been taught, particularly in the past generation of spy scares and Cold War, to think of secrets as secrets — varying in their sensitivity but uniformly essential to the private conduct of diplomatic and military affairs and somehow detrimental to the national interest if prematurely disclosed. By the standards of official Washington — Government and press alike — this is an antiquated, quaint and romantic view. For practically everything that our

Government does, plans, thinks, hears and contemplates in the realms of foreign policy is stamped and treated as secret — and then unraveled by that same Government, by the Congress and by the press in one continuing round of professional and social contacts and cooperative and competitive exchanges of information. . . . [The] reporter and the official trespass regularly, customarily, easily, and unselfconsciously (even unconsciously) through what they both know to be official "secrets". . . . The Government hides what it can — and the press pries out what it can. . . . Each side in this "game" regularly "wins" and "loses" a round or two.[20]

The Supreme Court ruled 6–3 that the government had failed to justify prior restraint against the press in the light of the First Amendment. So the *Post, Times, Globe,* and *Post-Dispatch* were free to publish the rest of the Pentagon Papers. However, in the process of reaching the decision the opinions of various justices contained ominous warnings for the press that future prior restraint was not barred nor was criminal prosecution under the Espionage Act. Justice White, joined by Justice Stewart (both of whom had supported the majority opinion), cited sections of the espionage laws and stated that the standards in a criminal prosecution would have been quite different.

Justice White in his opinion said:

. . . terminating the ban on publication of the relatively few sensitive documents the government now seeks to suppress does not mean that the law either requires or invites newspapers or others to publish them or that they will be immune from criminal action if they do. . . . [He went on to say that the newspapers] were now on full notice of the position of the United States and must face the consequences if they publish. . . . [That] the government mistakenly chose to proceed by injunction does not mean that it could not successfully proceed in another way. . . . [Referring to the espionage laws he said,] I would have no difficulty sustaining convictions under these sections. . . .

All of the concurring opinions dealt with the problems of prior restraint, and none took issue with Justice White.

Among the dissenting opinions Justice Harlan, with Justices Burger and Blackmun concurring, concluded that the Court should restrain publication if it was satisfied that the subject matter "does lie within the proper compass of the President's foreign relations power," and if the responsible cabinet officer concerned determined that disclosure "would irreparably impair the national security." It is clear that if the government had chosen the course of criminal prosecution the three dissenting Justices might have joined White and Stewart, and perhaps others, in a far-reaching decision against the newspapers.

During the course of the various Watergate trials and hearings there has been no authoritative discussion of the tactics used by the government in New York Times Company v. United States. However, a good guess is that the reason the government didn't attempt criminal prosecution of the press was that it had decided a more effective criminal prosecution could be made against Daniel Ellsberg. In fact, the Grand Jury in Los Angeles, which had been impaneled in March 1971 issued a two-count indictment against Ellsberg on June 25, 1971, just five days before the Supreme Court decision. The indictment charged the defendant with

> . . . unauthorized possession of, access to, and control over copies of certain documents and writings relating to national defense . . . willfully, knowingly and unlawfully retaining the same and failing to deliver them to the officer or employee of the United States entitled to receive them [and] Daniel Ellsberg did willfully, knowingly and unlawfully convert to his own use copies of certain documents and writings . . . the aforesaid documents and writings being things of value to the United States. . . .

In other words, Ellsberg was indicted for stealing government property and failing to return it. At that time nothing was said about transmission of the information to unauthorized persons.

Months later, in a superseding indictment of fifteen counts, both Ellsberg and Anthony Russo were charged with conspiracy to commit offenses against the United States including "defrauding the United States and an agency thereof by retaining Government property, but also impairing, obstructing, and defeating its lawful Governmental function of controlling the dissemination of classified Government studies, reports, memoranda and communications. . . ." Judge Byrne ruled to strike some of the language of the indictment before the trial, including the applicability of

Subsection 793 (d). The trial eventually got under way on January 17, 1973.

In the meantime, just after the first indictment of Ellsberg and the Supreme Court decision at the end of June, the White House "plumbers" were created to conduct domestic covert operations with the principal goal of destroying the reputation and credibility of Daniel Ellsberg, but always relating their activities to the broader objective of protecting Richard Nixon's Vietnam War objectives. Hence there were such operations as Howard Hunt's forging of a State Department cable in order to deceive the public into believing that President Kennedy had planned the assassination of Diem. There were also operations such as ordering some of the Cuban-Americans, who later were caught in the Watergate break-in, to beat up Ellsberg at a peace rally in Washington.

It was felt that the "plumbers" should be in the White House, partly, at least, because the FBI had refused to cooperate with the "Huston Plan" the year before. It supposedly was not appropriate for CIA to conduct such operations since Congress had forcefully stated in the National Security Act that, "the agency shall have no police, subpoena, law enforcement powers, or internal security functions." However, Howard Hunt and others associated with the "plumbers" operations had CIA backgrounds and there was close cooperation with the Agency — in fact, highly illegal cooperation, as subsequent revelations disclosed. The CIA had for years experimented with psychological profiles of foreign leaders put together by panels of psychiatrists based on information available to the Agency. For example, before the summit meeting in Vienna in 1961, a profile of Khrushchev was prepared for Kennedy's use. So the "plumbers" asked CIA to prepare a psychological profile of Ellsberg, which was rejected by John Ehrlichman as not being hard-hitting enough. In order to prepare a better profile the psychiatrists needed better information.

This led to the most notorious of the "plumber" operations — the break-in of the office of Daniel Ellsberg's psychiatrist on September 4, 1971. It was also the most damaging to the government. The CIA was involved, providing special equipment used for clandestine operations, including disguises, cameras, and photographic equipment. Pictures were made of the psychiatrist's office, hallway, parking lot, etc. Apparently some of the prints of this film are in CIA files, even today. The "plumbers" were given a remarkable degree of independence if the testimony of their bosses Ehrlichman and Colson is to be believed. Whatever the truth, it is certain that Richard Nixon was astounded by the stupidity of the break-in. The following is taken from the edited transcripts of the White House tapes released by President Nixon April 30, 1974:

Meeting of the President and John Dean in the Oval Office, March 17, 1973:

DEAN: . . . The other potential problem is Ehrlichman's and this is —

PRESIDENT: In connection with Hunt?

DEAN: In connection with Hunt and Liddy both.

PRESIDENT: They worked for him?

DEAN: They — these fellows had to be some idiots as we've learned after the fact. They went out and went into Dr. Ellsberg's doctor's office and they had, they were geared up with all this CIA equipment — cameras and the like. Well they turned the stuff back in to the CIA at some point in time and left film in the camera. CIA has not put this together, and they don't know what it all means right now. But it wouldn't take a very sharp investigator very long because you've got pictures in the CIA files that they had to turn over to (unintelligible).

PRESIDENT: What in the world — what in the name of God was Ehrlichman having something (unintelligible) in the Ellsberg (unintelligible).

DEAN: They were trying to — this was part of an operation that — in connection with the Pentagon Papers. They were — the whole thing — they wanted to get Ellsberg's psychiatric records for some reason. I don't know.

PRESIDENT: This is the first I ever heard of this . . . .[21]

While the President and John Dean were talking, the government was pursuing its criminal prosecution of Ellsberg and Russo in California. The White House wanted to win that one badly, so badly, in fact, that Ehrlichman, with the obvious knowledge of the President, offered the FBI directorship to Judge Byrne, to take effect after he finished the trial. The White House also sent

Army Vice Chief of Staff General Alexander Haig, in uniform with all his medals, as a witness for the prosecution to attack the credibility of two defense witnesses.

But is was all to no avail. Judge Byrne dismissed all the charges against Ellsberg and Russo because of prosecutorial misconduct, including, but not limited to, failure to produce wire-tap logs of Ellsberg's telephone conversations, and failure to report at the prescribed time that burglars employed by the White House had been sent to break into Ellsberg's psychiatrist's office files. The whole shabby story was part of the larger conspiracy of deception in the two succeeding governments of Johnson and Nixon, starting with U.S. military intervention in Vietnam and, it is hoped, ending with Watergate.

Unfortunately, neither New York Times Company v. United States nor United States v. Ellsberg settled some very important legal questions which were surfaced in both cases. The fundamental question of the extent to which the First Amendment protects the press and the citizenry from criminal prosecution in matters of secrecy was left dangling. In the New York Times case some Supreme Court justices indicated that the press might have been subject to criminal prosecution based on the theft-conversion statute or the espionage laws. In the Ellsberg case, though the timing of the indictment was just prior to the New York Times decision, Ellsberg was not charged for having released information or materials to the press or anyone else. He was first indicted only under the "retention" section of the espionage laws and the "conversion" law.

Undoubtedly, the surprisingly limited first indictment reflected that, in support of the policy of secrecy and deception, the White House wanted Ellsberg charged immediately. There was no time to wait until all facts could be obtained. And it can be safely concluded that the reason Ellsberg was not indicted for any sort of disclosure to the press was that it would have been necessary to include the press in the criminal charge. That course would have required hard, admissible evidence and an above-board objective that the White House did not have. This conclusion is virtually confirmed by the fact that six months after Supreme Court justices made comments about possible action against the press, the superseding indictment charging both Ellsberg and Russo with violation of law regarding conspiracy, conversion, and retention of documents relating to the national defense did not include or even refer to any newspaper or individual member of the press.

It is worth examining the specific criminal case against Ellsberg and potentially against the *Times*. Ellsberg was charged under 18 U.S. Code, Section 641, which makes it a crime to steal, embezzle, or convert government property. This was the first time in history that information, referred to in the indictment as reports, writings, documents, etc., had been claimed as government property. There is a question of how government ownership of information is legally established. It is interesting that in the *New York Times* case the government did not make this claim. If all defense information which had a classification marking were considered as the property of the government then what would the courts do about all the information that has been given intentionally to the press or published, after retirement, for commercial profit by government officials, including many former presidents?

Also as a historical first, the government charged Ellsberg, in one count, with conspiring to defraud the United States by defeating its lawful governmental function of controlling the dissemination of classified government studies, and so forth, which really constituted *information*. But the system of classifying official information was established by Executive Order, not by act of Congress. The order applies only within the executive branch of our government. As will be discussed in the chapter dealing with Congress, one of the important failings in the control of government secrets is that the system has not been established by law. Violators of the classification regulations are only subject to certain disciplinary procedures, including dismissal.

The only "classified information" expressly covered by the espionage laws makes it a crime to willfully disclose classified information pertaining to codes, ciphers, and cryptographic systems. Also, in 1950 Congress made it a crime for "government employees to communicate classified information to foreign governments or communist organizations or their agents" [50 U.S. Code Subsection 793 (d)]. The other type of protected information is "Restricted Data," as defined and controlled by the Atomic Energy Act. There is no law upon which to base a conclusion that all information classified by the government is protected by criminal sanction.[22] Judge Byrne emphasized this fact repeatedly in the Ellsberg-Russo case.

But the government stressed that the information in the Pentagon Papers was not ordinary classified material, but was "Top Secret," the highest category in the classification system. Yet William Florence, the retired Defense Department security classification specialist who served as consultant to defense counsel, in testifying as an expert witness said he had reviewed all twenty exhibits charged against the defendants, and, using the definition of national defense interests contained in Executive Order 10501 (the authority at that time), he concluded that none of the information required any classification when Ellsberg reproduced them.

David Nissen, the prosecuting attorney had said: "Your Honor, we are confident that the only question concerning classification is whether the documents were actually classified by someone with authority to do so. . . ."[23] Morton Halperin, who had responsibility under the Secretary of Defense for the preparation of the Pentagon Papers, has stated that he was not even aware of the contents of Executive Order 10501. Leslie Gelb, who supervised the study and who routinely used the "Top Secret" classification on the papers, did not even have "Top Secret" classification authority.[24]

In addition to the section of the espionage law dealing with codes (Section 798) the two other most important sections are 793 and 794. Section 794 punishes for transmitting information relating to national defense to foreigners if it is done "with intent or reason to believe that it is to be used to the injury of the

United States or to the advantage of a foreign nation." It also covers, in time of war, information about troop movements and military plans which are intentionally "communicated to the enemy.

It was Section 793 of the espionage law that was used for the criminal charges drawn against Ellsberg and Russo and was the section which the Supreme Court justices had in mind in the *New York Times* case. Subsections (c), (d), and (e) are generally interpreted to make it a crime to receive material in the "knowledge that it has been obtained in violation of other provisions, or to communicate defense-related material to any person not entitled to receive it, or to retain such material." These provisions would seem to make it a crime for any individual or newspaper to receive, retain, or communicate defense-related material without authorization by the government.[25]

According to Mr. Benno Schmidt, of Columbia University Law School, an authority on the espionage laws, the subsections of 793 pose the greatest potential threat to newspapers and reporters who obtain and print national defense information. These statutes are in "almost certain conflict with the First Amendment." Some of the language in these subsections were amendments in the Internal Security Act of 1950 to deal with what was perceived to be a "substantial threat of domestic communism." Subsection 793(e) was extended to nongovernment workers expressly because of the alarm caused in Congress by the "pumpkin papers" found in the Whitaker Chambers–Alger Hiss case.[26]

As we have seen, the early fifties were emotional days — the height of the Cold War, the fears of a communist "fifth column," and the spy scares. Since then Congress has refused time and again to place criminal sanctions in support of a classification system based on Executive Orders. Professor Schmidt concludes that

. . . the confusion in legislative history constitutes a clear invitation to the courts to declare subsections 793(d) and (e) unconstitutional on grounds of vagueness and overbreadth. . . . These two subsections are virtually incomprehensible. . . . In my reading of the Espionage

Statutes, publication of defense information not animated by a purpose to communicate to a foreign country is not prohibited, except for the narrow range of cryptographic information.[27]

Whether Professor Schmidt is correct or not, there can be no doubt that there is a requirement in both the executive branch and the Congress to develop a much clearer set of ground rules to guide the nation in striking a balance between freedom and security of information.

The Nixon Administration, frustrated by its inability to control leaks to the press and troubled by the weak case against Ellsberg, decided after the landslide election to tilt the balance of information control far in the direction of secrecy. Nixon and his lawyers felt it was time for the United States to adopt something like the British Official Secrets Act of 1911. The British have always had much more comprehensive control over government information than the United States. Section 2, the so-called "catch-all" section of the British Act, provides for criminal prosecution of any government employee or former employee who communicates official information to unauthorized persons. It also provides for prosecution of those who receive official information "knowing, or having reasonable ground to believe, that it has been communicated . . . in contravention of the Act." In other words, though it is called the Official Secrets Act it provides for criminal prosecution for the unauthorized distribution or reception of all official information whether classified or not.

In 1972 the British Government appointed a Commission under the chairmanship of Lord Oliver Franks, former British Ambassador to Washington, to review Section 2 of the Official Secrets Act. The Franks Commission recommended that Section 2 be repealed and replaced by an entirely new Official Information Act, while retaining the Official Secrets Act with its espionage provisions. The new Act would no longer provide for controlling all official information, but would be limited to

. . . cabinet documents, information likely to assist criminal activities or to impede law enforcement. . . [and] classified information relating to defense or internal security, or to foreign relations, or to the currency or to the reserves, the unauthorized disclosure of which would cause serious injury to the interests of the nation.[28]

Even this language permits a much more broadly based control of information than that covering the classification of national security or national defense information in the Executive Orders of the United States. The Franks Commission recommendations did not go very far toward relaxing information control in Britain, but even they have not been adopted yet and the prospects do not look bright.

The British have another remarkable device for controlling sensitive information in the press known as the "D Notice." The D Notice is an administrative procedure with no legal authority which is run by the Defense, Press, and Broadcasting Committee, a nonstatutory body composed of government officials dealing with defense and national security and representatives of press and broadcasting. The D Notices are sent to the press and broadcasters informing them that specific items of information are regarded by the government as secret and requesting that the media not publish. The press has with very few exceptions obeyed all D Notices since the system was inaugurated in 1912, perhaps because in practice, though not legally binding, the Notices were in fact an alert for the risk of prosecution under the Official Secrets Act.[29]

It is not surprising, therefore, that the Nixon Administration looked enviously at the British system and pressed aggressively to try to emulate it. In March 1973 Nixon sent Congress a massive revision of the Federal Criminal Code, contained in a 600-page bill which included revival of the death penalty, attenuation of the insanity defense, and a proposal for official secrecy more drastic than anything required in World Wars I and II, the Korean War, the Vietnam War, and the Cold War.[30] The proposed law was modeled on the Franks Commission recommendations and made it a federal crime for *current and former government personnel* merely to disclose classified information. The bill provided also to make criminal *any* person who disclosed *any* national defense information to another person not authorized by the government to receive it. Any recipient of such "national defense information," including, of course, the media, would be subject to criminal prosecution unless such information was returned to the government immediately. The "reason to believe" and injury factors in current law were dropped. The proposed law also provided that the unauthorized communication of classified information by current and former government employees could be punished even if the information has been improperly classified. Thus any information marked "Top Secret," "Secret," or "Confidential" by the thousands of government officials with such authority could lead to a $100,000 fine and fifteen years in jail during war or a "national-defense emergency." In peacetime the law called for $50,000 and seven years and $25,000 and three years for minor offenses.

Among other things, the Nixon proposals were designed to overcome the law established by the Supreme Court in the United States *v.* Gorin. The Gorin decision gave the jury the right to make a determination whether information which had been communicated to unauthorized persons truly pertained to national defense. The Justice Department has alleged that the Gorin decision makes it necessary to disclose the very information which the government seeks to protect and that, therefore, the government has had to forgo prosecutions because security prevented the disclosure of information to juries.[31] In the Ellsberg case, however, the government introduced into evidence *eleven* "Top Secret" documents which retained that security classification throughout that public trial. After the trial the government put them back in "Top Secret" storage.

If the Nixon proposals had been adopted, the government would have had absolute power to make unchallenged determination concerning what information should be classified, with prosecution and conviction virtually guaranteed even if the information were classified in error.

David Wise, a journalist and author who has long been concerned about government secrecy, had this to say about the Nixon proposals:

Such legislation would of course give the Government total control over information, instead of, as is now the case, only partial control. Its passage would mean the effective repeal of the First Amendment, and the early arrival of 1984 in time for the American Bicentennial. What is truly shocking about such legislation is not its terms and its provisions, which are totalitarian, but the fact that the legislation would have been drafted and proposed at all. It reveals a quality of mind . . . frightening to anyone who respects truth and values freedom.[32]

Fortunately, Watergate has made the enactment of any such legislation most unlikely, but that does not mean that the pressures for greater security control are not continuing.

CIA and the Press

The relations of CIA with the press need to be looked at from several standpoints, including the maintenance of essential secrecy by keeping sensitive information away from the press, public relations and the image of CIA, the manipulation of the press through leaks and briefings to advance foreign policy objectives, and the clandestine use of the press for operational purposes. By its very nature CIA abhors publicity, which it usually receives when something has gone wrong but understandably very seldom when things are going well. Allen Dulles used to emphasize to his staff that successful CIA employees had a passion for anonymity, getting their satisfaction from a job well done in a very closed community, but never from public recognition.

Several years after they had retired, former CIA Director Allen Dulles and former deputy for operations Richard Bissell appeared in May 1965 in a remarkable NBC TV News program narrated by John Chancellor called "The Science of Spying." The program dealt explicitly with the "dirty tricks" side of CIA, with emphasis on the overthrow of the Guatemalan government in 1954 and the Bay of Pigs in 1961. Richard Bissell, speaking of our struggle against communism, said that

. . . most of our conflict is in the non-military dimension. . . . [We] are rivals in a whole variety of activities that are not public, that are not open, including espionage, subversion, which more precisely I suppose could be described as the effort to influence the course of events in other countries covertly.

Speaking of the dilemma confronted by the United States in attempting to block left-wing governments supported by the communists, Bissell said: ". . . we find ourselves supporting the right, not because we are rightest, but because there are literally no other alternatives to chaos, or to encouragement of those who have made themselves explicitly our enemies."[33] That dilemma has continued to trouble the government in exactly the same way, most recently in the uproar over CIA covert operations in Chile. In 1974 and 1975 a growing segment of Congress urged that CIA phase out most of its secret political activities, and that none should be undertaken without the express approval of Congress. In order to check this tide, CIA Director William Colby had more direct contact with the media than any of his predecessors, including TV interviews, press conferences, participation in a public debate, and a *Time* magazine cover story. In the latter interview Colby said: "The CIA's cloak-and-dagger days have ended." But he defended the continuing need for a capability to operate covertly, saying that to prohibit such operations would "leave us with nothing between a diplomatic protest and sending in the Marines."[34]

Through the years of the Cold War, at least until the U-2 incident of 1960, CIA had what it considered an excellent press, i.e., almost nothing. Even the U-2 affair brought mixed reaction, because CIA was given well-deserved praise for planning the high-flying plane with its precision cameras which permitted us to learn such valuable intelligence about the Soviet strategic weapons. It was not until the Bay of Pigs operation of 1961 that CIA received its first very bad press. But even then the impact was short lived. The next serious blow didn't come until the exposé published in 1967 in *Ramparts,* a leftist magazine. The so-called establishment press had been very gentle to CIA until recently — the era of the "big lie." The revelations about CIA's illegal domestic operations against U.S. citizens and the possible involvement of CIA in assassination plots were given very extensive press coverage.

As we have seen, during the Cold War the press was part of the anti-communist establishment. Those members of the press who were sought out by CIA welcomed the opportunity to receive special briefings and leaks clearly directed against the communists. Sometimes newsmen received an exclusive newsbreak of a sensational story; sometimes there would be a de-briefing of a recently defected KGB agent or an agent from one of the other communist espionage services. Allen Dulles was a master of the effective use of the world press against the communists. In addition to appreciating the usefulness of their contacts with CIA, most members of the press were persuaded of the need for essential secrecy — not only to keep information out of the hands of the communists, but also to protect the lives of CIA agents. Despite its remarkably good treatment from the press, CIA has become progressively concerned about control of secret information.

In 1969 a former CIA official wrote in *Foreign Affairs:*

The disclosure of intelligence activities in the press in recent years is a clear national liability. These disclosures have created a public awareness that the U.S. Government has, at least at times, resorted to covert operations in inappropriate situations, failed to maintain secrecy and failed to review ongoing operations adequately. The public revelation of these weaknesses, even though they are now partially corrected, hampers CIA (and the U.S. Government) by limiting those willing to cooperate with it and increasing those opposed to it and its activities. . . . Legislation, whether regarded as desirable or not (and even ignoring the Constitutional problems), is impossible to achieve in the present climate, and it would be unwise to count on improved prospects in the future.[35]

He was right; attempts to legislate further controls did not succeed. However, CIA leaders have continued to press for more protection of sensitive secret information. In 1974 CIA Director William Colby pressed for legislation which would permit stiff penalties for the crime of revealing information about CIA's methods or sources. Obviously there are methods and sources that need to be protected, but unless the definition is precise and the sources are specific there is danger that the First Amendment rights of the citizen and the press would be violated. This is a vicious circle, because CIA does not feel that it can go from the general to the specific without compromising its own security requirements. Unfortunately essential secrets are now much more difficult to maintain because of the gross irresponsibility of the government during the past decade when national security was used as cover for "big lies" to deceive the public.

The most sensational and highly publicized controversy over CIA information control has been the Victor Marchetti case, Marchetti, a former high-ranking CIA employee, had written a novel about his CIA experiences and was drafting a nonfiction book about the Agency which was inadvertently discovered by CIA. In 1972 Judge Albert Bryan issued an injunction prohibiting Marchetti from "disclosing in any manner (1) any information relating to intelligence activities, (2) any information concerning intelligence sources and methods, or (3) any intelligence information." Marchetti thus became the first American writer to be served with an official order of censorship by a U.S. court.[36] Marchetti appealed the prior-restraint ruling all the way to the Supreme Court, which refused to hear the case.

Anyone who works for CIA, as a condition of employment, must sign a secrecy agreement promising not to reveal any information learned while at CIA relating to sources or methods without first securing authorization from the Agency. So, when Marchetti completed his manuscript in 1973 it was delivered to CIA. The Agency required that 339 sections of the book be deleted on security grounds, between fifteen and twenty percent of the whole. Marchetti's lawyer, along with Knopf, the publisher, filed suit challenging CIA's censorship. By trial time, early in 1974, CIA had reduced the number of deletions from 339 to 168. At the trial all five of the Agency's highest-ranking officers testified about the importance of maintaining the secrecy of the remaining items. But Judge Bryan was not persuaded, ruling that only 27 of the 168 items required continuing classification. The CIA appealed the judge's decision to higher courts. The Fourth U.S. Circuit Court of Appeals reversed Judge Bryan's decision, ruling that Marchetti and Marks had failed to prove that the 168 deletions were improperly excised. Judge Clement Haynsworth, writing for the court, said that there was "a presumption of regularity in performance by public officials" who have the job of keeping government secrets. As we have seen in the Vietnam involvement and Watergate, such "presumptions of regularity" are very dangerous in a democracy which has insufficient accountability. Only Congress can resolve this matter by the process of remedial legislation.

The least known of CIA's relations with the media has been its covert use for operational purposes. In November 1973 the *Washington Star-News* carried a story reporting that CIA had thirty-six American newsmen on its payroll, including five who worked for general circulation news organizations.[37] Aroused by this story and concerned about its implications for freedom of the press, Stuart Loory, former Washington correspondent for the *Los Angeles Times,* investigated the subject in depth, publishing the results in the *Columbia Journalism Review.* He found:

CIA contracts with 30 journalists (by the Agency's own count) who work overseas as stringers, free-lance writers and full-time correspondents for small publications;

CIA efforts to plant fake or misleading news stories in world-wide news services;

CIA requests for information often accompanied by cash payments, made to U.S. newsmen in such diverse places as Spain, Italy and Eastern Europe, and to newsmen at home awaiting foreign assignments;

CIA access to information in the home offices of some large U.S. news organizations.

Loory concludes that

. . . if even one American overseas carrying a press card is a paid informer for the CIA, then all Americans with those credentials are suspect. We automatically — and with good reason — consider Soviet and Chinese newsmen as mouthpieces for their governments, while at the same time congratulating ourselves for our independence. Now we know that some of that independence has, with the stealth required of clandestine operations, been taken from us — or given away. Whether they work for large publications or small, whether they are full-time correspondents or stringers, any American journalist overseas who takes money from the CIA contaminates the reputation of all foreign correspondents.[38]

In other words, the end of defeating communists does not justify the means of adopting communist methods. The free press should be 100 percent free.

In summary, during the Cold War the American press was too willing to accommodate the government and not sufficiently jealous of its freedom and its First Amendment privileges and responsibilities. Recently, nearly too late, that has begun to change. Writing in *Foreign Policy* in the fall of 1974 Charles Bray, the State Department spokesman from 1971 to 1973, said:

> In sum, the public can reasonably expect the Government and the media to have another go at redefining their adversary relationship. . . . Nobody would suggest that reporters should lower their standards, but we can ask reporters to ask themselves whether their only role is to challenge . . . challenge . . . challenge.[39]

Possibly the pendulum has swung too far, but Mr. Bray is insufficiently aware that the era of the "big lie" probably would not have occurred if the press had adequately performed its adversary role and had challenged the veracity and the judgment of the government. Even today Henry Kissinger enjoys a remarkably benign and passive press.

6

Congress and Executive Secrecy

If the press can be faulted for its inadequate challenge to Executive secrecy in national security affairs, the Congress must be given even lower marks. A major reason that our system of checks and balances has not worked effectively, especially in the past decade, has been the failure of Congress to exercise its authority and responsibility in matters of national security. One of the reasons the secrecy system has been successfully used to cover up White House conspiracy and lying without check has been the passive acceptance by most members of Congress of Executive Branch domination. The Congress simply has not insisted on presidential accountability in matters of defense and foreign affairs.

As we have seen, starting in 1947–48 with the bipartisan approach to foreign policy enunciated by Senators Tom Connally (D.–Tex.) and Arthur H. Vandenberg (R.–Mich.), there has been a widely accepted myth that partisan politics should remain at home. In matters of national security, especially where communism was involved, the patriotic thing to do was always to support the President and, if outright support were not acceptable, at least to give him the benefit of the doubt and keep your mouth shut. This bipartisanship, this consensus, ensured virtually no opposition until Vietnam, and even then the congressional power of the purse was not used until very late, in response to public outcry. Throughout the Cold War, members of Congress eagerly passed every Defense budget, invariably granting more money than the President had requested. The astronomical outlays for the escalation of U.S. involvement in Vietnam, going as high as 27 billion dollars in 1967, were passed with only token opposition. The habits of the Cold War consensus did not readily change.

Today, after the worst decade in our history, there is a surge of congressional interest in the perils of excessive secrecy and lack of executive accountability. But there is a real question, even now, whether the necessary majority will be mustered to buffer executive branch freewheeling and to pass such laws as are needed to provide a better balance. Even after reading the Pentagon Papers and absorbing the full implications of the Watergate conspiracy there is a reluctance in Congress to change the old comfortable ways — a reluctance to insist through law that the executive branch be made accountable to congressional oversight in matters of national security.

There are many explanations for this situation. For years the Senate and House Armed Services Committees have been dominated by conservatives who have been strong supporters of the Pentagon and the CIA. In this role they had the full support of those agencies and the incredible power derived from such support. Since the power was shared both ways there was never a problem about secrecy. The more liberal Senate Foreign Relations and House Foreign Affairs Committees, with authorization responsibility for the State Department, USIA, and Foreign Aid, deal with budgets which are only a small fraction of the Defense budget, and have had, until recently, only limited impact on the conduct of foreign affairs.

There has been an understandable reluctance on the part of many members of Congress to be burdened with secret information. Congressmen thrive on public debate and don't like to be restrained about the information they discuss. Some of them feel that if they had access to considerable secret information they would be hampered as lawmakers and politicians. Some others just prefer not to know about some of the secret foreign policy plans because that way they don't have to take a position of responsibility one way or another.

Members of the House state that they just don't have the time for national security affairs. They are so busy representing the people in their individual districts, most of whom don't pay much attention to national security affairs (except when a Vietnam War comes along), that they don't have time to keep adequately informed about the details of national security. Furthermore, they are expending a substantial part of their time on the process of getting reelected every two years. Even in the Senate there is generally a lack of national security know-how except for some members of the Foreign Relations and Armed Services Committees, and those senators with presidential ambitions. Another important reason for the lack of congressional oversight has been the inadequate professional, research, and investigative staffing. The trust of and cooperation with executive branch agencies inspired by the Cold War consensus meant that Congress never gave priority to creating the necessary staff in the national security field.[1]

Until recently there has been limited attention to the dangers implicit in national security secrecy's threatening the foundations of our democratic system and the Constitutional rights of Congress. Several individual members have tried to alert their fellows, but for the most part a substantial majority of Congress has succumbed to the wishes of succeeding presidents. The twin tragedies of Vietnam and Watergate and the new interest in surveillance of the CIA may have changed those habits and we may be on the verge of a new era of congressional action.

There are four major areas of congressional concern for secrecy in the executive branch, each interrelated with the others, but for various reasons usually treated separately. These are executive privilege, the secrecy system and the classification of information, the secret operations of CIA, and espionage laws.

Executive Privilege

The nation can no more tolerate presidential withholding of documents when the Executive Branch is under Congressional investigation than it can afford to let a bank president dictate to a bank examiner what books he may see. Unhappy are a people whose suspected officials can lay down the terms of investigation, for then the investigation becomes a dead letter.

These are the words of Raoul Berger, one of the great scholar-authorities on executive privilege writing in the *Washington Post*.[2] The principle of executive privilege is a relatively new phenomenon. Even during the height of the Civil War President Lincoln met every request from Congress for information needed for its investigation of the conduct of the war.

One of the first instances of the assertion of executive privilege came as a result of a confrontation between President Eisenhower and Senator Joseph McCarthy during the Army-McCarthy hearings. The President sent a letter to Secretary of Defense Charles Wilson instructing him and his subordinates not to testify before McCarthy.[3] In 1957 Attorney General William Rogers spelled out the basis for the principle of executive privilege, noting that the Constitution vests "executive power" in the President and charges him to "take care that the laws be faithfully executed." He linked this with the doctrine of separation of powers. The Attorney General specified five categories of information that the President was privileged not to disclose to Congress:

1. military and diplomatic secrets and foreign affairs;
2. information made confidential by statute;
3. investigations relating to pending litigation and investigative files and reports;
4. information relating to internal government affairs privileged from disclosure in the public interest; and
5. records incidental to the making of policy, including interdepartmental memoranda, advisory opinions, recommendations of subordinates, and informal working papers.[4]

In 1962 President Kennedy in response to a request for a clarification of his position on executive privilege from Congressman John Moss, then chairman of the House Subcommitte on Government Information, said:

Executive privilege can be invoked only by the President and will not be used without specific Presidential approval. Your own interest in assuring the widest public accessibility to governmental information is, of course, well known, and I can assure you this Administration will continue to cooperate with your subcommittee and the entire Congress in achieving this objective.[5]

Both Johnson and Nixon affirmed Kennedy's view that executive privilege could be invoked only by the President himself. However, Nixon's pledge rapidly disintegrated. During his first four and a half years in office there were nineteen claims of privilege, only four of these made by the President himself.

And then came the unfolding revelations of the Watergate crimes, followed by the most extraordinary assertion of executive privilege in our history. Attorney General Richard Kleindienst, speaking for the President, proclaimed that Congress could not order any employee of the executive branch to appear and testify without the consent of the President. This finding did not limit privilege to White House staffers or policy makers but extended to all Federal employees. Kleindienst did not explain in any detail the Constitutional or legal basis for this sweeping privilege. He asserted that the President's judgment whether to produce witnesses or documents would be final and that neither the Congress nor the courts had the Constitutional authority to interfere.[6]

Raoul Berger said:

Against the assumption that, "confidentiality" is "indispensable" to the operation of the entire government must be weighed the undeniable need of Congress for information, the cost of concealing confirmatory evidence of a conspiracy to corrupt the political process and the loss of confidence in the President which has shaken the nation. Concealment in these circumstances is too high a price to pay for the preservation of "confidentiality" in the White House.[7]

Writing about this problem of executive privilege and the Congress, Senator Charles Mathias (R.–Md.) said:

In particular, the role of Congress cannot continue to be — as it has increasingly become — a function of Executive "good will" and "generosity." In short, while relations between the two branches must, in some degree, depend upon and be determined by the good will that exists or does not exist between the humans involved, it must above all depend upon and be determined by a clear understanding and acceptance by both branches that each is a coordinate branch of government and that neither is superior or subordinate to the other. And the time may well be at hand when the courts have to be called upon to settle the "boundary disputes" and clarify the ground rules governing relations between the two branches.[8]

Not long thereafter, Senator Mathias and others who had been clamoring for a court decision to spell out the boundaries of executive privilege got their wish — at least part of it — in what may turn out to be one of the most controversial Supreme Court decisions in history. In a unanimous decision, 8–0 (Rehnquist abstaining), the Court on July 24, 1974, sealed the fate of Richard Nixon by forcing him to give up the tapes and records of 64 White House conversations requested by the special prosecutor and Judge John Sirica. One of the tapes contained the so-called "smoking-gun" information which precipitated Nixon's historic resignation. The Court found that Nixon's claim for executive privilege was not strong enough to override the claims of a "demonstrated, specific need in a criminal trial." But the Court also established, for the first time, the validity of the doctrine of executive privilege. In the excitement over the demise of Nixon and the transition to Ford there has been very inadequate attention paid to the potentially dangerous implications of the Court's decision.

Chief Justice Burger's opinion on behalf of the unanimous Court said:

Nowhere in the Constitution . . . is there any explicit reference to a privilege of confidentiality, yet to the extent this interest relates to the effective discharge of a President's powers it is constitutionally based. . . . The privilege can be said to derive from the supremacy of each branch within its own assigned areas of constitutional duties. Certain powers and privileges flow from the nature of enumerated powers: the protection of the confidentiality of Presidential communications has similar constitutional underpinnings.

Elsewhere the Court said, "a presumptive privilege for Presidential communications [is] fundamental to the operations of government and inextricably rooted in the separation of powers." The doctrine of executive privilege has thus been endowed with solid Constitutional grounding and great political weight. Supporters of the doctrine now have the backing of a unanimous Supreme Court decision which has added force because it was given in a single opinion by the Chief Justice himself.[9]

In his opinion Chief Justice Burger made it clear that the

Court accords the highest degree of privilege to presidential claims "of need to protect military, diplomatic, and sensitive national security secrets." Commenting on the significance of this ruling Tom Wicker of the *New York Times* said:

> The problem is that, in the doctrine of executive privilege now certified by the Supreme Court to have "constitutional underpinnings," a President apparently could determine the scope of that area of secrecy for himself and the privilege he asserted for it would be absolute — except in the unlikely event that it came into conflict with a higher, competing interest. It is possible even to read the Burger decision as saying that had Mr. Nixon been able to claim that the tapes concerned "military, diplomatic or sensitive national security secrets," the privilege he could claim for them would have outweighed the fundamental demands for due process of law in the fair administration of criminal justice.[10]

The Court, in granting such sweeping powers of executive privilege in the maintenance of diplomatic and military secrets, has clearly failed to give sufficient attention to the danger of alleged national security being used as a tool of presidential deception. In view of the "big lie" technique employed during the past decade under cover of national security the Court's myopia must be viewed as a stunning setback to democracy and freedom. The powers granted the President in this decision would not only give consent to the secrecy maintained in the bombing of Cambodia, but the secrecy of a Bay of Pigs or a future secret invasion required in the "interest of national security." The unchecked power to deceive the people is a danger our system of government cannot safely accommodate.

The entire Watergate conspiracy is chock-full of the most dramatic evidence of this danger. A chilling example is manifest in the following conversation taken from the infamous March 2, 1972, tape. Nixon, Haldeman, and Dean are discussing how to handle Howard Hunt's threat to tell the story of the burglary of the office of Daniel Ellsberg's psychiatrist and the role of John Ehrlichman:

DEAN: You might put it on a national security grounds basis.
HALDEMAN: It absolutely was.

PRESIDENT: National security. We had to get information for national security grounds.

DEAN: . . . Why wouldn't we have the FBI or CIA do the job rather than the White House "plumbers?

PRESIDENT: Because we had to do it on a confidential basis.

HALDEMAN: Because we were checking them.

PRESIDENT: Neither [FBI and CIA] could be trusted.

DEAN: . . . I think we could get by on that.

The Cold War consensus was so profound that some of the tragic distortions about national security linger on even in the Supreme Court. In the Pentagon Papers case, New York Times Company v. United States, Justice Stewart with Justice White concurring spoke about the "related areas of national defense and international relations." He said:

> For better or for worse, the simple fact is that a President of the United States possesses vastly greater constitutional independence in these two vital areas of power than does, say, a prime minister of a country with a parliamentary form of government. In the absence of governmental checks and balances present in other areas of our national life, the only effective restraint upon executive policy and power in the area of national defense and international affairs may lie in an enlightened citizenry — in an informed and critical public opinion which alone can here protect the values of democratic government.

Certainly an informed and critical public opinion becomes even more important, as does the related role of the press and educational institutions in contributing to such informed opinion. Justice Stewart in saying, in effect, that the people must be so enlightened that they elect presidents who can be trusted. However, in the face of two presidents in a row who have engaged in extensive deception of the public under the cover of secrecy Justice Stewart's opinion seems entirely too risky.

Fortunately, there are other opinions. In the same *New York Times* case, Justice Black with Justice Douglas concurring said:

> The word "security" is a broad, vague generality whose contours should not be invoked to abrogate the fundamental law embodied in the First Amendment. The guarding of military and diplomatic secrets at the expense of informed representative government provides no real security for our Republic.

This important point was apparently lost sight of when Justice Douglas concurred in the unanimous opinion presented by Justice Burger in the Nixon tapes case. It is completely at odds with the executive privilege powers for national security granted in the Burger opinion.

Probably the best way to resolve this dilemma was suggested in a later portion of Justice Stewart's opinion. Stewart said,

> [It] is clear to me that it is a constitutional duty of the executive — as a matter of sovereign prerogative and not as a matter of law as the courts know law — through the promulgation and enforcement of executive regulations, to protect the confidentiality necessary to carry out its responsibilities in the fields of international relations and national defense. This is not to say that Congress and the courts have no role to play. Undoubtedly Congress has the power to enact specific and appropriate criminal laws to protect Government property and preserve Government secrets. . . . Moreover, if Congress should pass a specific law authorizing civil proceedings in this field, the courts would likewise have the duty to decide the constitutionality of such a law. . . .

The time has come for congressional action.

The Secrecy System and the Classification of Information

Since publication of the Pentagon Papers there has been a burst of draft legislation in both Houses of Congress to do something about excessive secrecy in government. Unfortunately, most of the attention of Congress has focused on measures to curb the volume of secrecy and techniques to provide for the declassification and disclosure of information that does not merit classification.

There has been insufficient attention to the more difficult and much more important problem of how to provide the checks and balances necessary to ensure the adequate participation of Congress in the major decisions of national security involving war and peace. The question that remains to be answered is how can Congress be satisfied that it is fully informed so that it can carry out its legislative responsibilities — especially its budgetary and oversight responsibilities? It has become abundantly clear that for years Congress has not been given the full story, usually on grounds of national security. During the years of the Cold War consensus this lack of information was acceptable to most of Congress. It is hoped that is no longer true.

Certainly there is a need to cut down the quantity of secrecy too, but the more important job is to make the executive branch accountable for its acts. The evidence of the massiveness of excessive secrecy is abundant. In hearings before the House Foreign Operations and Government Information Subcommittee of the Committee on Government Operations, William Florence estimated in 1971 that there were "at least 20 million classified documents including reproduced copies in the Department of Defense." He went on to say that

. . . less than one-half of one percent of the different documents which bear currently assigned classification markings actually contain information qualifying even for the lowest defense classification in Executive Order 10501. In other words, the disclosure of information in at least 99½ percent of those classified documents could not be prejudicial to the defense interests of the United States. . . . [As an indication of the absurd extent to which the classification reflex oversteps the bounds Florence noted:] Not so very long ago someone in the Navy Department placed the "Secret" marking on some newspaper items of particular interest to the Navy. . . . [That] action caused some embarrassment in the Department of Defense. As a result a special directive had to be published to tell people not to classify newspapers.[11]

Describing the dimension of the problem Congressman William Moorhead (D.–Pa.), former chairman of the Government Information Subcommittee, said:

There are 55,000 arms pumping up and down in Government offices stamping "Confidential" on stacks of government documents; more than 18,000 government employees are wielding "Secret" stamps, and a censorship elite of nearly 3,000 bureaucrats have authority to stamp "Top Secret" on public records. These are not wild estimates. These numbers were provided by the Government agencies, themselves.[12]

Testifying before the Moorhead subcommittee in June 1971,

former U.S. Ambassador to the United Nations Arthur Goldberg said:

> I have read and prepared countless thousands of classified documents and participated in classifying some of them. In my experience, 75 percent of these never should have been classified in the first place; another 15 percent quickly outlived the need for secrecy; and only about 10 percent genuinely required restricted access over any significant period of time.[13]

In addition to all of the classified documents in the government there are millions of classified papers in the files of industries throughout the country who have government contracts and operate under the Executive Order classification rules that are written by the Defense Department. Once information becomes classified it is extraordinarily difficult to declassify it, mainly because of the sheer bulk of documents and the administrative barriers to sorting through the jungle of overgrowth. Today, almost thirty years after the end of World War II, there are still 100 million pages of classified war records in the U.S. Archives. The total classified holdings of the Archives are currently at least one billion.

The major proposals to do something about these problems have stemmed from hearings held before the Government Operations subcommittees dealing with information in the Senate and the House. One concept of Senator Edmund Muskie (D.–Maine), Chairman of the Senate Subcommittee on Intergovernmental Relations, cosponsored with Senator Jacob Javits (R.–N.Y.) was a Government Secrecy Control Act. In presenting the bill on the floor of the Senate in 1974 Muskie said the bill was designed "to restore the balance between secrecy and accountability by restoring the balance between the powers of the Executive and Legislative branches over national security policy and the information necessary to its determination." Senator Javits said, "The classification reform policies of the Nixon Administration have been only partially successful. It is time that legislation was enacted to enforce those classification policies in practice and to give Congress a stronger voice in the crucial decisions about what secrecy our national security interests truly require."

The Muskie-Javits proposals called for a new Registrar of National Defense and Foreign Policy Information with authority to review and revise classification practices throughout the executive branch. They also wanted a new Joint Congressional Committee on Government Secrecy. The Registrar was to be required to prepare and transmit to the Joint Committee a detailed monthly index of records being classified by each agency. No government documents which did not appear on the index were to be withheld from disclosure under the Freedom of Information Act. The Joint Committee was to have authority to review the index and direct its revision, including the immediate or speeded-up declassification of secret information. It would have had specific authority to go to court to enforce its subpoenas and its directives that documents be declassified.

The Joint Committee could have judged whether document classification conformed to the policy that information be permitted to be kept secret

. . . only when the disclosure of such information would harm national defense or foreign policy, and not in order to impede access by Congress to such information or to conceal incompetence, inefficiency, wrongdoing or administrative error, to avoid embarrassment to any officer or agency, or to restrain competition or independent initiative.

The Joint Committee according to Senator Muskie

. . . would act as arbiter between members or committees of Congress seeking access to classified information and [government] agencies seeking to withhold it or to dictate the terms of its disclosure. More broadly the Joint Committee would have the role of overall Congressional monitor of national security policy. With the information available from the index the Committee will be in a position to steer other committees, Foreign Relations and Armed Services most obviously, into areas of inquiry and oversight they might otherwise miss.[14]

The reactions to the Muskie-Javits bill were not enthusiastic, especially from those speaking for the executive branch. Robert Dixon, the Assistant Attorney General, said,

[We] have serious doubts about those aspects which will confer on a joint congressional committee the power to declassify national security documents. . . . [The] executive branch has exclusive constitutional authority to enforce the laws, except in the rare circumstances where Congress has authorized an independent establishment to exercise limited enforcement power as incidental to its quasi-legislative or quasi-judicial power.

Dixon also said that any provisions for a joint congressional committee to determine whether national security information should be classified or declassified would be unconstitutional. He said that "national security information is entitled to even a stronger privilege than presidential conversations" (a view that seems to have been confirmed by the unanimous decision of the Supreme Court in the Nixon tapes case). Finally, speaking of the question whether Congress has the constitutional right to determine if the executive has properly classified an item of information, Dixon said [this] is a gray area of law. . . . Courts lack the range of experience and expertise to determine whether [disclosure of] information may cause damage to the national security."[15]

Both the Department of Defense and the Department of State expressed the view that Nixon's Executive Order 11652 has improved the classification system so that no legislative reform is required. Carol Laise, Assistant Secretary of State for Public Affairs, said,

[A] register of the scope proposed would be a giant undertaking . . . and would impose burdens on the reporting agencies far beyond their present or anticipated means. . . . [Responsibility] for the detailed design and implementation of a natural security classification system can be effectively and properly assigned only to the executive office and agencies responsible for the conduct of our national security affairs.[16]

Arthur Schlesinger, Jr., former special assistant to President Kennedy and authority on American history, had this to say about the proposed legislation:

The way to do this, given the by now ample and irrefutable demonstration that the President cannot be trusted to run a rational secrecy system, is for Congress to establish the criteria for and control of such a system by statute. There can be no constitutional question of the power of Congress so to act. Former Chief Justice Warren said on December 13, 1973, "Whatever secrecy is to be permitted concerning governmental records in the highest as well as in the lower echelons should be fixed by law." Former Justice Goldberg told the House Government Information Subcommittee in 1972, "I have no doubts that Congress is authorized to enact such legislation," and Justice White made the same point in the *Mink* decision. Indeed, Congress did exactly this when it passed the Atomic Energy Act and established a statutory classification system for the Atomic Energy Commission.

Speaking specifically about the merits of the Muskie-Javits proposals Schlesinger said,

A Registrar of National Defense and Foreign Policy Information located in the White House is not likely to defy a President who has a mania about secrecy. A Joint Committee on Government Secrecy is all too likely to become an instrument rather than a critic of executive secrecy. We know all too well the sweetheart relationships that so often grow up between the executive and privileged groups in Congress. I can easily see such a body reinforcing rather than restraining the Presidency in this field.[17]

Schlesinger felt that an independent commission would provide more effective control.

The most comprehensive and important work in the field of government secrecy has been accomplished by the House Subcommittee on Government Information, which started its work on the classification system in 1956 under the chairmanship of Congressman John Moss (D.–Calif), who became the father of the Freedom of Information Act. As noted in Chapter 2, that Act does not cover information required by Executive Order to be kept secret in the "interest of national defense or foreign policy." Since 1966, when the Act was passed, there has been growing concern in Congress that it has not sufficiently protected the rights of citizens seeking information.

After years of hearings and investigations of citizens' complaints, seventeen amendments to the Freedom of Information Act were passed in November 1974, by a large majority in both Houses of Congress over Ford's veto. One of the amendments permits a citizen or a newspaper requesting specific classified foreign policy or national defense records to seek judicial review before the records can be withheld by the government. A petitioner can ask that a Federal judge privately review the information and rule whether it should remain classified or be made public. When President Ford vetoed the proposed amendments, he said he objected to the courts' being permitted to make "classification decisions in sensitive and complex areas where they have no expertise."[18] This question of expertise will be examined further. One of the reasons it comes up so frequently is that the so-called experts in the government have tipped the balance so extremely in the direction of security that the pressures for disclosure are inevitably growing. On November 21, 1974, both Houses of Congress voted overwhelmingly to override the President's veto. Thus, the amendments became law and another small advance on behalf of information freedom was taken.

Though the Freedom of Information Act has been significantly improved by the new amendments there is still a basic need for Congress to enact a law to control national security information. In 1974 Congressman Moorhead, then Chairman of the Government Information subcommittee, joined by 24 House co-sponsors, attempted to grapple with the problem. Their bill did not reach the House floor for a vote, but it did advance considerably the prospect for useful legislation dealing with government secrecy. Moorhead proposed to amend the defense and foreign policy provisions of the Freedom of Information Act.

The Amendment contained a recommendation to create a new independent regulatory body within the executive branch to be called the Classification Review Commission (CRC). The CRC was to be given wide regulatory and quasi-adjudicatory powers over the day-to-day operations of the security classification system. The CRC was to established the regulation for security classification and police the implementation of those regulations including penalties for violations. It was to rule on requests for declassification and to investigate charges of improper classification made by Congress, the press, or private citizens. The CRC was to be empowered to hold hearings and to settle disputes between Congress and the executive over access to classified information. The CRC decisions were to be subject to judicial review if either party requested such review. The CRC was to have nine members appointed by the President with the advice and consent of the Senate. In addition, the Moorhead proposals called for a schedule of rapid declassification of information mandated by law. No information was to remain classified more than three years, with "Top Secret" to move to "Secret" after one year, "Secret" to "Confidential" after one year, and "Confidential" to a declassified status after one year.

Commenting on his proposals Chairman Moorhead said:

> [We] cannot depend on individual Executive Agencies having classification authority to police themselves against massive abuses of the system. It has not happened during the past two decades under two major presidential Executive Orders. . . . It is for precisely this reason that I feel we need a completely hard-nosed, powerful, and dedicated regulatory body to make any security classification law really work the way Congress intends. . . . This legislation strikes that delicate balance between the conflicting needs of the Congress and the Executive and the public as a whole in this vital area.[19]

The Moorhead proposals do provide a basis for dealing with most of the requirement for congressional checks and balances. The Classification Review Commission is an ingenious and politically realistic arrangement to tighten up the controls over the secrecy system which will ensure Congress better access to information, but which also recognizes that any workable machinery must be located within the executive. The Commission could and should provide the bridge between Congress and the executive which could begin to restore public trust, especially if the President accepts its role. There is a need, however, to go beyond the Moorhead proposals by expanding the functions of the Commission to include responsibility for distributing National Intelligence Estimates and serving as an advocate of openness and freedom of information.

The Secret Operations of CIA

The most controversial aspects of executive secrecy and congressional oversight, or lack thereof, are provoked by the clandestine operations of CIA. As we have seen, succeeding administrations have maintained that CIA covert operations are authorized by the so-called "fifth function" of the powers granted CIA in the National Security Act of 1947. It reads, "to perform such other functions and duties related to intelligence affecting the national security as the National Security Council may from time to time direct." Many members of Congress, including some who voted for the Act in 1947, have maintained that they do not consider covert political and paramilitary operations as "related to intelligence," and that they had no intention of authorizing such operations. Nevertheless, it has been common knowledge through the years that CIA engages in such operations.

In 1949 the Central Intelligence Act was passed by Congress to authorize the Director of Central Intelligence (DCI) to hire and fire personnel without regard to Civil Service regulations. The Act also exempts CIA from any laws requiring disclosure of the "organization, functions, names, official titles, salaries or numbers of personnel employed." The Act exempts the Bureau of the Budget from reporting to Congress on these matters. For "objects of a confidential, extraordinary, or emergency nature" the DCI is authorized to spend funds on his special voucher. Reportedly about half of the money spent by CIA is audited by the General Accounting Office, the rest is so sensitive that it is audited by a special secret procedure.[20]

In order to clarify authority for special political and military operations, the National Security Council since 1948 has issued a series of special directives know as NSCID's. These documents, in time, have come to be known as the "secret charter" of CIA.[21] So CIA is able to operate with a secret budget which provides funds for secretly authorized operations which are not revealed to most members of Congress. The entire CIA budget is hidden, most of it in large categories of the Department of Defense budget. Thus the normal legislative control of the power of the purse does not apply to the operations of CIA. This is an extraordinary example of the power of the Cold War consensus, especially because CIA has engaged in military operations involving the potential commitment of the United States to war.

As a means of dealing with its congressional relations, CIA has given an annual budget briefing to special five-member subcommittees of the House and Senate Appropriations Committees. These subcommittees always include the chairman of the committee. The other four members are carefully selected and almost without exception are very conservative. General W. Bedell Smith and Allen Dulles extended the briefings to special committees from both the House and Senate Armed Services Committees. Again, the chairman of the senior committees served on the special subcommittees and the other members were selected in close collaboration with the Director of CIA, thus ensuring security and a conservative point of view.

These informal CIA "watchdog" committees have continued to serve as the basis for congressional oversight through the years. The members do not share their information with the rest of Congress, nor had they ever launched an investigation of CIA activities until the recent furor over CIA involvement in Watergate and the break-in of the office of Ellsberg's psychiatrist. Those developments did inspire several "watchdog" committee meetings, especially of the House Armed Services subcommittee chaired by Lucien Nedzi (D.–Mich.). But, for the most part, CIA oversight through the years has been vested in an elite group of about twenty essentially passive and friendly members of Congress.

Lyman Kirkpatrick, former Executive Director of CIA, reporting on a briefing by General Smith in 1951, recalls Clarence Cannon, Chairman of the House Appropriations Committee, saying, "Thank you, Mr. Director. Now it is understood that everything that has been said here today is secret, even the fact that this meeting was held." Speaking further of Congressman Cannon, Kirkpatrick says he

. . . never lost his keen interest in the CIA and indeed seemed to feel a proprietary interest in the organization throughout his life. I remember that he expressed an interest in the case of Edward Bancroft who had been Benjamin Franklin's secretary in Paris. . . .

It was discovered more than half a century later that Bancroft had been a British Intelligence agent the entire time and that everything Franklin and his colleagues did in Paris was known in London within days. Congressman Cannon was fascinated with this episode and was keenly interested in a study that we had prepared on it.[22]

Unfortunately, those members of Congress responsible for watching CIA were more interested in such CIA-prepared historical studies than in current covert operations. At a meeting with top CIA leaders preparing for one of the sessions before the appropriations subcommittee, Allen Dulles indicated that there wouldn't be any difficulty. "I'll just tell them a few war stories," he said.[23] Senator Leverett Saltonstall (R.–Mass.), who was for years the senior minority member of the Senate Armed Services subcommittee on CIA, said in a speech in 1966: "It is not a question of reluctance on the part of CIA officials to speak to us. Instead it is a question of our reluctance, if you will, to seek information and knowledge on subjects which I personally, as a member of Congress and as a citizen would rather not have."[24] That this was a commonly held view was confirmed by Allen Dulles on a nationwide TV program when he said: "When I appeared before them, again and again, I have been stopped by members of Congress saying, 'we don't want to hear about this. We might talk in our sleep. Don't tell us this.'"[25]

Senator John Stennis (D.–Miss.), currently chairman of the Senate Armed Services Committee and also the CIA "watchdog" subcommittee, said in 1971, "As has been said spying is spying . . . You have to make up your mind that you are going to have an intelligence agency and protect it as such, and shut your eyes some and take what is coming." The late Senator Allen Ellender (D.–La.), who was chaiman of the CIA Subcommittee of the Appropriations Committee in 1971, claimed that his group went over the CIA budget line by line. He was pursued on this matter on the Senate floor by Senator J. William Fulbright (D.–Ark), who was concerned about CIA involvement in Laos. The follow ing colloquy ensued:

MR. FULBRIGHT: It has been stated that the CIA has 36,000 there [in Laos]. Would the Senator say that before the creation of the

Army in Laos they [the CIA] came before the committee and the committee knew of it and approved it?

MR. ELLENDER: Probably so.

MR. FULBRIGHT: Did the Senator approve it?

MR. ELLENDER: It was not — I did not know anything about it . . . I never asked to begin with, whether or not there were any funds to carry on the war in this sum the CIA asked for. It never dawned on me to ask about it.[26]

It is clear that the informal arrangements for congressional oversight of CIA have provided no control at all. In fact, these arrangements have undoubtedly given executive leadership a sense of license rather than restraint.

In 1955 the Hoover Commission took a look at CIA and concluded that there was a need for outside surveillance, especially from Congress. The Hoover Commission was concerned that an agency which was protected by law from disclosing details about its budget, functions, and personnel would be subject to abuses of power. This concern inspired more than twenty bills in Congress, the most important of which was introduced by Senator Mike Mansfield (D.–Mont.), with 34 Republican and Democratic cosponsors. The proposal called for a joint congressional committee composed of six members from each House to have legislative oversight of CIA. The committee was to have a permanent staff, a broad investigative authority with the power to hold hearings and subpoena witnesses.[27] The committee was to be formed primarily of members who had served on the informal committees and was to maintain full security. In many ways the legislation was similar to that establishing the Joint Committee on Atomic Energy.

The Senate Rules Committee, which had favorably reported the bill by a vote of 8–1, set forth the major arguments for passage:

(a) Congressional surveillance has existed, since 1946, in the atomic energy field, an area equally as sensitive as foreign intelligence.

(b) A specialized joint committee would promote new confidence between Congress and CIA.

(c) Studies of CIA by ad hoc temporary groups are not sufficient.

(d) A policy of secrey for the mere sake of secrecy invites abuse and prevents Congress and the nation from knowing whether we have a fine intelligence service or a very poor one.[28]

Senator Carl Hayden (D.–Ariz.), who was the only dissenting member, filed the following minority report:

(a) Existing surveillance by members of the Appropriations and Armed Services Committees is adequate.

(b) Functions of the CIA are essentially executive in character.

(c) CIA has been intensely, repeatedly and adequately investigated by various special commissions.

(d) The proposal to create a joint committee raised a constitutional issue of separation of powers between executive and legislative branches.

(e) To compare CIA with the Atomic Energy Commission, or to use the atomic energy analogy is invalid.

Ironically Senator Hayden supported this last argument by claiming that while atomic energy is a legitimate subject for congressional control the CIA is "peculiarly the prerogative of the Executive and intimately associated with the foreign relations of the country."[29]. Undoubtedly Senator Hayden was correct about the link with foreign relations, but he and other friends of CIA consistently fought any attempt to involve the Senate Foreign Relations Committee in the oversight of CIA.

During the debate on the floor of the Senate, Richard Russell (D.–Ga.), speaking as Chairman of the Armed Services Subcommittee on CIA, said, "We have asked [Allen Dulles] very searching questions about some activities which it almost chills the marrow of a man to hear about."[30] Senator Alben Barkley (D.–Ky.), who had served for four years on the National Security Council during his tenure as Truman's Vice President, said:

Some of the information gathered by the Central Intelligence Agency and laid before the National Security Council itself was so confidential and secret that the very portfolios in which it was contained were under lock and key. . . . I would lose my right arm before I would divulge it to anyone, even to members of my own family.[31]

Another argument used by several senators was the fact that

CIA agents serving overseas are often in great physical danger, making security about their operations absolutely essential. Another argument was that greater congressional surveillance might block sharing of intelligence information with our allies, all of whom had immunity from detailed legislative supervision.[32] As a result of the debate and strong lobbying by members of the Eisenhower Administration, 8 of the original sponsors of the bill defected and it was defeated 59 to 27, with 10 not voting.

Despite more than 200 proposals for systematic congressional surveillance of CIA in both the Senate and the House, the issue did not muster sufficient support for another vote until 1966. Senator Eugene McCarthy (D.–Minn.), with the strong backing of J. William Fulbright, Chairman of the Senate Foreign Relations Committee, proposed "A full and complete study with respect to the effects of the operations and activities of the Central Intelligence Agency upon the foreign relations of the United States." The investigation was to be conducted by the Senate Foreign Relations Committee.[33] This proposal immediately caused jurisdictional problems with Senator Russell, who had become the most powerful man in the Senate and was now Chairman of the Senate Armed Services Committee as well as chairman of the CIA "watchdog" committee.

As a result of Russell's opposition, McCarthy compromised his resolution, asking merely that the "watchdog" committee be expanded to include three members of the Foreign Relations Committee. The "watchdog" committee had been reorganized to include three members from the Appropriations Committee, three members from the Armed Services Committee, as well as Chairman Russell, but no members from Foreign Relations. Russell considered this proposal as a challenge to his power, an attempt to "muscle in" on his jurisdiction. The CIA indicated that it was unwilling to discuss its sources and methods with the Foreign Relations Committee and the word was circulated that if the surveillance mechanism were broadened to include Foreign Relations members there would be a danger of leaks endangering the lives of CIA agents overseas.[34] There could be no doubt that the Johnson Administration, which was being vigorously criticized by Fulbright and his Foreign Relations Committee on Vietnam policy, would prefer to limit oversight to Russell, a strong supporter of U.S. involvement in Vietnam, including the activities of CIA.

When the resolution got to the Senate floor the vote was almost the same as it had been a decade before, 61 against and 28 for. The real issue was the confrontation of power between Russell and Fulbright. After his crushing victory Russell moved in January 1967 to invite three members of the Senate Foreign Relations Committee, including Fulbright and Mansfield, to attend all meetings of the "watchdog" committee. This moved Mansfield, after the *Ramparts* revelations about CIA secret subsidies to student and labor organizations, to join with Senators Dirksen and Russell and House Minority Leader Gerald Ford in a statement saying, "there is enough Congressional surveillance of the CIA."[35]

This contentment in Congress did not last long. After the death of Russell, John Stennis (D.–Miss.) became Chairman of the Senate Armed Services Committee and the CIA "watchdog" committee. When Fulbright and Stuart Symington (D.–Mo.), who were invited to attend the "watchdog" meetings, intensified their criticism of U.S. Vietnam policy, and CIA activities in general, Stennis decided to stop the sessions. During 1971 and 1972 there was not a single meeting of the "watchdog" group. Neither Symington nor Fulbright

> . . . was trusted at the time by either the CIA or by the conservative Senators who have kept oversight of the CIA as their own private preserve. In the absence of any joint subcommittee meetings, the five senior members of the Appropriations Committee, all of whom were stanch hawks and Administration supporters, met privately to go over the Agency's budget.[36]

Symington on November 23, 1971, challenged this arrangement by offering an amendment on the Senate floor which would limit the Federal expenditures for intelligence to $4 billion, about $2 billion less than requested. The Symington Amendment was defeated 51 to 36.

A a result of the CIA links to Watergate, and more recently the revelations of CIA's programs to "destabilize" the government of Salvador Allende in Chile and illegal domestic operations, there has been new demand for better congressional oversight. Growing doubts about CIA operations have emerged from the general mistrust of the executive caused by the conspiracy and perjury oozing from the White House. The fact that a former CIA agent, Howard Hunt, had such a key role in the "plumbers," the Watergate break-in, and the break-in of the office of Ellsberg's psychiatrist was very damaging. But it became more damaging when word came out that CIA, at White House instruction, had assisted Hunt with equipment and CIA-owned houses to be used for sensitive meetings. The active participation of former CIA Director Richard Helms in drawing up illegal domestic operations contained in the Huston Plan shocked many members of Congress. There was ample press coverage of CIA involvement in Chile, especially the collaboration between William Broe, the Chief of Western Hemisphere Operations, and the leadership of ITT. Members of Congress became angered though when details of CIA Chilean operations were admitted by the Administration, only a few months after Kissinger and other State Department officials had informed congressional committees that there were no such operations.

Congressman Michael Harrington (D.–Mass.), who first revealed the details of the Administration's deception regarding CIA operations in Chile, said:

The role of the CIA in foreign policy, as authorized by the highest officials of the executive branch, must be fully and openly reexamined. The fiction that Congress exercises any real control and scrutiny over CIA activities must be dispelled and the existing mechanisms replaced by an effective Congressional review structure, consistent with the democratic process. The arbitrary exclusion of CIA oversight from the normal foreign policy deliberations in Congress must be ended. More fundamentally, the future direction of intelligence policy must be wrested from the exclusive and secret control of special interests in both the executive branch and in Congress and forced to face the more demanding test of free and open debate that our system of government requires.[37]

The growing criticism of Congress did not appear to have much impact on President Ford and his advisors, however. At his press conference in late September Ford was asked: "Under what international law do we have a right to attempt to destabilize the constitutionally elected government of another country? Ford replied: "I am not going to pass judgment whether it is permitted or authorized under international law. It is a recognized fact that historically as well as presently, such actions are taken in the best interest of the countries involved."

Time magazine, commenting on the President's reply said:

That blunt response by President Gerald Ford at his press conference last week was either remarkably careless or remarkably candid. It left the troubling impression which the Administration afterward did nothing to dispel, that the U.S. feels free to subvert another government whenever it suits American policy. In an era of detente with the Soviet Union and improving relations with China, Ford's words seemed to represent an anachronistic, cold-war view of national security reminiscent of the 1950's.[38]

Ford's position was exactly the sort of rhetoric that gives comfort to the hawks in Moscow and perpetuates the archaic and unproductive struggle between the CIA and KGB.

On October 2, 1974, it was revealed in the *Washington Post* that Kissinger and CIA Director Colby had made an "unprecedented" agreement to keep the House Foreign Affairs Committee informed on CIA covert political operations. Kissinger and Colby reportedly said that no covert operations comparable to those which had occurred in Chile were presently being undertaken anywhere in the world. They did not guarantee, however, that the United States would never engage in such an operation in the future. Congressman Nedzi, Chairman of the Armed Services Subcommittee on CIA, said that Kissinger and Colby had also agreed to brief his committee on any pending covert activities before they were undertaken. "Nobody said we're going to give you veto power," Nedzi commented, "but my understanding is that we would be told before rather than after."[39]

The most far-reaching proposal ever initiated in Congress came on October 2, 1974, in an amendment to the Foreign Aid

Bill initiated by Senator James Abourezk (D.–S. D.), who called for a complete ban on CIA covert political operations. The amendment was defeated 68–17 and thus, for the first time in history, the Senate in a sort of backhanded way gave its approval to the continuation of such operations. However, the Senate did adopt an amendment by Senator Harold Hughes (D.–Ia.) requiring the President to justify covert operations as being in the interest of national security in a written report to the appropriate committees of the House and Senate. If the President failed to give such notice, the amendment says, "All covert CIA activities now in progress would be forced to cease, and no new operations could be initiated." Senator Hughes said, "This is only the beginning toward the imperative of imposing some order and structure to the means by which the American people can exercise a measure of control over the cloak-and-dagger operations of our intelligence."[40]

A day later Senator Stennis announced that Majority Leader Mike Mansfield and Minority Leader Hugh Scott had agreed to "sit and participate in the activities" of the Senate oversight subcommittee on CIA.[41]

In December 1974 the *New York Times* headlined "Huge CIA Operation Reported in U.S. Against Antiwar Forces, Other Dissidents in Nixon Years." Shortly thereafter the CIA Chief of counterintelligence and his deputies resigned. President Ford moved rapidly to appoint a citizens' panel headed by Vice President Nelson Rockefeller to investigate the charges. There was a steady stream of revelations about how both the CIA and FBI were used to penetrate, spy on, and manipulate the activities of thousands of U.S. citizens who were actively opposing American involvement in the Vietnam War. Actually, the illegal activities went back to the Cold War days, but they were at their height during the Vietnam War, especially the period from 1970 to 1972.

The Senate and House both established their own independent investigating committees with wide-ranging authority. The Senate Select Committee under the chairmanship of Senator Frank Church was asked to investigate the charges against both the CIA and the FBI, including the illegal domestic operations and the assertions that CIA had been involved in assassination plots. The House Committee was chaired by Lucien Nedzi who was already chairman of the CIA watchdog committee. But the most significant development was in the Senate, where for the first time in 28 years a strong committee was created, by a decisive vote, to investigate the activities of CIA. The formation of this committee paved the way for the long-overdue congressional legislation to ensure adequate oversight of CIA.

Congress and the Espionage Laws

In the previous discussion we have seen, especially in the *New York Times and* Ellsberg cases, that there are significant unresolved matters of law relating to the disclosure of defense information, One reason the law is unresolved is the ambiguous language of Subsections 793(d) and 793(e) of the Espionage Law.
According to Benno Schmidt,

These two provisions are undoubtedly the most confusing and complex of all the federal Espionage Statutes. They are also the statutes posing the greatest potential threat to newspapers' and reporters' obtaining and printing of national defense information. The legislative drafting is at its shotgun worst precisely where greatest caution should have been exercised. Moreover, legislative history suggests a basic and continuing Congressional misunderstanding of the effects actually achieved.[42]

As noted in Chapter 5, 18 U.S. Code, Section 641, originally drafted in 1917, to apply to government employees only, was amended in 1950 to extend the same liabilities to all persons. The amendment was attached to the Internal Security Act as part of a series of measures, generated by the hysteria of those days, to block communist subversion.

Since the Pentagon Papers case and various other leaks, the Justice Department and the CIA have increased the pressure on Congress for laws to permit prosecution of unauthorized disclosure of defense information. In connection with plans for a revision of the criminal provisions of the U.S. Code a bill has been prepared in the Senate Judiciary Committee, originating with John McClellan (D.–Ark.), Chairman of the Subcommittee on Criminal Laws and Procedures, and Roman Hruska (R.–Neb.), the ranking minority member. These men, two of the most conservative and secrecy-oriented in the Senate, prepared their legislation in close collaboration with the Justice Department.

The bill contains a subchapter entitled "Espionage and Related Offenses" which is supposed to clarify and improve the espionage laws. Espionage is defined as follows:

A person is guilty of an offense, if knowing that national defense information may be used to the prejudice of the safety or interest of the United States, or to the advantage of a foreign power, he:
   (1) communicates such information to a foreign power;
   (2) obtains or collects such information knowing that it may be communicated to a foreign power. [The penalty for this crime could be life imprisonment if the offense is] (A) committed in time of war or during a national defense emergency or (B) if the information directly concerns nuclear weaponry, military space craft or satellites, early warning systems or other means of defense or retaliation against large scale attack, war plans, communications intelligence or cryptographic information, or any other major weapons system or major element of defense strategy.[43]

For all other categories of national defense information the penalty is not more than thirty years in jail.

National defense information is defined as relating to:

   (1) the military capability of the U.S. or of an associate nation;
   (2) military planning or operations of the U.S.;
   (3) military communications of the U.S.;
   (4) military installations of the U.S.;
   (5) military weaponry, weapons development; or weapons research of the U.S.;
   (6) intelligence operations, activities, plans, estimates, analyses, sources, or methods of the U.S.;
   (7) intelligence with regard to a foreign power;
   (8) commmunications intelligence information or cryptographic information;
   (9) restricted data as defined in section 11 of the Atomic Energy Act of 1954;
   (10) in time of war, any other matter involving the security of the U.S. that might be useful to the enemy.

If a person communicates any such information "knowing that it may be used to the prejudice of the safety or interest of the U.S. or to the advantage of a foreign power to a person who he knows is not authorized to receive it" he will be liable to a penalty of not more than fifteen years in time of war, and not more than seven years at other times.

For mishandling national defense information a person is guilty of an offense if, being in authorized possession or control of such information, he causes its loss, destruction, theft or communication to a person not authorized to receive it, knowingly fails to report what has happened to it, or intentionally fails to deliver it on demand to a Federal public servant who is authorized to demand it. The penalty for this offense is up to seven years in jail. It would very clearly have applied to Ellsberg had it been law at the time. The same crime with the same seven-year penalty applies to persons "being in unauthorized possession or control of national defense information who communicate it to another person not authorized to receive it, or fail to deliver it promptly to a federal public servant who is entitled to receive it." Such a law would have applied to those named in the *New York Times* and *Washington Post* staffs in the Pentagon Papers trial.

Finally, the legislation establishes that a person

. . . is guilty of an offense, if, being or having been in authorized possession or control of classified information or having obtained such information as a result of his being or having been a federal public servant, he knowingly communicates such information to a person who is not authorized to receive it. [Classified information] means any information, regardless of its origin, that is marked or designated pursuant to the provisions of a statute or an executive order, or a regulation or rule issued pursuant thereto, as information requiring a specific degree of protection against unauthorized disclosure for reasons of national security.

In other words all government employees, former government employees, or employees of businesses, universities, or scientific research organizations having access to classified information, as defined, are subject to criminal prosecution for communicating such information to someone not authorized to receive it. The penalty is up to seven years if the information is communicated to an agent of a foreign power, and not more than three years in all other cases. Had such a law been in existence Victor Marchetti could have been prosecuted.

The legislation does expressly exclude those who receive unauthorized classified information from prosecution. Thus, while Marchetti might have gone to jail his publisher Knopf would not have been liable. The bill doesn't say anything about intentional leaks from the White House or the Defense Department, nor about Presidents and other high-ranking officials who publish national defense information in books, after they retire from the government.

McClellan and Hruska have produced a bill which covers the various types of security information more broadly than ever before. Their language moves in the direction of more secrecy and greater control of information, rather than toward openness and greater freedom of information. The McClellan-Hruska definitions of national defense information and classified information are so sweeping and comprehensive that almost anything could be included, and would be if one of the thousands of government personnel authorized to use classifying stamps decided to stamp it classified. The bill provides no standards, and sets no limits. There are not even time limits controlling the period a document may be considered as defense information or classified information. In fact, the proposed law in the section dealing with classified information says, "It is not a defense to a prosecution under this section . . . that the information was not lawfully subject to classification at the time of the offense." In other words if an Ellsberg could prove that the so-called "Top Secret" information was so old or so misclassified at the time of its disclosure as to be not lawfully subject to classification, he would still be subject to a potential jail sentence because the document still had a classified mark on it.

No, this legislation will not correct the ambiguities of the existing espionage laws. It is the work of men who served under Richard Nixon and who still serve Jerry Ford in collaboration with two of the most conservative members of the U.S. Senate. It would be better to leave the espionage laws in their present ambiguous state than to adopt these proposed changes which would represent a long step backward. However, the mood in Congress has been changing and there is a genuine possibility for constructive revamping of the espionage laws.

7

Conclusions and Recommendations

The sickness that has infected the U.S. government in recent decades, and most seriously since the Vietnam War, has some grim symptoms, but nothing that can't be cured by employing the essential strengths of our democratic system. In order to find the remedies we need to understand what went wrong and why. The most important reason for the breakdown was the grant of extraordinary powers to the executive branch for the intended purpose of protecting the nation's security. The American people, responding to the fear of Soviet-led communism and nuclear weapons, willingly acquiesced in the need for secret decisions, secret operations, and secret information to protect our national security. It was generally accepted that the American public would be deprived of certain information in order to prevent our enemies from obtaining our secrets. This broad national security consensus was dependent on the public's trust of its government. When that trust was violated, the consensus crumbled. The trust can be restored again, but only by insisting on the accountability and the constitutional checks and balances essential for the health of our democracy.

Hannah Arendt, writing about the Pentagon Papers, said, "When we talk about lying among active men, let us remember that the lie did not creep into politics by some accident of human sinfulness; moral outrage, for this reason alone, is not likely to make it disappear." Arendt is certainly correct, and the more totalitarian the society the more likely that the lie will be successful. The way to impede the spread of totalitarianism in the United States is not through "moral outrage," but by limiting the secrecy system through accountability so that those who lie know they are being watched — so that the public, if so inclined, can throw the rascals out at the ballot box. Secrets are necessary, but as Justice Potter Stewart said in his opinion in the Pentagon Papers case, "Secrecy can best be preserved only when credibility is truly maintained." Anthony Lake, a former member of the National Security Council staff, says: "The essential first step is for the government to realize that it cannot lead the public while misleading it."[1] The use of secrecy to mislead the American people destroys the democratic process and, at the same time, the validity of any legitimate secrets.

The Cold War machismo made Americans vulnerable to the manipulators of patriotism. If a person were insufficiently aggressive in his anti-communism he was suspected of being unpatriotic. This kind of superficial, oversimplified approach to the issue of national security became especially dangerous under the umbrella of secrecy because the public, not being able to look at the information or the assumptions, had no opportunity to rein in the wild horses of anti-communist extremism. Worst of all, the public can be frightened by those phony patriots who are willing to use the "big lie" to promote nonexistent dangers in order to get their way. James Madison knew about this when he wrote to Thomas Jefferson on May 13, 1798: "Perhaps it is a universal truth that the loss of liberty at home is to be charged to provisions against danger, real or *pretended,* from abroad" (emphasis added).

The end of defeating communism has never justified adopting totalitarian, conspiratorial means. The present secrecy system should be abolished and replaced by a new program which protects a very small amount of sensitive information. The new program should be established by law by Congress in such a manner that full accountability is guaranteed. Those responsible for controlling the very limited amount of classified information should be made fully aware of the great public trust they have been given. A policy should be established that it is better to err on the side of openness than on the side of excessive secrecy, especially in dealing with Congress. Former Attorney General and Under-secretary of State Nicholas Katzenbach has said:

Today there can be no substitute for a general rule of openness with Congress. Congress must become truly involved in decisions and programs for action, and it must be told what the problems are, what the apparent options for action are, and why the Executive has come forward with particular proposals. If, in the process, nations abroad come to know somewhat more about the way an Administration's mind is working, I think the price — if it is that — eminently worth paying.[2]

Congressional Action

Many important measures can and should be taken by the executive branch to revise and curb the secrecy system, but even if sweeping changes are adopted it will still be essential for Congress to act. In order to guarantee the required accountability for national security secrets Congress should by statute provide for oversight of security classification of information, oversight of CIA, and revision of the espionage laws.

One of the difficulties impeding congressional action, until recently, has been that most members of Congress have been insufficiently aware of the degree to which their own responsibilities have been usurped by the secrecy system. Too many of the senior members of powerful committees dealing with national security were content with the secrecy system and, as reported earlier, preferred not to have responsibility for knowing national security secrets. Even now, Congress is giving too much attention to the administrative aspects of the classification system, such as number of classified documents, number of authorized classifiers, and the number of years before a document is declassified. The much more important goal should be to establish a mechanism to ensure that Congress has oversight of secret information, and to ensure that Congress is receiving the information essential to its legislative responsibilities.

The House Subcommittee on Government Information, presently chaired by Bella Abzug (D.–New York), has done the most thoroughgoing work on this subject. The Subcommittee has concentrated on further amending the Freedom of Information Act to include classified defense and foreign policy information in its provisions.

The Freedom of Information Act does provide the best legislative framework for dealing with national security secrecy. Some of the ideas suggested by Congressman Moorhead for amending the Act would go far toward providing the essential checks and balances. What is needed, in addition to basic lines of communication and time links on secrecy, is some form of high-level independent commission within the executive branch, with members appointed by the President with the advice and consent of the Senate. Such a Commission would provide a basis for the essential compromise between Congress and the executive which will be necessary if any new system is to work.

Despite Administration protestations to the contrary, it is clear that the system of Executive Orders controlling secrecy classification does not work. Too many lies, too many errors, too much waste, and too little freedom of information have resulted from that system. On the other hand it is a fact that Congress cannot manage a security system — the executive implements the laws. Congress can and should establish the boundaries by law, and should also create by law an executive agency reporting to the President which will monitor the new system.

One of the weaknesses in the Moorhead amendment was that it said that the Commission shall furnish to Congress, committees of Congress, and the Comptroller General, upon request, certain classified information necessary for Congress to discharge fully and properly all of its constitutional responsibilities. The trouble with that language is that it is limited to information which gets to Congress "upon request." If Congress is limited to having information it knows enough about to request it will miss much of the important information. Obviously there are many national security matters Congress doesn't know about and therefore cannot request, even though it is important information affecting the work of Congress. One recommended step would be to considerably expand the staffs of the key committees in Congress dealing with national security matters. These expert staff members could provide advice on the sort of information they think should be requested from the Commission.

But a more fundamental step would be to broaden the concept of the Commission's role. In addition to adjudicating requests for classified information from Congress, the Commission should serve in an advisory role to the President, affirmatively indicating to him information it thinks the Congress should have. In this way, the Commission could serve as a bridge between the executive and Congress, improving the flow of information. Clearly the Commission would not substitute for congressional relations and informational briefings by the State Department, Defense Department, or CIA; but when it observed information being withheld by those agencies which it thought should be available to Congress it could serve in an advocacy role within the Administration. The President, of course, would make the final decision to settle such differences of opinion. Such concepts are very frightening to most national security managers inculcated with the habits of the past thirty years, but they will be essential if trust and the effective working of our democracy are to be restored. The Commission would be serving to balance the needs of freedom of information and essential secrecy.

One way to strengthen the Commission along these lines would be to make its chairman a member, or at least an observer, of the National Security Council. Another very important step would be to make the Commission the channel for reviewing and transmitting national intelligence estimates to the appropriate committees of Congress. As will be discussed later, the national intelligence-estimating machinery is now inadequate for this purpose, but it should be rejuvenated and restructured. In 1972 Senator John Sherman Cooper (D.–Ky.) proposed legislation which would have brought the intelligence estimates to Congress, but nothing was done. But something could be done now, either through the proposed amendment to the Freedom of Information Act and the new Classification Review Commission, or through separate but related legislation.

Thomas L. Hughes, former Assistant Secretary of State for Intelligence and Research, has proposed a Permanent Joint Committee [of Congress] on Intelligence Estimates.

The purpose would be to feed the intelligence community's own estimates in an orderly and timely way into an Executive-Legislative leadership relation . . . [Such] a move could promote fruitful consultation instead of destructive confrontation between the branches, while simultaneously enhancing the role of the National Estimates process as a servant to both. [According to Hughes the advantages would be:]

. . . the vehicle of organized intelligence is almost ideal for making a serious multi-purpose inroad on the secrecy/democracy issue in the Executive-Legislative framework.

— The Congress and the intelligence community have a similar stake in institutionalizing skepticism and in assuring that the products of an expensive and elaborate process are not ignored. Their joint countervailing power could help compel greater Executive articulation of its own rationale for proposed international action.

— With the supposed distillation of national intelligence, vouchsafed to the Congress, the credible use of secrecy to undermine Constitutional checks and balances in other areas should decline.

— Once the National Intelligence Estimate (NIE) base is available to the Congressional leadership, some protection is afforded against organizations habitually manipulating partial information on Capitol Hill to protect their interests or promote their programs.

Since NIE's are encapsulations and do not disclose sources they are different in kind from, and more secure than, raw intelligence reports. Likewise, since no attribution is made to diplomatic or other official conversations, diplomatic discourse is protected and another of the normal arguments for minimum disclosure is overcome.

— Institutionalizing these arrangements with the Congress could have the accompanying effect of heightening attention to the NIE system within the Executive Branch and protecting it against further institutional erosion there. . . .

— The joint Committee's access to National Estimates might serve as an indirect check and reference point against the selective and slanted intelligence often sped to the Appropriations and Armed Services Committees by means of end-runs around budget time.

— Focusing on intelligence estimates probably avoids the Executive privilege issue. Estimates are supposed to be expert evaluations and predictions. Until the Nixon Administration they have been considered beyond policy control. Authors of estimates are not advisers to Presidents. Hence, both they and their products should be outside the assertion or protection of a claim of Executive privilege. . . .

— The Congress would have the advantage, which it now lacks, of knowing that its leadership has access to the coordinated wisdom of the Executive Branch's own experts after those experts have sifted the Executive's information. The alternative of building a comparatively miniature but none-the-less expensive Congressional service of competitive experts, with all the consequent confrontations, duplications, and inconclusiveness, could be avoided.[3]

As in some of the other proposals that are put forward in this chapter those of Hughes involve risks and might offend bureaucratic sensibilities.

A somewhat different approach to this subject has been suggested by former National Security Council Adviser McGeorge Bundy, who believes that instead of having access to the executive national intelligence estimates it would be better for Congress to request its own estimates from CIA. He thinks the executive branch should permit CIA to carry out such a service for Congress. According to Bundy,

The CIA has a well deserved and scrupulously defended reputation for integrity in its assessments and care in its use of uncertain data. It also has plenty of experience in presenting its assessments in ways that do not compromise either its sources of information or the policy options of the Executive Branch. . . . [In] a few critical matters like strategic strength the American intelligence community is the world's leading primary source of data, and in many other fields it competes with the best available elsewhere. The Congress as a whole would be greatly reinforced by easy access to this major source of responsible and wide-ranging information on the rest of the world.

Anything which tends to widen both the range of attention and the readership of the government's best information agency is desirable. Opening CIA to the Congress should do both. Indeed my personal view is that all these matters would come into better focus if the name — though not the initials — of the CIA were changed to Central Information Agency. For its real business is information, and intelligence is only part of that. As its covert activities properly contract, and as the problems on which the American Government needs good world-wide information increase, I think the CIA has an extraordinary opportunity to transmute itself — with help from the

Congress — into a great national *informational* resource. . . . Therefore it would be critical to the success of this proposal that Congress should employ its own political power to protect the access of CIA analysts to relevant information gathered by other agencies. Presidents and Secretaries of State who are engaged in sensitive diplomatic negotiations may well insist, at least for brief periods of time, that their diplomatic conversations not be shared with intelligence analysts. In my own experience, it nearly always proved possible to protect the privacy of particularly sensitive diplomatic exchanges by sharing them with selected senior intelligence officers, who then assumed the responsibility of insuring that their implications were absorbed into the estimating process as a whole.

The role I am suggesting for the CIA, in short, is one of serving as a membrane through which things which are properly secret can be honestly reflected in analyses which are not. In this sense the Agency can become a means by which the ordinary dangers of the classification system are reversed. Ordinarily the existence of a single piece of top secret information can impose this classification on every document in which it is mentioned, thus creating a chain reaction in which cautious officials spread the classification epidemically to every new document with any relation to the old one. But a systematic process of informing Congress could have the reverse effect: officials with an interest in maximizing the flow of information could and would find ways of transmuting what is important about legitimately secret information into a form which is not dangerous. I know from my own experience that this process is entirely practicable in the vast majority of cases. What has been lacking in the intelligence community is the incentive to apply it. This incentive the Congress has in its power to supply.[4]

Given the crescendo of criticism swirling around CIA, some of Bundy's remarks may sound unrealistic, but it should be remembered that both Bundy and Hughes are talking about the intelligence-estimating process, not the clandestine operations of CIA. Part of this problem is public relations and agency image, but another part is the question of proper organization. In any case, there are very persuasive arguments for making major intelligence estimates available to Congress in one form or another. If the proposed Commission becomes law, one of its important functions could be the arrangements for making appropriate estimates available to Congress.

It is important for Congress also to establish boundary lines for government secrets. One fairly simple part of the legislation should be a provision that all classified information should be declassified if it is more than ten years old. Such an arbitrary time limit may risk the publication of some information which could be politically or personally embarrassing to individuals or governments, but it certainly would not threaten the security of the United States. The classification system is for the protection of security, not for protection against political embarrassment. The Moorhead amendment specifically notes this point in defining the authority of individuals empowered to classify, saying: "Such individuals shall not classify official information in order to conceal incompetence, inefficiency, wrong doing, administrative error, to avoid embarrassment to any individual or agency, or to restrain competition or independent initiative."[5]

The ten-year limit would free hundreds of millions of classified documents going back to World War II. It would save millions of dollars spent each year to maintain secure storage facilities for these mountains of documents. It would save many more millions paid in salaries to the personnel given the preposterous assignment of sifting through all these documents on a case-by-case basis to determine which can be declassified under present regulations. As has been reported frequently elsewhere in this book, the mass of classified information has been outrageously excessive, at least at a ratio of nine out of ten documents.

The only way to deal with the problem of the past is to set a firm limit and legislate to declassify information beyond that limit. There is no magic about ten years as the limit; it could be eight. The statute could provide for certain exemptions such as cryptographic systems, intelligence sources, and war plans where release would cause grave damage. The release of all other information after ten years would be a boon for technological advancement, historians and scholars, and would contribute to a better understanding of the workings of our government.

The sharp debate continues between members of Congress who are trying to revise the secrecy system and the national security managers of the executive branch over the question of how long information should remain classified. Nixon's Executive Order 11652 provides that, unless exempted from the schedule, "Top Secret" shall be downgraded to "Secret" after two years, to "Confidential" after two more years, and declassified after ten years. Information originally classified "Secret" shall be downgraded to "Confidential" after two years and declassified after eight years. Information originally classified "Confidential" shall be declassified after six years. The Moorhead bill provided that "Top Secret" be downgraded to "Secret" after one year, from "Secret" to "Confidential" after one more year, and declassified after another year, a span of three years.

It is recommended that a compromise be made which would accept the government period of two years from "Top Secret" to "Secret," two years from "Secret" to "Confidential," but only one year from "Confidential" to declassification for a total span of five years. There is absolutely no justification for the current government practice of keeping "Confidential" information classified for six years. The lower the classification the stronger the case for early declassification. Occasionally there will undoubtedly be disputes between Congress and the executive about the continuing classification of certain information, but these can be resolved by the Classification Review Commission, and failing that, by the courts.

Morton Halperin, a former member of the National Security Council staff who has been studying the secrecy system, believes that Congress should go even further in its reform of the secrecy system. He recommends that Congress establish three categories of information: that which must be made public, that which should be kept secret, and a middle category that would be classified only after balancing the possible harm to national defense against the advantages to public understanding. The courts would be charged under the provisions of the Freedom of Information Act with policing the implementation of all three categories. Halperin believes Congress should establish by statute the types of information that must be public and the types that will remain secret. He has suggested the following:

Types of information that should be released — Commitments to employ American forces; American combat advisers; American civilians or foreign mercenaries in combat or as combat advisers; financing of combat operations; U.S. troops abroad; nuclear weapons abroad; military assistance programs; research on a new weapons system, current and estimated costs of weapons systems, existence of budgets and authorized functions of intelligence organizations, and executive branch financing or ownership of private organizations.

Types of information which should be kept secret — Details of advanced weapons systems design and operational characteristics; details of plans for military operations; diplomatic negotiations; code making and breaking, the detailed operational characteristics of intelligence gathering systems, and the identity of spies.[6]

Mr. Halperin's approach is ingenious, but it is difficult to imagine Congress's mandating by statute what information needs to be protected and what does not. Based on the opinions of the Supreme Court until now, it is highly likely that they would rule such action unconstitutional if this issue were tested. Another, much smaller, difficulty with the Halperin proposals is that no time limits are recommended. As has been emphasized throughout this book, most diplomatic secrets should be declassified in a relatively short period of time. It would probably be much more feasible to have the Commission, already described, take on the responsibility for determining categories of information that need classification protection. There is considerable merit in Halperin's notion that any U.S. military involvements relating to combat or potential warfare abroad should be public. If Congress is inclined to legislate this matter it might be handled in an amendment to the War Powers Act.

Another important area which should be included in the legislation is oversight for the industrial secrecy system. There is a long-standing need for Congress to investigate the entire fabric of the military-industrial complex, but in the specific area of classification one of the major responsibilities of the Classification Review Commission should be to review and then establish the standards for industrial security. As of early 1975 there were more than 11,000 industrial and research facilities cleared to handle defense contracts controlled by the Pentagon security system. Most of these arrangements should be abolished. As we have seen, research and inventiveness are impaired by secrecy as are sound economic competition and productivity. The millions of documents held in expensive classification storage which are more than five years old should be declassified at once.

In 1970 the Pentagon asked its Defense Science Board to establish a task force to study and make recommendations on Defense secrecy. Among its findings, ". . . it is unlikely that classified information will remain secure for periods as long as five years, and it is more reasonable to assume that it will become known by others in periods as short as one year." The panel also estimated that the volume of scientific and technical information that is classified could be reduced "by perhaps as much as 90 percent. [Because of secrecy] . . . the laboratories in which highly classified work is carried out have been encountering more difficulty in recruiting the most brilliant and capable minds." A member of the task force said that "if present trends continue for another decade, our national effort in weapons research will become little better than mediocre." Another member concluded that "while secrecy is an effective instrument in a closed society, it is much less effective in an open society in the long run; instead the open society should recognize that openness is one of its strongest weapons. . . ."[7] The evidence is strong that most of the industrial security program inhibits our national security and endangers our democracy. The Congress should certainly empower the Classification Review Commission with authority to correct this unfortunate and vast extension of the secrecy system.

A significant additional advantage in establishing a Classification Review Commission within the executive branch is that it will tend to limit the potential problems of executive privilege in the national security field. If the President accepts the view that it is in his interest and that of the nation to compromise with Congress in the establishment of a Commission many of the elements required to restore public trust will have been achieved. It will also go a long way toward striking a balance for the sweeping powers of executive privilege in the maintenance of diplomatic and military secrets contained in the unfortunate unanimous decision of the Supreme Court on July 24, 1974, concerning the Nixon tapes. The proposed congressional legislation may force a showdown in the courts, or perhaps the Commission, in trying to resolve a dispute between the executive and the Congress, will inspire such a showdown. As reported earlier, Justice Potter Stewart has stated that "if Congress should pass a specific law authorizing civil proceedings in this field [secrecy in international relations and defense] the courts would likewise have the duty to decide the constitutionality of such a law." Let's hope the persuasiveness of the arguments and the spirit of compromise in the recommended legislation will avoid such a collision, but if it doesn't, the sooner it comes the better.

David Wise, a long-time student of government secrecy, says:

> My own view is that the present classification system should be junked. I doubt there is any need for a formal system of official secrecy in the United States. We have only had such a system for a bit more than two decades, and there is nothing in our history that requires its continuation. It is a relic of the Cold War. It breeds concealment and mistrust; it encourages the government to lie. It is unrealistic, however, to think that Congress and the Executive Branch would agree to end all official secrecy.[8]

Yes, it is unrealistic. Furthermore, there are a few essential secrets. If there is adequate control and accountability ensuring that the secrets are legitimate, then trust will grow and the necessary secrets will be better protected. The recommendations discussed here, if implemented, should go a long way toward that goal.

In summary, the Congress should enact legislation which would emphasize its needs for being aware of national security information. An important aspect of this would be to provide by statute for congressional access to National Intelligence Estimates. The Congress should establish a Classification Review Commission within the executive branch to provide oversight of the classification system and to ensure that Congress has access to information that it ought to have in the conduct of its legislative responsibilities. The Commission would serve as an advocate for greater freedom of information. The statute should reflect the strong sense of the Congress that government secrecy should be reduced to the absolute minimum consistent with genuine security requirements. In this connection, all classified information more than ten years of age should be declassified. All current information should be declassified after a period of no more than five years. Certain clearly sensitive information should be exempted from this provision. The Classification Review Commission should be empowered to revamp and drastically reduce the industrial security program.

Congress and CIA

The CIA involvement in Watergate, the ousting of the Allende government in Chile, and the illegal domestic operations against U.S. citizens have inspired a public outcry of such proportions that Congress has been forced to action it should have taken twenty years ago. In 1974 and early 1975 CIA received a drumbeat of adverse publicity far exceeding that stemming from the *Ramparts* revelations in 1967 or the linkage with Watergate and the Ellsberg psychiatrist break-in. The crescendo of criticism against CIA added to the fear and mistrust in government which has pervaded the country.

As we have seen, Congress has had a most shabby record in dealing with the issues of adequate oversight and accountability for clandestine operations. In 1956 a Senate proposal for a joint congressional committee to have legislative oversight of CIA was decisively defeated; and, in 1966, a Senate proposal for a full study of the effect of CIA operations and activities on U.S. foreign relations was rejected by a large margin. Congress through the years has tolerated the informal system of CIA "watchdog" committees whose members were carefully selected and were almost without exception uncritical supporters of CIA who preferred not to be told too much.

In 1975 the situation changed profoundly. The Cold War consensus of 1956 and 1966 was dead. Most congressional leaders finally acknowledged that the informal oversight did not work. President Ford saw that his case for restricting congressional oversight was weak. He agreed to cooperate with a thorough investigation of the extent of CIA involvement in domestic affairs and ordered that all such operations be banned. Even most clandestine CIA foreign operations have been archaic and inappropriate for over a decade, overtaken by the new technology of information gathering and by a relaxation of tensions between the United States and the Soviet Union.

It is ironic that when Congress got around to establishing adequate legislative oversight most of the CIA covert political and paramilitary operations had been phased out. However, there remains a substantial clandestine espionage organization. If for no other reason than public trust, there should be a permanent joint congressional committee of oversight for CIA. Most of the proposals so far have called for very limited and exclusive membership on such a committee, perhaps no more than six members from each House. There is a good case for a small committee, but a membership of eighteen would provide more effective coverage. There is good precedent for this number in the Joint Committee on Atomic Energy, which had eighteen. The CIA committee might have three members drawn from the Senate Foreign Relations Committee, three from the House Foreign Affairs Committee, six from the Senate and House Armed Services committees, and six from the two Appropriations committees.

It is essential that the Foreign Relations and Foreign Affairs committees be strongly represented. One of the most ridiculous arguments, unfortunately sustained through the years, has been that CIA is an armed services function and not a foreign relations function. This has been rationalized because most of the CIA budget is hidden in the Defense budget, but the main reason has been political opportunism — friends of CIA leadership like Senators Russell and Stennis were running Armed Services, while some of the critics of CIA such as Senator Fulbright were at Foreign Relations. Whatever the politics, there can be no question that CIA operations have basic foreign policy ramifications and should be reviewed by foreign policy experts in the Congress. A much more exacting oversight of the CIA budget is needed. The security requirements for that budget have been exaggerated, and certainly the full details should be reviewed by the Committee members and audited by appropriately cleared representatives of the General Accounting Office.

The joint committee should be given responsibility for the entire U.S. intelligence community coordinated by CIA, including the Defense Intelligence Agency, the National Security Agency, the National Reconnaissance Office, and the Bureau of Intelligence and Research of the State Department. This range of committee responsibility would be important to ensure budgetary control, to set priorities, and to ascertain that CIA coordination of the entire intelligence effort is being satisfactorily fulfilled. There is precedent, again, for a joint committee with responsibilities which deal with budgeting and functions cutting across several agencies in the Joint Committee for Atomic Energy. Once Congress establishes the Joint Committee on CIA it should turn its attention to the following priorities:

1. A review of the entire U.S. intelligence-gathering effort to determine the adequacy of its performance and organization.

2. A review of the intelligence-estimating process to determine the adequacy of its results and their utilization. In this connection the Committee could play a useful role in the arrangements for making National Intelligence Estimates available, in appropriate form, to Congress.

3. A review of the clandestine operations program of CIA to determine the extent to which such operations should be reduced or phased out and the relationship of such cutbacks to similar cutbacks by the Soviet KGB.

4. After the studies above have been completed, the Committee should propose new legislation to modify the National Security Act of 1947 to reflect the realities of CIA functions and responsibilities of today.

The Congress should appropriate an adequate budget in support of the Joint Committee on CIA to ensure a sufficiently large staff to carry out the studies mentioned and the other continuing functions.

It was unfortunate that the investigations of CIA illegal domestic activities were conducted by select committees in both the Senate and the House. Partly because of the sensitivity of this work, but also because of the desirability of avoiding duplication of effort, it would be much better to have CIA oversight handled by a joint committee. The Select Senate Committee headed by Frank Church (D. – Idaho) investigated the activities of both the CIA and the FBI. If a new oversight committee for the FBI is established, it should be separate from the joint committee for CIA oversight. The functions of the two agencies are vastly different. Only the FBI should deal with domestic intelligence operations as already established by law. The CIA is expressly excluded from such operations.

Congress and the Espionage Act

As reported in the last chapter, the legislation modifying the U.S. Code and the espionage laws proposed by the Justice Department and joined by Senators McClellan and Hruska is a retrogression. The new language is far more repressive and restrictive than any criminal laws dealing with this subject in our entire history. What is needed today is clarification and simplification of the espionage laws to eliminate some ambiguous sections. In order to accomplish this objective it is recommended that sections 793 and 794 be rewritten, and that Subsections (d) and (e) of 793 be eliminated. These last contain the ambiguous language discussed in earlier chapters which challenges the First Amendment and threatens freedom of the press.

Before these sections of the espionage laws are recast, however, it would be preferable to wait for passage of legislation, discussed earlier in this chapter, which would amend the Freedom of Information Act to provide for a statutory classification system and a Classification Review Commission. Once the classification system is established by a statute replacing the present Executive Order, all such information should be covered by the revised espionage law. Section 794 makes it a crime to transmit, without authority, information relating to national defense to foreigners if it is done "with intent or reason to believe that it is to be used to the injury of the U.S. or to the advantage of a foreign nation." As already discussed, that intent clause is difficult to prove. Section 794 would be improved if it provided that the unauthorized transmission of information, classified by law, to a representative of a foreign government would be subject to criminal sanction. The unauthorized transmission of secret information to foreign agents is clearly a form of espionage. The penalty in time of war would be greater than at other times.

However, leaking classified information to the press or to a member of Congress is certainly not espionage, nor is publication of such information by a newspaper, book publisher, or TV network. One of the difficulties about punishing such leaks is the fine distinction between authorized and unauthorized disclosure. When the President, the Secretary of State, or of Defense leaks security information no questions are raised, nor are they raised when a President or a Secretary of State, after retirement, includes "Top Secret" information in his memoirs. Because high-ranking officials have used classified information for political or personal purposes, it is difficult to draw a firm line for low-ranking officials. Undoubtedly, there should be administrative penalties for unauthorized disclosure of classified information. Penalties could range from public reprimand and loss of one grade in pay all the way to loss of job and possibly loss of eligibility for future government jobs and for a U.S. passport. A Classification Review Commission could establish administrative sanctions.

The new system of classification would need protection, especially since the amount of classified information would be carefully limited and involve legitimate secrets. But the best way to protect it would be to improve administration and respect for the system. We have never had criminal penalties for violations of Executive Orders authorizing the classification system through the Cold War to the present. There are fewer grounds for criminal sanctions today than at any time since the beginning of the Cold War. If the approach recommended here were adopted, the espionage laws would be revised to cover information which was illegally transmitted to agents of a foreign power and would eliminate the vague subsections which seem to provide criminal sanction for certain transmission, publication, or unauthorized retention of government defense information. If these subsections were removed the questions raised by Justices White and Stewart in the United States *v.* the New York Times Company would be resolved, as would be most of the issues left dangling when Judge Byrne dismissed charges against Daniel Ellsberg and Anthony Russo.

This still leaves unresolved the question of a former government employee who has signed a secrecy agreement and then proceeds to publish information the government claims is still classified, as in the Marchetti case. According to various decisions already rendered by the courts, the government does have the right to require employees who work in agencies handling sensitive information to sign a secrecy agreement. If the recommendations in this chapter are adopted, a former government employee could publish any information that is ten years old, "Confidential" information after one year, "Secret" information after three, and "Top Secret" information after five. If he or she wished to publish any current information sooner, under the terms of his secrecy agreement he would have to obtain permission of his former agency. If permission were not granted he could appeal and obtain a court decision under the amendment to the Freedom of Information Act passed by Congress in the fall of 1974. This procedure might cause certain additional administrative burdens for the government but should provide adequate protection for government interests as well as for former government employees who are budding authors.

The principle to be remembered in considering all these measures is the desirability of providing greater openness and freedom of information while protecting essential secrets. We should be careful not to mix considerations of espionage with issues of freedom of information, as Congress did in 1950 acting under the influence of McCarthyism and Stalinism.

The Future of CIA

More attention has been given to CIA in this book than to any other part of the national security establishment because that Agency was given such a major role in waging the Cold War and because the clandestine nature of its operations made it such an important part of the secrecy system. Personnel and techniques of the CIA were responsible for bringing clandestine operations into Watergate and, for the first time, into American politics and a national election through the Committee to Re-Elect the President (CREEP). In the minds of most Americans the sickness that has infected the U.S. government is profoundly linked with CIA.

As discussed in the chapter on CIA, the most severe criticism has centered on the so-called "department of dirty tricks," the covert political and para-military action. There had been relatively little complaint about espionage and counter-espionage operations in the Establishment press until late 1974 when the *New York Times* reported large-scale CIA domestic operations, especially penetration of the U.S. anti-war movement from 1969 to 1971. There has been general agreement that the United States should have a strong intelligence program, but as CIA publicity has increased a growing sophistication has emerged making the distinction between political "dirty tricks" and the intelligence needed to make sound foreign policy and defense decisions. In this concluding section on CIA I want to recommend courses of action for dealing with the future of clandestine operations and measures for strengthening the intelligence-estimating machinery.

There has been a growing clamor for bringing covert CIA action to an end. Former Attorney General Nicholas Katzenbach, a member of the three-man panel established by President Johnson to investigate CIA in 1967 after the *Ramparts* story, says:

We should abandon publicly all covert operations designed to influence political results in foreign countries. Specifically, there should be no secret subsidies of police or counter-insurgency forces, no efforts to influence elections, no secret monetary subsidies of groups sympathetic to the United States, whether governmental, non-governmental or revolutionary. We should confine our covert activities overseas to the gathering of intelligence information.[9]

Morton Halperin and Jeremy Stone go even further than Katzenbach:

We believe that the United States no longer needs a large establishment whose function is to conduct covert operations and gather intelligence covertly. Accordingly the entire covert-operations section of the CIA should be dismantled. The CIA should become what it was originally meant to be — an intelligence evaluation and coordinating organization with no operating responsibilities.[10]

Victor Marchetti and John Marks agree:

[The] best solution would be not simply to separate the Clandestine Services from the rest of CIA, but to abolish them completely. The few clandestine functions which still serve a useful purpose could be transferred to other government departments, but for the most part, such activities should be eliminated. This would deprive the Government of its arsenal of dirty tricks, but the republic could easily sustain the loss — and be the better for it.[11]

Despite the sweeping recommendations for abolition of covert operations by most of those who have studied the subject, it is improbable that either the executive branch or the Congress will take such action, at least for some time. As reported in Chapter 6, Senator James Abourezk (D.–S.D.) initiated an amendment in late 1974 calling for a complete ban on CIA covert political operations, which was defeated in the Senate by the decisive vote of 68–17. Perhaps after a new joint committee on CIA oversight is created and it has taken a thorough look at clandestine operations, there will be a conclusion in Congress that such operations should be abolished. In the meantime, a majority of Congress will probably heed the cautionary remark of CIA Director Colby who says the elimination of covert operations would "leave us with nothing between a diplomatic protest and sending in the marines." But the strongest argument for continuing the clandestine operation will be that the Soviet KGB is still conducting such operations.

Allen Dulles writing about the KGB said: "It is a multi-purpose, clandestine arm of power . . . more than an intelligence or counter-intelligence organization. It is an instrument for subversion, manipulation, and violence, for the secret intervention in the affairs of other countries." According to Marchetti and Marks, "his description was a correct one, but he could — just as accurately — have used the same terms to describe his own CIA."[12] The point is that both CIA and KGB have been rationalizing the continuing existence of certain operations on grounds that the other is conducting such operations. As discussed in Chapter 4, both organizations are flawed, both are dated, and both are still conducting political and psychological operations which tend to run counter to the objectives of their governments' foreign policies. Yet, the continuing existence of these operations is used as a sort of litmus paper, by both sides, to test the true motivation and relative hostility of the other.

It is recommended therefore, that clandestine operations be added to the agenda of United States–Soviet Union negotiations on detente with the objectivity of mutually phasing out such operations. There will be some who will call this proposal naive and totally impractical, but such critics are misguided or inexperienced. It is true that by their very nature covert operations are supposed to be secret and are never acknowledged in official diplomacy. However, it can be asserted authoritatively that there is a long, but mostly unpublicized, history of arrangements made by both the U.S. and the U.S.S.R. in this field. Some of the arrangements have had considerable publicity, such as the exchange of U-2 pilot Gary Powers for KGB master spy Colonel Rudolf Abel. There are several forms of negotiation, both formal and informal, official and unofficial — for example, the crucial negotiation during the Cuban Missile Crisis between newsman John Scali (former U.S. Ambassador to the United Nations) and a representative of the KGB.

If the United States and the Soviets are inclined to explore the mutual reduction of clandestine operations there are practical ways of going about it. Undoubtedly, both the CIA and the KGB will find strong reasons why such talks should not be held, especially the KGB. There is an immense difference between the KGB and the CIA. The KGB is a gigantic organization with responsibility for all Soviet internal security. The Soviet Union is a police state because of the power and control of the KGB. What we are talking about here are only the external operations of the KGB. However, all bureaucracies by their nature resist diminution of their authority and responsibility and the leaders of the KGB will fight any reduction in their operations, especially because they will fear a trend. If external operations are cut back, internal operations may be, too.

It is far more difficult for a totalitarian police state to modify its ways in these matters than for a democracy, even one which has had a massive secret government program for as long as we have had. For this reason we will need to give the Soviet leadership strong incentives. Certainly one of the strongest incentives will be our demonstration of an intent to measure the progress of detente, at least in part, by evidence of the Soviets' joining us in phasing out covert operations. One approach in this process would be to let the Soviets know, through appropriate channels, that we were unilaterally phasing out certain operations and that we would be carefully watching to observe evidence of their taking similar steps. If, after a reasonable period of time, there was no such evidence we would publicize the fact. We would also begin to publicize the existence of certain KGB operations, KGB agents among Soviet diplomats, and KGB espionage. We might, when useful, declare certain Soviet diplomats known to be KGB persona non grata.

We should make it very clear to the Soviets that this sort of harassment, exposure, and publicity would occur only if they refused to cooperate in the reduction of such covert operations. In order to carry out this policy effectively it would probably be necessary, at least for a while, to step up CIA counter-intelligence abroad and FBI counter-intelligence in the United States, dealing with operations of the KGB. There would undoubtedly be some risk, as there is in any negotiation with the Soviets, that the hard liners in the Kremlin would use this issue to block further progress of detente. Instead of a gradual reduction of covert operations the hawks in Moscow would press for counter-harassment against the United States. This would be a calculated risk, but it seems a good one because detente has already moved so far that any turning back would be just as harmful, perhaps more so, for the Soviet Union. As for the United States, the other very important consideration is that Soviet leaders as well as U.S. leaders are beginning to realize that clandestine operations, by their nature, run exactly counter to the mutually expressed goal of reducing tensions and the risks of war. A program for the joint reduction of covert operations would advance the prospects for detente. It would also have the strong support of Congress and the American people.

National Intelligence Estimates

As discussed in Chapter 4, there has been a retrogression in the national intelligence-estimating process in the last few years. The most important role assigned to the Director of Central Intelligence has been substantially diluted. The DCI was supposed to be the intelligence adviser of the President with direct and independent access. As Chairman of the United States Intelligence Board (USIB) he had the final word on the intelligence estimates that went to the President to guide his decisions. There was in CIA a Board of National Estimates which had the principal role in drafting the estimates. That has all changed through a series of actions largely controlled and inspired by Henry Kissinger. The Board of National Estimates has been abolished. The National Intelligence Officers (NIO's) who replaced it are enmeshed in the machinery of the NSC; Kissinger as Secretary of State dominates the NSC. With his other hat as National Security adviser and chief of the NSC staff he controls not only the agenda of the NSC, but also the intelligence briefings. Most of the briefings of the President are handled by Kissinger, rather than by Colby.

There is a great need to restore the independence, objectivity, and prestige of the intelligence-estimating process. Chester Cooper, a former member of the CIA national estimates staff who later became a member of the NSC staff, suggested removing "the estimating responsibility from CIA and placing it within the NSC structure." Cooper noted that long-standing practice had insulated the intelligence estimators from face-to-face confrontation with policy and decision makers. He felt that placing the estimators within the NSC policy-making framework would give them a more sensitive feel for policies under consideration and that estimates would be more relevant and more influential.[13] Cooper's proposals have been partially implemented because the NSC staff does have a larger role in the estimating process, but the estimating responsibility has been only partially removed from CIA.

The result of all of these moves is that the fundamental principle of keeping intelligence producers separate from intelligence users has been violated many times over. The other important principle of keeping intelligence estimators separate and independent from the influence and control of policy makers has also been dissipated. One of the important criticisms of the CIA organization has been that the DCI is responsible for both covert operations and intelligence estimates and therefore cannot have truly independent judgment. The linkage of operators and policy makers with the estimators has become even closer during the past two or three years.

What is needed is an entirely new approach which will implement the sound principles of independent intelligence estimating, for the first time. It is recommended that a new Office of National Intelligence Estimates (ONE) be created as part of the office of the President. The ONE would be entirely separate from CIA. The National Security Act would be revised to place the intelligence-estimating responsibility in ONE. The director of ONE would report directly to the President. The national intelligence estimates would still go to the National Security Council, but ONE would not be part of the NSC machinery. It would be a separate White

House office, just as the NSC office is separate, or the Office of
Management and Budget (OMB) is separate. Henry Kissinger, or
his successor, would no longer have any control over the estimating process. The Secretary of State as a member of NSC would
be a consumer of the products of ONE, but the President's National Security Adviser would have no role in the estimating
process.

The Board of National Estimates would be restored with a
membership of twelve to fifteen men and women who would be
selected on the basis of their wisdom, judgment, expert knowledge, and experience in estimating. In addition to the Board of
National Estimates the ONE would have a small staff of senior
intelligence experts with specialized knowledge of functional matters such as strategic weapons, energy, space technology, agriculture, etc., or of the Soviet Union, China, the Middle East, and
the other geographic areas of the world. The ONE would be
established by statute at the apex of the intelligence community.
Its function would be limited exclusively to the preparation of
intelligence estimates to assist the President and the members of
the NSC in making U.S. foreign and defense policy decisions.

The ONE would be serviced by all of the intelligence agencies
of the U.S. government, including CIA, the Defense Intelligence
Agency, the National Security Agency, the State Department's
Bureau of Intelligence and Research, the National Reconnaissance Office, and reports of the FBI and the Secret Service of the
Treasury relating to foreign affairs. The staff of the ONE would
be fully cleared for access to the most sensitive intelligence information. The United States Intelligence Board (USIB) would no
longer approve national intelligence estimates, in accordance with
the principle that operating agencies such as State and Defense,
who are also the dominant members of the National Security
Council, should not also be members of the body which prepares
the national intelligence estimates.

The Director of Central Intelligence would be replaced by the
Director of ONE as the man with final authority for national
estimates. The CIA, with an admittedly diminished role, would

continue to have responsibility for coordinating the entire intelli-
gence-collecting effort and the DCI, as chairman of USIB, would
have final authority to ensure the adequacy of that effort. The
CIA would continue to have responsibility for current intelligence
reports and the preparation and circulation of the daily intelligence digest. The CIA would continue to have major responsibility
for research and intelligence about such subjects as the progress
of the Soviet and Chinese economies, including reporting on
industrial development and agriculture. The CIA would also continue to have a major role in various aspects of scientific intelligence. While negotiations with the Soviets are progressing for the
gradual phase out of clandestine operations, CIA would continue
to have responsibility for those assets. In other words, CIA would
continue to carry out responsibilities that have been part of the
Agency's function for years.

In addition, the move of the national estimates to the White
House would accomplish something that was always intended,
but never implemented — it would make the national estimates
the most important part of our vast intelligence apparatus, with
the kind of prestige and authority needed to ensure maximum
attention from the policy makers. It we had had a ONE of this
sort in 1964 and 1965 we might not have gone into the Vietnam
War. A completely independent, highly prestigious body such as
this would be able to report the facts about Soviet strategic
weapons or Soviet military intentions without any pressure from
the Pentagon or others who have time and time again exaggerated
the dangers we were facing. One of the important early contribu-
tions of the ONE might be a probable significant cut in the U.S.
defense budget. The public relations specialists of the Pentagon
and the wolf callers among the pundits would have little impact
in competition with a powerful body such as the ONE.

This will be especially true if arrangements are made to transmit the national intelligence estimates to Congress. As Thomas
Hughes noted, making the NIE's available to Congress will
strengthen the system in both directions. They will certainly
strengthen the work of Congress in both budgeting and lawmak-

ing. Congress will be much better informed about national security dangers and will not have to rely on speculation in the press or possibly biased briefings from bureaucrats supporting a particular piece of the budget. On the other hand, the fact that Congress is receiving the NIE's should guarantee that they receive most careful attention from the President and the National Security Council. It the NIE's are used in this manner the decision-making process should be strengthened, executive-legislative relations should be strengthened, and the stifling impact of the secrecy system should be significantly reduced. The danger of tragic blunders, such as U.S. involvement in Vietnam, would be diminished and public trust would be greatly increased.

It is high time that the United States make the most of its intelligence system which costs the taxpayer about six billion dollars a year. It won't happen though unless the appropriate prestige and power are given to those responsible for the national estimates. If this proposal is adopted with a ONE established in the executive office of the President it should be possible to attract the finest talent in the United States. The Director of ONE would be second only to the secretaries of State and Defense in U.S. national security affairs. Such a step should bring greater sanity and stability to our national security after all the frenzy and imbalance of the past decade. It would contribute too to the checks and balances of our democracy.

The Press and Other Media

The press has been rejuvenated by Watergate, but most of the regained reputation must be credited to a few writers and editors of one paper, the *Washington Post*. In the field of national security affairs the press has a long way to go. There is still a willingness passively to accept the backgrounders of Henry Kissinger without challenge. The White House press corps seldom comes up with fresh insight, and the networks night after night peddle the handouts of Ron Nessen. One of the most shocking failures of the press has been its coverage of the Pentagon. Secretary Schlesinger is able to make pronouncements about the strategic importance of "perceptions" while most of the press sit nodding their heads in affirmation. This is the theory that even though we have more than adequate defense we should continue to build new weapons so that no one will *perceive* that we are behind. In other words, we build more weapons than we need merely because some people have a perception that we are not strong enough. (There is an element of "Catch 22" in all this!) Yet, in the course of more than twenty interviews with members of the Washington press corps, I found that only one seemed to have any grasp of the "perception" concept. That concept is costing the American taxpayer billions of dollars and makes no sense. The press has done almost nothing about the workings of the military-industrial complex as discussed in Chapter 3, and the industrial secrecy system is an unknown subject.

Why is this so? After Vietnam and the near-miss of Watergate one would think the press would be bounding forward to fill its adversary role as established by the First Amendment. Sure, after the *New York Times* story about CIA domestic spying there was a flurry of competent investigative reporting, but where is the investigative reporting of the much bigger, more important stories of our foreign and defense policies, our national security apparatus? Who among the press is taking on the adversary role and doing the investigation of the assumptions and policies of Henry Kissinger, James Schlesinger, and Senator Henry Jackson? The story of the post-Vladivostok SALT negotiations has policy implications involving perhaps 100 billion dollars of taxpayers' money, but who in the press is investigating the facts which may challenge the conventional wisdom and the policy assumptions of the government?

Part of the trouble is that so much of the Washington press, as was the case during the early years of the Vietnam War, has accepted the conventional wisdom. In the fields of foreign and defense policy editors are still too willing to give the government the benefit of the doubt. Not only has the secrecy system been inadequately challenged, but the rationale for the major policies has often been left unexposed. There has been too much willingness to accept the explanations of the policy makers at face value. For example, I referred in Chapter 1 to a *New York Times* article about Schlesinger which says his critics think he "has gone mad" because he continues to advocate increasing strategic weapons. Yet the details of why his critics think that way have been only superficially investigated and assessed. Policies may be perfectly sound and well thought out, but they should be under constant challenge by the press — that is the only way they will remain sound. If the press does not fulfill its adversary role it will not be fulfilling its obligation to the American people which was guaranteed protection under the First Amendment.

Speaking of the First Amendment, the press should mount an aggressive campaign in support of the amendment to the Freedom of Information Act and the establishment of a Classification Review Commission discussed earlier in this chapter. Now that the other amendments to the Freedom of Information Act have been passed over the President's veto the press should move aggressively ahead to request needed information, and if turned down should take advantage of the opportunity for a court ruling. If several of the tests are made successfully the government will be encouraged to relax and facilitate the release of legitimate claims for information. Finally, the press should encourage Congress to revise the espionage laws as discussed earlier, especially to eliminate those ambiguous sections which might subject the press to criminal prosecution for publishing certain information.

The press should have a paramount role in changing the secrecy system and contributing to more open and effective process of foreign and defense policy.

Notes

1
NATIONAL SECURITY — REALITY AND HOAX

1. Walter Lippmann, *U. S. Foreign Policy: Shield of the Republic* (Boston, 1943), p. 51.
2. Arnold Wolfers, "National Security as an Ambiguous Symbol," *Political Science Quarterly*, Vol. 67, No. 4, December 1952.
3. Frank N. Trager and Frank L. Simonie in *National Security and American Society: Theory Process and Policy*, edited by Trager and Philip Kronenberg (Lawrence, Kansas, 1973), p. 36.
4. Clark Clifford, quoted in Arthur Krock's *Memoirs* (London, 1968), pp. 228–229.
5. Dean Acheson, *Present at the Creation* (New York, 1969), pp. 374–375.
6. *Ibid.*, pp. 376–377.
7. *Ibid.*, pp. 378–379.
8. Townsend Hoopes, *The Devil and John Foster Dulles* (Boston, 1973), p. 198.
9. Jack Raymond, *Power at the Pentagon* (New York, 1964), pp. 248–249.
10. Gordon B. Turner and Richard D. Challener, *National Security in the Nuclear Age* (New York, 1960), in a chapter by Turner entitled "Strategic Concepts," p. 7.
11. Robert Strausz-Hupé, quoted in Arthur Herzog, *The War-Peace Establishment* (New York, 1963), pp. 6–7.
12. Edward Teller, quoted in *ibid.*, pp. 25–26.
13. Raymond, *op. cit.*, p. 251; and Herman Kahn, *On Thermonuclear War* (Princeton, New Jersey, 1960).
14. Albert Wohlstetter, quoted in Herzog, *op. cit.*, pp. 64–65.
15. Nikita Khrushchev, *Krushchev Remembers* (Boston, 1970), p. 500.
16. Arthur Herzog, quoted in Raymond, *op. cit.*, p. 251.
17. John Newhouse, *Cold Dawn* (New York, 1973), pp. 220–221.
18. Graham Allison, "Cool It: The Foreign Policy of Young America," *Foreign Policy*, Winter 1970–71, p. 144.
19. Richard Barnet, "The Illusion of Security," *Foreign Policy*, Summer 1971, p. 80.
20. *Ibid.*, p. 82.
21. Maxwell D. Taylor, "The Legitimate Claims of National Security," *Foreign Affairs*, April 1974, p. 577.
22. Lincoln P. Bloomfield, "Foreign Policy for Disillusioned Liberals," *Foreign Policy*, Winter 1972–73, pp. 66–67.

23. James Schlesinger, quoted in Leslie Gelb, "Schlesinger for Defense," *New York Times Magazine,* August 4, 1974.

24. Andrei D. Sakharov, quoted in a dispatch by Moscow correspondent Robert Kaiser, *Washington Post,* April 29, 1974.

25. Roy Medvedev, quoted in a dispatch by Moscow correspondent Peter Osnos, *Washington Post,* October 8, 1974.

26. Schlesinger, quoted in Gelb, *op. cit.*

27. Schlesinger remarks reported in a column by Michael Getler, editorial page, *Washington Post,* June 6, 1974.

28. Robert McNamara, in a speech to the American Society of Newspaper Editors, May 1966, quoted in Arthur M. Cox, *Prospects for Peacekeeping* (Washington, 1967), p. 30.

29. Gelb, *op. cit.*

30. Thomas J. McIntyre, U.S. Senator (D.–N.H.), in a speech at the Kennedy Center, "National Town Meeting," June 26, 1974.

31. Flora Lewis, "Strategic Debate and Secrecy," *New York Times,* July 9, 1974.

32. McIntyre, speech cited above.

33. Richard Barnet, *Roots of War* (New York, 1972), p. 341.

2

THE GROWTH OF THE U.S. SECRECY SYSTEM

1. For an excellent study of secrecy in the United States see "The Evolution of Government Information Security Classification Policy: A Brief Overview (1775–1973)" by Harold C. Relyea, Congressional Research Service, The Library of Congress, September 11, 1973.

2. "Executive Classification of Information — Security Classification Problems Involving Exemption (b)(1) of the Freedom of Information Act," 5 U.S.C. 552, Third Report of House Committee on Government Operations, May 22, 1973 (Washington, 1973), p. 3.

3. U.S. Congress, Senate, *Executive Journal,* Vol. I (August 4, 1790), p. 55.

4. Arthur Schlesinger, Jr., *The Imperial Presidency* (Boston, 1973), p. 332.

5. *A Compilation of the Messages and Papers of the Presidents 1789–1897,* Vol. I, edited by James D. Richardson (Washington, 1896), p. 194.

6. National Archives, "Origin of Defense Information Markings in the Army and Former War Department," mimeograph (Washington, 1972), p. 44.

7. Arthur Schlesinger, Jr., testimony before Senate Subcommittee on Intergovernmental Relations, Committee on Government Operations, May 23, 1974.

8. Relyea, *op. cit.*, p. 12.

9. Schlesinger, *The Imperial Presidency*, pp. 338–339.

10. National Archives, "Defense Information Markings in the Army" (Washington, 1935), p. 24.

11. Relyea, *op. cit.*, p. 30.

12. Robert Haydn Alcorn, *No Bugles for Spies* (New York, 1962), p. 134.

13. R. Harris Smith, *OSS* (Berkeley, California, 1972), p. 11.

14. Stewart Alsop and Thomas Braden, *Sub Rosa* (New York, 1946), p. 26.

15. National Security Act of 1947, Public Law 80–253, July 26, 1947.

16. Richard H. Rovere, *Senator Joe McCarthy* (New York, 1959), p. 4.

17. *Ibid.*, p. 5.

18. Executive Order No. 10290, *Federal Register*, September 27, 1951.

19. Relyea, *op. cit.*, p. 36.

20. Rovere, *op. cit.*, p. 15.

21. Executive Order No. 10501, *Federal Register*, November 9, 1953.

22. Senate Foreign Relations Committee, "Security Classification as a Problem in the Congressional Role in Foreign Policy" (Washington, 1971).

23. Atomic Energy Act of 1954, Public Law 83–703 as amended.

24. House Report 1884, 85th Congress, p. 152.

25. David Wise and Thomas B. Ross, *The Invisible Government* (New York, 1964), p. 123.

26. David Wise, *The Politics of Lying* (New York, 1973), p. 35.

27. Schleslinger, *The Imperial Presidency*, p. 343.

28. House Report 1257, 87th Congress (September 22, 1961), p. 57.

29. Freedom of Information Act, Public Law 89–487, July 4, 1966.

30. Mink VEPA 410 US (1973), Hearings "U.S. Government Information Policies and Practices — Administration and Operation of the Freedom of Information Act" (92d Congress, 2d session).

31. Relyea, *op. cit.*, p. 70.

3
EXECUTIVE SECRECY

1. William Macomber, Hearings before Subcommittee on Government Information, Committee on Government Operations, 92d Congress, 1st Session (June 30 and July 7, 1971), p. 900.

2. *Ibid.,* p. 901.

3. Andrew Berding, *Dulles on Diplomacy* (Princeton, New Jersey, 1965), p. 142.

4. Macomber, *op. cit.,* p. 900.

5. McGeorge Bundy, "Toward an Open Foreign Policy," editorial page, *Washington Post,* October 2, 1974.

6. Alfred Friendly, "Confessions of a Code Breaker," *Washington Post,* November 9, 1974.

7. Edward Teller, testimony before the Senate Subcommittee on Intergovernmental Relations, June 10, 1974.

8. John McPhee, "The Curve of Binding Energy," piece on Theodore Taylor, *New Yorker,* December 10, 1973, p. 67.

9. *Ibid.,* December 3, 1973, p. 116.

10. David O. Cooke, Deputy Assistant Secretary of Defense, Hearings on Government Secrecy, Senate Subcommittee on Intergovernmental Relations, May 31, 1974.

11. Edward Teller, *ibid.*

12. Edward Teller, "Problems of Secrecy," *Journal of the National Classification Management Society,* Vol. VI, No. 1, 1971.

13. Joseph J. Cody, Major General, USAF, Deputy Director, Contract Administration Services, Department of Defense, in a letter to Congressman William Moorhead, Chairman, House Subcommittee on Government Information, August 26, 1974.

14. David Cooke, *loc. cit.*

15. William Florence, "Executive Classification of Information," Third Report, House Committee on Government Operations, May 22, 1973.

16 Jack Raymond, *Power at the Pentagon* (New York, 1964), pp. 155–156.

17. Cody, *loc. cit.*

18. Joseph J. Liebling, "Classification Management — Current and Future Trends," *Journal of the National Classification Management Society,* Vol. VI, No. 1, 1971.

19. Raymond, *op. cit.,* pp. 138–139.

20. David O. Cooke, in a letter to Congressman Moorhead, Chairman, House Subcommittee on Government Information, August 29, 1974.

21. Cooke, *ibid.*

4
CIA AND THE INTELLIGENCE COMMUNITY

1. George F. Kennan (X), "The Sources of Soviet Conduct," *Foreign Affairs*, July 1947.

2. E.H. Cookridge, *Gehlen: Spy of the Century* (New York, 1972), pp. 116–118.

3. *Ibid.*, p. 158.

4. See *Memoirs of General Gehlen* (New York, 1972), Chapter 3; also Cookridge, *op. cit.*, pp. 41–58.

5. Cookridge, *op. cit.*, p. 5.

6. Heinz Hohne and Herman Zolling, *The General Was a Spy* (New York, 1972).

7. William Colby, Director, Central Intelligence Agency, interview in *Time* magazine, September 30, 1974, p. 19.

8. For more information on the operations listed in these paragraphs, see David Wise and Thomas Ross, *The Invisible Government* (New York, 1964), and Victor Marchetti and John Marks, *The CIA and the Cult of Intelligence* (New York, 1974).

9. Harry Howe Ransom, *The Intelligence Establishment* (Cambridge, Massachusetts, 1970), p. 185.

10. Richard Deacon, *A History of the British Secret Service* (New York, 1970), p. 399.

11. *Ibid.*, p. 398.

12. Kim Philby (H.A.R.), *My Silent War* (London, 1968).

13. Deacon, *op. cit.*, p. 408.

14. Cookridge, *op. cit.*, p. 284.

15. *Ibid.*, pp. 320–329.

16. Hohne and Zolling, *op. cit.*, p. 179.

17. Paul Blackstock, "The CIA and the Intelligence Community," *Forums in History* (St. Louis, Missouri, 1974), p. 2.

18. Ransom, *op. cit.*, p. 21

19. Much of the material for the discussion of technological intelligence is obtained from an excellent piece by Herbert Scoville, Jr., "The Technology of Surveillance," *Society* magazine, March–April 1975, pp. 58–63. Scoville was formerly Deputy Director for Research and Assistant Director of CIA for Scientific Intelligence. The article was a paper submitted at a conference on CIA in September 1974, which was organized by the Center for National Security Studies in Washington.

20. *Ibid.*, p. 61.

21. *Ibid.*, p. 62.

22. *Ibid.*, p. 63. See also Hebert Scoville, Jr., *SALT — The*

Moscow Agreements and Beyond (New York, 1974), the chapter entitled "A Leap Forward in Verification."

23. John Barron, *KGB* (New York, 1974), p. 71.

24. *Ibid.*, p. 4.

25. Joseph Alsop, column in *Washington Post*, December 10, 1969.

26. Barron, *op. cit.*, pp. 58–59.

27. "Bonn's Spy: Mr. Available," *Washington Post*, May 6, 1974.

28. Sherman Kent, *Strategic Intelligence for American World Policy* (Princeton, New Jersey, 1966), pp. 180–182.

29. Marchetti and Marks, *op. cit.*, p. 317.

30. Kent, *op. cit.*, p. 60.

31. Thomas L. Hughes, in a chapter entitled "The Power to Speak and the Power to Listen," in *Secrecy and Foreign Policy*, edited by Thomas M. Franck and Edward Weisband (New York, 1974), p. 30.

32. Ransom, *op. cit.*, p. 147.

33. Laurence Stern, "Nixon Zeroes In on CIA Unit," *Washington Post*, September 9, 1973.

34. *Ibid.*

35. Tad Szulc, "Inside the Intelligence Establishment," *Washingtonian*, March 1974.

5
SECRECY AND THE MEDIA

1. New York Times Company *v.* United States 403 US 713 (1971).

2. Stewart Alsop, *The Center* (New York, 1968), p. 193.

3. Chalmers Roberts, *First Rough Draft* (New York, 1973), p. 171.

4. Victor Marchetti and John Marks, *The CIA and the Cult of Intelligence* (New York, 1974), pp. 357–358.

5. From a speech by Clifton Daniel of the *New York Times*, quoted in Arthur Schlesinger, Jr., *The Imperial Presidency* (Boston, 1973), p. 343.

6. Marchetti and Marks, *op. cit.*, p. 358.

7. Max Frankel, Editor, *New York Times Magazine*, writing in *Columbia Forum*, Winter 1973.

8. Roberts, *op. cit.*, p. 200.

9. Alsop, *op. cit.*, pp. 182–183.

10. Roberts, *op. cit.*, p. 341.

11. Benjamin Bradlee, "Withholding of Story Defended," *Washington Post*, March 25, 1975.

12. David Wise, *The Politics of Lying* (New York, 1973), p. 39.

13. Roberts, *op. cit.*, p. 229.

14. Wise, *op. cit.*, p. 42.

15. Haynes Johnson, in a chapter entitled "Conflicts Between Press and Government" in *Secrecy and Foreign Policy*, edited by Thomas M. Franck and Edward Weisband (New York, 1974), p. 169.

16. Wise, *op. cit.*, p. 51.

17. William Greider, *Washington Post*, July 19, 1974.

18. Roberts, *op. cit.*, p. 322.

19. David Wise, in a chapter entitled "Pressures on the Press," in *None of Your Business: Government Secrecy in America*, edited by Norman Dorsen and Stephen Gillers (New York, 1974), p. 225.

20. Max Frankel affidavit quoted in Wise, *Politics of Lying*, pp. 105–106.

21. *The Presidential Transcripts* (New York, 1974), p. 91.

22. Leonard Boudin, in a chapter entitled "The Ellsberg Case: Citizen Disclosure," in Franck and Weisband, *op. cit.*, p. 308.

23. Transcript of Proceedings, United States *v.* Russo and Ellsberg, Friday, March 16, 1973, U.S. District Court, Los Angeles, California.

24. Defense brief, "Classification Allegations in the Ellsberg-Russo Trial."

25. Benno Schmidt, in a chapter entitled "The American Espionage Statutes and Publication of Defense Information," in Franck and Weisband, *op. cit.*, p. 184.

26. *Ibid.*, p. 198.

27. *Ibid.*, pp. 200–201.

28. Franks Report, Vol. 6 (London, 1972).

29. Harry Street, in a chapter entitled "Secrecy and the Citizens' Right to Know: A British Civil Libertarian Perspective," in Franck and Weisband, *op. cit.*, p. 337.

30. Schlesinger, *op. cit.*, p. 350.

31. *Ibid.*, p. 351.

32. Wise, in Dorsen and Gillers, *op. cit.*, p. 232.

33. John Chancellor, "The Science of Spying," NBC-TV News transcript, May 4, 1965.

34. William Colby, CIA Director, interview in *Time* magazine, September 30, 1974.

35. William Barnds, "Intelligence and Foreign Policy: Dilemmas of a Democracy," *Foreign Affairs*, January 1969.

36. Marchetti and Marks, *op. cit.*, from the introduction by Melvin Wulf, Legal Director, American Civil Liberties Union, who was legal counsel for Marchetti.

37. Oswald Johnston, *Washington Star-News,* November 30, 1973.

38. Stuart Loory, "The CIA's Use of the Press — 'A Mighty Wurlitzer,' " *Columbia Jornalism Review,* September–October 1974.

39. Charles W. Bray, "The Media and Foreign Policy," *Foreign Policy,* Fall 1974.

6
CONGRESS AND EXECUTIVE SECRECY

1. The findings in these paragraphs are based on interviews conducted by the author with more than sixty members of Congress and their staffs.

2. Raoul Berger, Harvard Law School, in *Washington Post,* October 18, 1973.

3. Hearings before Special Subcommittee on Investigations, Committee on Government Operations, U.S. Senate, 83rd Congress, 2d Session (1954), pp. 1169–1172.

4. William Rogers, "Constitutional Law: The Papers of the Executive Branch," 44 *American Bar Association Journal* 941 (1958).

5. Clark Mollenhoff, *Washington Cover-Up* (Garden City, New York, 1962), p. 239.

6. *None of Your Business,* edited by Norman Dorsen and Stephen Gillers (New York, 1974), p. 30.

7. Berger in *Washington Post,* October 18, 1973.

8. Charles Mathias, U.S. Senator (R.–Md.), in a chapter entitled "Executive Privilege and the Congress," in *Secrecy and Foreign Policy,* edited by Thomas M. Franck and Edward Weisband (New York, 1974), p. 84.

9. Carrie Johnson, editorial page staff writer, *Washington Post,* July 26, 1974.

10. Tom Wicker, *New York Times,* July 26, 1974.

11. William Florence, "Executive Classification of Information — Security of Classification Problems Involving Exemption (b)(1) of the Freedom of Information Act," Third Report of the House Committee on Government Operations, May 22, 1973, pp. 34 and 46.

12. William Moorhead, "Executive Classification of Information" (see note 11 above), p. 33.

13. Arthur Goldberg, "Security Classification as a Problem in the Congressional Role in Foreign Policy," U.S. Senate Committee on Foreign Relations, Legislative Reference Service, The Library of Congress (December 1971), p. 20.

14. Edmund Muskie, U.S. Senator (D.–Maine), press release, April 29, 1974.

15. Robert Dixon, Assistant Attorney General, statement before Senate Intergovernmental Relations Subcommittee of the Committee on Government Operations, May 30, 1974.

16. Carol Laise, Assistant Secretary of State for Public Affairs, statement before Senate Subcommittee on Intergovernmental Relations, May 30, 1974.

17. Arthur Schlesinger, Jr., statement before Senate Subcommittee on Intergovernmental Relations, May 30, 1974.

18. Martin Arnold, "Ford Vetoes Effort to Improve Access to Government Data," *New York Times*, October 18, 1974.

19. William Moorhead, Member of Congress (D.–Pa.) *Congressional Record*, House, June 10, 1974, H 4970.

20. Harry H. Ransom, *The Intelligence Establishment* (Cambridge, Massachusetts, 1970), p. 87.

21. David Wise, "Covert Operations Abroad," a paper delivered to a conference on CIA organized by The Center for National Security Studies, Washington, September 1974.

22. Lyman Kirkpatrick, *The Real CIA* (New York, 1968), pp. 116 and 269.

23. Victor Marchetti and John Marks, *The CIA and the Cult of Intelligence* (New York, 1974), p. 345.

24. *Ibid.*, p. 344.

25. John Chancellor, "The Science of Spying," NBC-TV News transcript, May 4, 1965.

26. David Wise, *The Politics of Lying* (New York, 1973), p. 114.

27. Senate Conference Resolution Number 2, 84th Congress, 1st Session, January 14, 1955.

28. Senate Report No. 1570, "Joint Committee on Central Intelligence Agency," Committee on Rules and Administration, 84th Congress, 2d Session, February 23, 1956.

29. *Ibid.*

30. *Congressional Record*, April 9, 1956, p. 5298.

31. *Ibid.*

32. Ransom, *op. cit.*, p. 171.

33. *Congressional Record*, 89th Congress, 2d Session, July 27, 1966, p. 14930.

34. Ransom, *op. cit.*, pp. 174–175.

35. *New York Times*, February 25, 1967.

36. Marchetti and Marks, *op. cit.*, p. 343.

37. Michael Harrington, Member of Congress (D.–Mass.), "Democracy and Secret Operations," *Washington Post*, September 22, 1974.

38. *Time* magazine, "The CIA: Time to Come in from the Cold," September 30, 1974.

39. Laurence Stern, "CIA to Share Operations Data with Foreign Affairs Panel," *Washington Post*, October 2, 1974.

40. *New York Times*, October 3, 1974.

41. *Washington Post*, October 4, 1974.

42. Benno Schmidt, in a chapter entitled "The Espionage Statutes and Defense Information," in *Secrecy and Foreign Policy*, edited by Thomas M. Franck and Edward Weisband (New York, 1974), p. 196.

43. John McClellan and Roman Hruska, Committee Print, October 15, 1974. A bill to revise Title 18 of the U.S. Code, the Federal Criminal Code.

7
CONCLUSIONS AND RECOMMENDATIONS

1. Anthony Lake, quoted in David Wise, *The Politics of Lying* (New York, 1973), p. 347.

2. Nicholas Katzenbach, "Foreign Policy and Secrecy," *Foreign Affairs*, October 1973.

3. Thomas L. Hughes, "The Power to Speak and the Power to Listen: Reflections on Bureaucratic Politics and a Recommendation on Information Flows," in *Secrecy and Foreign Policy*, edited by Thomas M. Franck and Edward Weisband (New York, 1974), pp. 39–40.

4. McGeorge Bundy, in *ibid*.

5. William Moorhead et al., HR 12004, a bill to amend Section 552 of Title V of the U.S. Code (known as the Freedom of Information Act) to provide for the classification and declassification of information in the interest of national defense.

6. Morton Halperin, in testimony before House Subcommittee on Government Information, July 25, 1974.

7. 1970 Defense Science Board Task Force on Secrecy, Appendix 6, "Security Classification Reform," report of hearings before Government Information Subcommittee on HR 12004, 93rd Congress, 2d Session, July and August 1974.

8. Wise, *op. cit.*, p. 349.

9. Nicholas Katzenback, *op. cit.*

10. Morton Halperin and Jeremy Stone, in a chapter entitled Secrecy and Covert Intelligence Collection and Operations," in *None of Your Business*, edited by Norman Dorsen and Stephen Gillers (New York, 1974), p. 128.

11. Victor Marchetti and John Marks, *The CIA and the Cult of Intelligence* (New York, 1974), p. 376.

12. *Ibid.,* p. 370.

13. Chester Cooper, "The CIA and Decision-making," *Foreign Affairs,* January 1972.

Index

THE MYTHS OF NATIONAL SECURITY

THE PERIL OF SECRET GOVERNMENT

by Arthur Macy Cox

Drawing on his years of experience in the State Department, the White House, and the CIA, Arthur Macy Cox examines the unbridled power of the intelligence community and secret government — and how it grew to its awesome Watergate-era proportions.

Cox believes that, ironically, the very measures designed to achieve national security have provided its gravest threats: a secret government breeding totalitarianism, and a defense-oriented economy that has seriously weakened the nation's economic structure.

He views Watergate as a symptom of a wider malaise which developed over the past three decades as successive Presidents invoked national security to build a vast secrecy system. In a revealing chapter on the growth of secrecy, Cox shows that the emphasis in government until World War I was on broad disclosure of public policy and decisionmaking. Nowhere in the Constitution is there a provision for secrecy in the Executive and Judicial branches, and no significant system of secrecy emerged throughout the entire nineteenth century.

However, in 1917 the first system of official secrecy classification was adopted, and Congress passed the Espionage Act. In World War II, Roosevelt easily won broad public acceptance of the need for secrecy, and his successors manipulated Cold War hysteria to gain the nation's support for a rapidly multiplying intelligence network, and the secrecy mentality that led to Watergate.

Cox shows how major organizational changes were made in response to the need for "national security," although the term

(continued on back flap)